THE CHANGING TIMES

Ian Braybrook

REVISED EDITION

The Changing Times
Original edition published in 2011
This revised edition published in 2018 by
Marilyn Bennet Publishing
Maine Media
100 Brown Street
Castlemaine Victoria Australia 3450
Phone: 0409 333 513
Email: ianandmazza@gmail.com

Copyright © Ian Braybrook, 2011, 2018

ISBN: 978-0-9944370-3-7

A catalogue record for this book is available from the National Library of Australia

Photographs courtesy of:
The Author, Chris Rae, family collections & other sources.
Front Cover:
Back row: Alan, Mum & Dad. Front row: Ian, Maurie & Frank.
Back Cover:
Ian at Buninyong in 1940

On notification, any inadvertent copyright omissions will be corrected in a future edition.

Text design and layout by Level Heading – levelheading.com

Other book by the same Author:
    Gweneth Wisewould – Outpost Doctor
    Six Ha'pennies
    Bush Wireless
    Sarah's Search – A Silk Odyssey (with Marilyn Bennet)

Imperial measurements are used throughout as they were in use in the years written about.

Dedicated to my late mother, Veronica Amelia Ellison, who endured so much but always with a smile never far away and to my late, much loved brother, Alan James Braybrook.

My thanks to Marilyn Bennet for her help in many ways. It was she who encouraged me to complete this story which I began forty years ago. A special thank you to Bernard Schultz of Level Heading for his patient and thorough work in editing, lay up and general assistance.

Contents

Part One

Chapter One 13
    The way it was
Chapter Two 20
    Blackwood township ~ sausages ~ Barry's Reef and the Old Sultan Mine.
Chapter Three 25
    Basalt ~ Beaufort ~ Daylesford and a mouth organ band.
Chapter Four 35
    Eganstown ~ Roy Ellison ~ bush drive ~ the rifleman ~ a new home.
Chapter Five 39
    Stolen children ~ Ballarat Orphanage ~ The Depression ~ death of a son.
Chapter Six 45
    Black Friday ~ roof collapse ~ Ballarat ~ Bunninyong ~ Blakeville.
Chapter Seven 51
    Another move ~ goat's milk ~ Joe Callaghan ~ Barry's Reef.
Chapter Eight 56
    Gold by the ton ~ an unusual barber ~ death of a postmaster.
Chapter Nine 61
    Sunday's butter ~ Hobyahs and other scary things ~ Dr Gwen's delicate surgery.
Chapter Ten 66
    Blackwood Mineral Springs ~ radio comes to Barry's Reef.
Chapter Eleven 69
    Blue Mount ~ a boy goes to war ~ little boys lost.
Chapter Twelve 78
    Trentham ~ ferrets ~ grape picking ~ the Yankee Mine explosion.
Chapter Thirteen 85
    The War ~ death of a neighbour ~ Fitzroy ~ another school
Chapter Fourteen 91
    The times are changing ~ death calls on us.
Chapter Fifteen 98
    A funeral ~ new friends ~ South Kingsville ~ Spotswood.

Chapter Sixteen **104**
    Mum gets a job ~ leaving Trentham ~ a surprise wedding.
Chapter Seventeen **110**
    City life ~ beach bums ~ Lance Creek ~ a new ute.
Chapter Eighteen **118**
    Another school ~ snakes alive ~ the pig ~ Cudgee calls.
Chapter Nineteen **126**
    Panmure ~ Pop versus Mum ~ Melbourne by taxi.
Chapter Twenty **130**
    The city again ~ Footscray Tech ~ a farm in Dixie ~ back to Basalt.
Chapter Twenty-One **134**
    A baby brother ~ Austin car ~ Terang hospital ~ twins for Mum.
Chapter Twenty-Two **139**
    The 1937 Chev ~ North Melbourne ~ I get a job ~ childhood ends.

PART TWO

Chapter Twenty-Three **143**
    A working man
Chapter Twenty-Four **148**
    Excell's Employment Agency ~ Drouin ~ two quid a week
Chapter Twenty-Five **152**
    A taxi? ~ money bag ~ bad language ~ sacked
Chapter Twenty-Six **158**
    Back to Excell's ~ Doctor's Flat ~ Swifts Creek ~ Omeo.
Chapter Twenty-Seven **170**
    Excell's again ~ Whittlesea.
Chapter Twenty-Eight **175**
    Yarraville ~ a brush with the law ~ camping out ~ jobs, cars and a flying sausage
Chapter Twenty-Nine **182**
    Street dwellers ~ jobs ~ the Gypsy woman ~ the brown cliffs of Darley.
Chapter Thirty **190**
    Homeless ~ peach picking ~ goodbye city life ~ police ~ Purnim West.
Chapter Thirty-One **195**
    Back to the bush ~ railway cops ~ Warrnambool ~ welcome home

Chapter Thirty-Two **199**
   Lillian and me ~ my 15th birthday party ~ Warrnambool Hospital.
Chapter Thirty-Three **214**
   Tonsils ~ tin baths ~ Radio 3YB ~ leaving Purnim West.
Chapter Thirty-Four **223**
   Daylesford ~ a long walk ~ Lismore ~ Williamstown
Chapter Thirty-Five **234**
   Lots of jobs ~ shearing sheds ~ Muddamurra Mick ~ Old Cobran ~ Deniliquin.
Chapter Thirty-Six **258**
   My first car ~ grape picker ~ truckie and more.
Chapter Thirty-Seven **277**
   A hide out ~ a brother marries ~ back to the bush for good.

Author's note

THE LUCK OF THE DRAW

I've been lucky. I drew a marvellous mother and three fine brothers; and I drew a poor and struggling household which proved to be one of my biggest inherited assets. It taught me how to cope; showed me that 'life was not meant to be easy'.

I cannot write my story without briefly telling that of my mother and father. It was their circumstances that shaped the person I am today. It was their activities, sadness and abundant misadventures that had a profound effect on my life and that of my siblings. But I also drew a negative side as you will appreciate when you read my story.

I chronicled these, my growing up years, because I felt compelled to record just how it was for many poor Australian people in the days of the Great Depression and, in my case, beyond. I fear that such ordinary stories will be lost if not placed in writing.

Everybody has a story to tell. This is mine.

Part One

Chapter One

THE WAY IT WAS

The year is 1978. I stand beside the ruins of a tiny miner's cottage on the roadside at Barry's Reef. This long forgotten hamlet is home to just one person, the widow of a well known classical singer living alone, I'll call her Mrs Lieflin. It is difficult now to imagine that Barry's Reef was once a bustling town, home to seven thousand hardy gold seekers and their families.

In the 1940s, the pile of rubble I look upon was the home of Joe Callaghan, my childhood best friend. His home is now nothing more than a brick chimney and a pile of rusted corrugated iron, pieces of timber and the occasional glimpse of a hardwood shingle.

As I gaze upon this shambles my mind goes back to the time when I was living with my family in the tumbled down shack next door, itself teetering on its foundations, about 100 yards to the north. We arrived there early in 1940.

Both of these relics lie on the west side of the road that leads from Trentham to Blackwood. Four miles from Trentham there is Garlic's Lead, then Newbury, both almost deserted townships, a few miles further on is Barry's Reef.

In the yard next door I see four boys at play. The oldest is about ten years old, another about eight, the third about seven and the youngest not yet five. They are playing cricket. Their wicket is a dented, rectangular kerosene tin; their bat a broken shovel handle and they use an old tennis ball. They are laughing and cheering, thoroughly enjoying themselves.

Frank, the eight-year-old is bowling, with Alan, the oldest, having the bat. Maurice, the seven-year-old is the wicketkeeper. Neither of the boys is really athletic. Alan the eldest is troubled by stiffness in his feet, in later years diagnosed as inherited Marie Tooth Syndrome. Frank is more interested in reading than sport. Maurice is the lively one; the one who loves to run and chase; he possesses a strong determination to win. The lads are similarly dressed in handed down clothing, a little shabby but clean. Their feet are protected by heavy leather boots. Short pants are held up by braces over short-sleeved jumpers worn over coloured, long sleeved home-made blouses. The blouses are buttoned at the collar and at the wrist.

The youngest boy, age five, that's me, is standing about twenty feet from the batsman. My job is chasing the ball wherever it may go – 'foxing' we call it. It's the lowliest job on the team.

At the rear of the house, wearing a home-made hessian apron, hanging washing on the line is Veronica, my wonderful Mum. My father had erected the clothes line when we moved into the house three months before, using fencing wire, bush poles and a bush sapling for a prop. Veronica is a pocket-sized, energetic and handsome woman of 38 years.

My mother Veronica at age about 20, c. 1927.

At the south side of the house is Andrew, tending to his small vegetable patch. He is ten years older than Veronica; he wears a beat up felt hat covering his near bald head. He works happily on his knees pulling weeds as he smokes a pipe. His friends call him 'Shoog', a boyhood nickname. I call him Daddy, and I love him dearly.

My father Andrew. He played cricket for suburban club Northcote, c. 1928.

It's a sunny Saturday morning in 1941. Joe Callaghan, our next-door neighbour at Barry's Reef, called for me over the fence that separated our homes. This time it was special; he was taking me into town. It was my friend's pension week, the fortnightly occasion when he went into Blackwood to buy his provisions.

'C'mon, Ian me boy,' he yells. 'Get over here and give me a hand with Dolly. I'm off in a couple of minutes, so get a wriggle on. The shop shuts at twelve.'

I nearly fell over myself as I ran to the gate, shouting. 'Mum, Mum, I'm going with Joe. Mum, I'm going with Joe.' It was so exciting. Joe was taking me with him to Blackwood to do his shopping.

'Alright, Ian.' my mother called from the clothes line. 'You be good for Joe now.'

I waited impatiently in the yard beside Joe's dilapidated lean-to stable as he harnessed Dolly, his brown cart horse. I was far too small to be of any help to him.

'Alright, boy,' he said. 'It's time to go.' He lifted me under my shoulders and sat me firmly on the upholstered seat of the spring cart.

For a little boy living in an isolated, abandoned gold town in the central highlands of Victoria, these occasional trips to town with Joe were a real highlight. I loved riding in the spring cart, perched high beside Joe in the driver's seat. I thought I was 'just it' in a spring cart. It was far more comfortable and prestigious than the common dray that I sometimes rode in with Bill Bunt. I felt very important and was bubbling with excitement at the prospect of the trip and especially of eating the lollies that Joe always bought me.

The spring cart was painted Brunswick green, with the sides and

Barry's Reef about 1870-80. Both Sultan mines are visible. Blue Mount is in the background

shafts decorated with multicoloured scrollwork. It was a truly beautiful cart, Joe's pride and joy. A timber seat ran the width of the vehicle about two feet from the front. Forward in the shafts, was Dolly. The horse was getting old but she was a faithful servant and Joe thought the world of her. So did I.

We had a great view of Dolly's backside with a close-up when she farted and pooed, which was often.

My friend Joe was the typical Australian bushman, with calloused, work-worn hands and wrinkled, weather-beaten skin. His clean-shaven face showed that life had been tough on him. I thought he was very old but in fact he was only in his late fifties; forced to retire early from his timber worker job at Powelltown in Gippsland. Ten years before, a load of logs he was snigging had rolled on him crushing his right leg.

The doctor had to amputate it to save him and he now wore a 'cork' leg. A stiff-legged limp showed that he had some handicap, but most were unaware of the wooden leg. I knew, because I sometimes sat on his knee at his fireside and his leg was hard and inflexible. 'Joe, why have you got a wooden leg?' I asked him once.

Me, standing on the mullock heap of Old Sultan mine, Barry's Reef, c. 1956. Joe Callaghan's house and our old home are in the background.

'Sit still or you'll get splinters in your bum,' was his reply.

His dress was also typically Australian bushman; a navy bluey coat, the ubiquitous, felt hat, stained with sweat, a collarless striped shirt with a flannel singlet beneath and grey cotton work trousers. Heavy, hobnailed boots completed his ensemble. Joe was rough in speech and manner and swore a lot, but a kinder man never lived.

He had never married and lived alone in his tiny shingle-roofed, weatherboard shack on the west side of the twisting mountain road that wound from Trentham to Blackwood. Across the track was the towering mullock heap of the abandoned Old Sultan mine. The vast pile of crushed stone dominated the landscape of Barry's Reef township – a scattering of old homes set in a small clearing of the dense eucalyptus forest.

At this time, the tiny outpost had a population of eleven, including my family, a far cry from the seven thousand residents of its heyday. In modern days it rarely gets a mention on any maps and only a handful know of its existence, nestling in a valley high in the ranges about seventy miles north of Melbourne. At some time government surveyors had renamed it Bayup, but the name didn't stick.

In the 1880s it was a bustling town of hectic activity, an Eldorado, with deep reef mines that yielded gold that was to be eventually measured in tons! They say the Old Sultan alone produced sixty-five tons. Late in the century the gold petered out and the population vanished. When I was a child the area was still littered with the remains of numerous houses and shops in various stages of collapse.

Joe's spring cart lurched and bounced over the bumpy gravel road and we made slow progress to Blackwood, but I didn't care. The journey of about four miles took about an hour as we wended our way through some of the most beautiful bushland in Australia. In many parts the track teetered on the edge of seemingly bottomless gullies, whilst on the other side, great tree clad hills rose to the sky. The bush floor was strewn with native shrubbery and the gullies filled with huge tree ferns, some four or five meters high and perhaps a hundred years old. In winter the bush blazed with the pinks, reds and whites of heath and the gold of wattles. In spring and summer it was carpeted with the massed colour of native wild flowers. In all seasons the pure mountain air was filled with the aroma of eucalyptus. There was also the yellow of the cursed English gorse and broom and the dull green of the blackberry. The latter, allegedly introduced by the famed Baron Von Mueller, went berserk in the Australian climate and spread like wildfire.

A sharp bend at the Bayup post office on Anderson's Corner, run by Mr and Mrs Anderson, and the track wound downwards to the gurgling Lerderderg River, which was nothing more than a tiny mountain stream here at its source. It was spanned by a rickety, single lane timber bridge built eighty years before.

Across the bridge the track turned hard left and wound up a very steep climb into Blackwood. This climb was too much for Dolly so Joe always took a detour, and before the bridge he'd turn right, following a little used path that ran beside the river. Shortly, we would cross a stony ford, pass the sports ground and there ascend a less steep climb into town. It was still hard going and Dolly had to stop frequently for a spell, her sides heaving as she sucked in volumes of air.

'Why do you call her Dolly, Joe?' I asked.

Joe grinned. 'After me sister, little mate. Her name's Dolly and me horse is built like her, especially across the arse.'

That seemed reasonable to me.

Chapter Two

BLACKWOOD TOWNSHIP ~ SAUSAGES ~ BARRY'S REEF AND THE OLD SULTAN MINE.

'Whoa, Dolly.' Called Joe as we reached the front of the Blackwood Co-Op Store, the only shop in town. Dolly plodded gratefully to a halt and Joe climbed stiffly from the cart, reaching into the back for Dolly's chaff-filled nose bag, which he hung around her neck. The horse began eating immediately.

My driver lifted me down and we made our way into the store where we were greeted warmly by a smiling Maurice Richards, the Co-Op Manager.

The atmosphere in that store is with me still; the smells and sights still linger. From the bare Baltic pine floorboards to the beautiful tongue-and-groove timber ceiling were shelves, all stacked generously with packaged and canned food. Piled at the back of the shop were hessian bags filled with potatoes, sugar and grain and calico sacks of flour and porridge oats.

I'd watch enthralled as Mr Richards prepared Joe's order, weighing sugar, flour, biscuits and salt in heavy brown paper bags, which he bound with string that hung from a roll attached to the ceiling. He would twist the string around his fingers and with one sharp jerk, snap it cleanly. I was fascinated by this. It took me another thirty years to find out how he did it.

My favourite view was of the shelves stacked with the big tins of Brockhoff and Guest biscuits. Mr Richards kept any that were broken for kids like me and I usually scored a handful in a paper bag.

With four sixpenny plugs of almost black pipe tobacco and a loaf of bread added to the contents of the Colonial Refinery hessian sugar bag, which served as Joe's shopping bag, we had completed the grocery shopping.

Joe grinned at Mr Richards with a twinkle in his eye. 'I almost forgot. You'd better give young Ian some lollies, Maurice.'

This was the moment I had waited for and Joe handed me a penny. Mr Richards waited patiently as I made my selection from the jars that rested on the counter top. 'No need to hurry, Ian. Take your time,' said Mr Richards warmly.

I agonised over this important decision. Two boiled lollies, two humbugs, four aniseed balls and two barley sugar twists and my penny was spent.

Apart from the hotel, the Co-Op was the only business in town. The old building on the west side of the street, opposite the hotel, housed the butcher shop and the post office as well as the grocery and stock feed we had just left.

Joe didn't drink, so we didn't go to the pub. All that remained was the shopping for the meat in the meat department next door, the floor was an inch deep in fresh sawdust, as was the practice at the time.

The butcher was William Sweet, Bill to everyone in the district. He was a descendant of the first settlers in what had then been called Red Hill. He had worked for many years as the butcher and everyone knew and liked him.

'What'll it be today, Joe?' asked Bill as he honed an already razor sharp blade on a steel that hung at his hip. Joe handed him his written order.

Hanging all about were the cut down carcasses of pigs, cattle and sheep. There was no electricity in Blackwood for refrigeration or anything else, and I don't know how the meat was kept fresh, but probably by blocks of ice in a cool room.

Bill skilfully carved Joe's order; some beef for stew, lamb chops, steaks and some sausages. I still yearn for the taste of those sausages made by Bill; real meat, spiced and stuffed into gut skins. Joe knew I liked them and never missed making sure there were three or four extras for me. A pig's head was a standing order.

'See you next time, Joe,' said the butcher. 'Hope you enjoy the sausages, Ian.'

'Yes, thank you, Mr Sweet. I will.' My parents had taught me to always say 'thank you' and address adults politely.

The trip home was a happy one, Joe puffing contentedly on his pipe and me munching my lollies, bursting with stories for my brothers and Mum and Dad.

Joe inhaled deeply, a look of contentment on his face. 'Yer can't beat fresh terbaccer, son. And this is Havelock – it's the best there is.'

I would envy him being grown up and smoking a pipe. My Dad smoked a pipe sometimes, too, but mostly he rolled his own cigarettes, very thinly, to make the weed last as long as he could. It was a luxury item for both men.

'Don't forget to keep a couple of lollies for yer brothers, Ian,' Joe reminded me, flicking Dolly with the reins. 'Giddup, girl.'

'Yes Joe. I'll keep them one each,' making a mental note to keep three aniseed balls – the smallest.

The pig's head wrapped in the Argus on the seat beside me always frightened me and sent shivers up my back and made my hair prickle when I thought of it. One time Joe asked me to hand the parcel down to him as we unloaded at his place. I wasn't game to say no but I

Blackwood, where I went shopping with my mate Joe Callaghan. This is how it looks now.

remember the horror I felt as I picked up the head. But Joe loved pig's head, and pig's trotters were a favourite item on his menu too. Me, I loved sausages.

We wound our way home, climbing up the steep track from the gorge, with the usual stops for Dolly to catch her breath.

On this journey Joe showed me where Karl Guggenheimer had recently crashed his car over the edge.

'See. It's still down there,' Joe pointed down the gully

I stared in wonder. We had all heard the story of Karl's crash and miraculous escape from any injury. It was the talk of the district and now I had actually *seen* the spot and I felt specially privileged. I'll bet none of the other kids have seen it.

Hundreds of feet below I could make out the wreck of Karl's old car, battered to bits. It was still there years later; maybe it still is today.

'Good thing he jumped clear early or he'd a been killed for sure,' observed Joe.

Joe Callaghan's home, and to the north 'Taylor's' house (still standing in 2018) where we lived in the early 1940s. Picture taken in 1954 from the top of the Old Sultan mullock heap. Joe's house has now gone and almost the entire area has returned to forest.

We stopped at Anderson's Post Office, which was nothing more than a small cottage with a front room as the office. Joe yarned with Mr Anderson for a time, perched on the edge of the verandah, before we set out on the final leg to home.

We passed the long-deserted schoolyard where once a few hundred children played. In the remnants of the town, the only fully intact building was the timber Mechanics Hall and Library near the banks of the creek. We soon went past this lovely building, set among concealing bushes on our left, about fifty yards from the road.

Dolly plodded on, crossing the small creek before finally breasting the last big hill. On our right the Old Sultan mine mullock heap towered above us, fifty feet high. The blues and greys of slate and the brilliant white of quartz glistened, lit by the lowering sun. At the base of the mullock, only a few yards from the road's edge, was the terrifying shaft. Unfenced and wide open, it went nine hundred feet straight down.

On our left was Joe's tiny cottage and fifty yards on, below the small hill dominated by eucalyptus trees and a huge lightwood tree, was home.

I'll never forget Joe and his kindness to my family. He was our closest neighbour at Barry's Reef and my dearest friend.

Chapter Three

BASALT ~ BEAUFORT ~ DAYLESFORD
AND A MOUTH ORGAN BAND.

We arrived in the Blackwood district in 1938 after a six year stint around Daylesford. There was my mother Veronica, my father Andrew, Mum's brother, my Uncle Roy Ellison, and my three older brothers Alan, Frank and Maurice.

The Depression was supposed to be over, but if it was we hadn't noticed any difference. Dad couldn't have worked at any manual job, even if there had been any, as he was weak from a chronic heart illness and any real exertion left him breathless. I suspect he was a victim of rheumatic fever as a child. It was common among poor people in early times and frequently permanently damaged hearts. Often it laid him up for days, unable to walk, let alone work, but he never complained. In 1931, long before I was born, he had lost his light job as a lift driver and storeman. It was the height of the Depression and the prospect of him finding another job was nil.

Andrew and Veronica, with Mum's sister Dulcie and her husband Albert and their baby son Douglas, moved to the goldfields area of Basalt in March 1932 as a result of a newspaper advertisement.

At the time there was a plan where the government paid the dole and gave what they called 'accommodation assistance' to those who were willing to leave the city and search for gold. The applicants were given a second-hand World War One army tent, a pick, shovel and gold pan. They were also entitled to a small, fortnightly handout of foodstuffs. Everyone called it 'The Dole'. The advertisement that changed their lives had appeared in The Argus:

> Man seeking a partner to work a goldmine at Blanket Flat, near Daylesford. Write to Eric Parsons at Daylesford Hospital.

They wrote to the advertiser and soon received a brief reply, written with a shaky hand:

> Dear Sir
> I would like you to come and see me about this mine of mine its a good offer and a good mine what just needs a bit of working come up and see me soon
> Eric Parsons

Andrew was voted by the group to go to see the man at Daylesford and get the full details.

'It sounds pretty good to me. Better than nothin' anyway,' said Albert in his pommy accent. 'You can get a free train ticket and at least we may have a chance to find a bit of gold.'

So Andrew went. The reconnaissance trip by steam train to Daylesford was a lengthy journey in those days when there was a stop to change trains at Woodend.

Eric Parsons turned out to be an old man, a patient and resident of the Daylesford hospital. Andrew found him resting in bed in a large ward at the hospital and figured that he was a more or less permanent patient. The old man explained to Andrew that he was 'too crook to work the mine' himself and the deal was a split of all the gold uncovered fifty-fifty. 'I'll trust you mate. You look honest to me.'

Eric said that there was a small furnished hut on the site as well. It seemed a good offer and Andrew took it up without hesitation, surprised that Eric could be so trusting with someone he had never met before.

With a shake of hands to seal the contract the two said farewell.

'Just drop my share in to me when you come in to get the dole. You should pick up a fair bit,' said a beaming Eric, seemingly confident that he would soon be receiving a regular income from gold. Armed with a rough map of the mine's location, Andrew delivered the news to the excited household back in Melbourne.

Mum decided it was then a good time to announce that she was pregnant. Oh boy!

Two days later, the quartet collected their camping gear from the Essendon town hall, and staggering under their huge load of tent, shovels dishes, pick, blankets and luggage, made their way to Spencer Street (Southern Cross) station and took the government-financed seventy mile train trip to Daylesford. The train hissed and steamed its way north eventually arriving at Daylesford. Here the group spied a horsedrawn cab awaiting fares amongst the line up of several hire cars, all eager to take passengers. The cabby was old and sat with a resigned, dispirited look on his bearded face; obviously not doing much business with the advent of modern cars.

'Let's go in the old buggy,' said Andrew. 'It's a bit different, so why not, and there's a lot of room for our stuff.' The cabby was pleased to have paying passengers and happily delivered them to a spot beneath a massive old tree, outside a pub at the bottom of Vincent Street. As they drove, Veronica sang softly the words of a popular song of the time:

> The shabby old Cabby sits high on his shelf, calling to everyone there, if you've got a little lady you're fond of, just call for the shabby old cabby.

Andrew Arthur Braybrook, my Dad, about 1933. There are very few photos of him in my posession.

The group alighted, with the cabby helping unload their huge amount of baggage.

'We had better stock up with tucker,' ventured Albert. 'There's a big shop over the road.'

The women waited, seated on a circular seat beneath the tree, surrounded by their various belongings while the men crossed the road to Evans and Evans store diagonally opposite. Presenting their dole entitlement dockets, the men half-filled a sugar bag with provisions. Tinned food, bread, flour, sugar, salt, golden syrup, tea and dripping. The golden syrup was for baby Douglas. With that completed, and with the last of their money, they hailed a hire car for the trip to Blanket Flat.

The car was a 1928 Chevrolet sedan, driven by a whiskery, red-faced man in his fifties. 'Eric Parsons mine? Oh yeah. That's at Basalt not Blanket Flat. It's about five miles out. That'll cost yer three and sixpence.' He spoke with suspicion, making a judgment of the group by their raggedy appearance. Andrew produced the money and they loaded their mountain of gear into the car and on the luggage rack at the rear end.

The Chev lurched and bounced its way over the rough bush road to the site of the mine, a desolate, baked earth area alongside the road. Basalt was nothing more than a locality, there were no houses and no people – it was just a small clearing in the thick bush.

'There she is mates,' announced the driver. 'Old Eric's gold mine. It's all yours.'

The group stared in disbelief at a scattering of rubbish and remnants of buildings.

'Where's the house?' queried Dulcie.

The driver threw his head back and laughed. 'You mean Eric's humpy? Fell down bloody years ago. Hooroo, I'm off. Good luck!'

In the falling darkness the sorry group set up camp in the old army tent. Little Douglas slept in an abandoned motor car that was rotting beneath a gum tree. There was much consternation when morning daylight revealed it to be a retired hearse.

It's probably needless to say the mine was worthless; for a start the shaft was half-filled with water. The men's attempts to bail it with the rusted bucket attached to the rotting windlass were useless. There was nothing to it but make the best of the situation. It was tough. Meals were sparse, with camp pie, bread and dripping, very weak tea with a dash of sugar and precious little else. One day a nasty argument broke out when Dulcie accused Andrew or Veronica of using some golden syrup. Andrew protested innocence. 'We didn't touch it.'

'You did. I measured it. It's for Douglas, not for us.' She wept. Such was life that a small amount of golden syrup was highly valued.

Dulcie and Albert were not impressed by their circumstances and a few weeks later returned to Melbourne, hopeful of getting a job. They couldn't pack and leave the miserable camp to catch the train quickly enough. I don't know what they used for money. They were quite lucky, as Albert's former employer, the Glenburvie Timber Coy, was able to re-hire him part-time.

A month went by, not a gram of gold was to be found in spite of Andrew's painful efforts at digging at the bottom of the hole. Their situation was hopeless and Veronica shed many tears as they lay sleepless in their old tent.

'Oh what can we do?' cried Veronica, over and over again. 'What can we do?'

They had almost lost all hope when a local man, aware of the situation, called and offered them rooms at his home in nearby Eganstown.

'Just temporary mind you. Just until you find a place for yourselves.'

They gladly accepted and stayed with the man for a couple of months before moving to an abandoned, sparsely furnished hut a few hundred yards further along the road.

Life was a bit better now.

Then Andrew received a notice from the Social Service Department instructing him to report at once to a railway camp at Beaufort, north of Ballarat, where a job awaited him. The notice included a rail and bus travel voucher. The next day he packed a few belongings and caught the bus to Ballarat and thence to Beaufort by train.

It eventuated that he was to be part of a 'susso gang', as they were commonly known, laying new tracks on the Ballarat line. There was a camp on the edge of the town, and food plus a bed with blankets were supplied.

It was heavy work, and on the third day Andrew was helping to lift a redgum sleeper into place when he collapsed, clutching his chest. The head fettler put him on a hand operated trolley and pushed him into town and a doctor for examination. As a result he was sent on to Ballarat Hospital. His weakened heart was unable to cope with the strain of heavy lifting and he was diagnosed with a failing heart. After a week's stay he was discharged and made his way home to Eganstown.

It is an ill wind that blows nobody good and as result Andrew was taken off the dole and awarded an invalid pension. The pay was a little better and the constant pressure of trying to find a job was lifted.

Time passed and there was great joy when they received a rare visitor. It was Veronica's much loved brother, Roy.

Roy Ellison was a rough looking young bloke, only five feet five tall, but all muscle, with a body like a barrel. His grey eyes always twinkled with mischief and his hair stuck out at all angles. And he was as tough as old boots. Young, fit and healthy and, giving him twenty years, he contrasted to my Dad who was never strong. Dad's hair didn't stick out at angles either, probably because he had very little left. He called his dome a skating rink for mosquitoes. Roy's positive attitude and happy demeanour brought new hope to the household. Everybody loved my Uncle Roy.

Uncle had made his welcome appearance one wintry day when he walked in from Ballarat. He was taking a break from his job as 'Scotty The Fighting Whirlwind' with Jimmy Sharman's travelling boxing show and intended to stay only a few days. He ended up staying for several months

'It was a rough life with Sharman,' he told me years later. 'Getting the shit belted out of you by big, strong young farmers and living on cups of tea and smokes. We lived on boiled saveloys for two weeks one time. There was no money – no bloody customers. No bastard had any money. I'd get thirty bob for a win and nothing for a loss. More often than not I didn't even get the thirty bloody bob if I did win.'

Uncle worked hard scouring the district for gold but found nothing but small, valueless specks.

Like Mum and Dad before the pension, Roy existed on the dole; grocery and food vouchers worth about a pound a week. There was no cash money except what he and Dad earned on the side, maybe selling a few rabbit skins.

Late in November Mum went to Melbourne to stay with her sister Dulcie for the birth of Frank at the Women's Hospital, a journey she made again eighteen months later for the birth of Maurice. She went to the city for the births because of a fear that her unmarried state

My mother with me, c.1937.

would be revealed if her children were born locally. The attitude to unmarried mothers, especially those living in sin, was severe in those days.

I came along at the time when they were living for a time at Eganstown, long enough for Mum to be accepted as Mrs Braybrook, so I was born in Daylesford hospital.

Along the way Mum and Dad had gained Alan, my half brother, from the 'Toddler's Home' or somewhere and he had joined our family. Even Alan, as an adult, could not ascertain where he spent his first seven years! Don't ask me how they managed to secure his release from government care, considering their impoverished circumstances. I seriously suspect that they stole him. I'll attempt to explain how Alan fits into the picture later.

* * *

Over the years our family lived in all sorts of abandoned houses scattered throughout the Daylesford area, mostly humpies with surrounds overgrown with blackberries and scrub, and we were as poor as church mice. Our clothes were patched and ill-fitting; always handed down or homemade, but they were always clean. There were no opportunity shops back then.

Mum took her old Singer sewing machine everywhere and was forever darning, sewing and mending. Our diet was poor and of comfort we had little but we kids were always neat and clean, even in the lowliest bush hut, Mum saw to that.

In spite of our circumstances we were a happy family and I didn't feel at all underprivileged. I guess we knew no different and presumed everybody lived the same. At any rate, the people we had contact with shared our lifestyle, like Jack and Alice Porter with their daughter Betty, who was my age. They were neighbours at Eganstown for a time and Alice and Mum remained lifelong friends.

One of the rare opportunities to earn money came when Dad and Roy formed a mouth organ band with Len Lester. They weren't very good but scored a job playing each Saturday night at the Eganstown pub dance hall which was attached to the main building. They each got paid three shillings and all the cakes and scones that they could eat. No free beer though!

The trio also played cricket for the local side. Dad was a very good player, having previously played for suburban Northcote as a competent bowler and batsman. He loved the game, and under his tuition, Uncle and Lennie became quite useful players. Uncle hated the 'bloody Pommy game' as he called it, but played to keep Dad happy.

Lennie owned a 1920 Model T Ford, cut down into a buckboard type truck, and it was their mode of travel to the game on Saturdays. They were happily driving home one evening after a shock win that had infuriated their opponents, a talented Creswick team, jammed into the tiny cabin with Uncle sipping on a precious bottle of beer. The hot exhaust pipe was touching a pile of straw in the back and eventually it caught alight. Our boys were quite oblivious to the growing conflagration behind them as they rattled happily along.

Behind them, a startled motorist in a sleek 1930 Chevrolet, tried desperately to warn them by leaning on his horn button.

'Listen to that smart bastard,' grumbled Lennie. 'Wants all the bloody the road. I'll show the bloody mongrel,' and he planted the foot. The old car wobbled and lurched as it topped forty miles an hour, the speed fanning the blaze until it was almost engulfing the entire rear end.

The driver behind, unable to overtake on the narrow road, and partly blinded by smoke and embers, pressed more frantically on the horn. Lennie cursed and went even faster careering downhill at a breakneck speed.

Dad twisted his body in the confined space and glanced backwards. To his horror he spotted the inferno, scarcely able to believe his eyes.

'Lennie! Lennie!' he shouted. 'For God's sake stop! We're on fire. We're on bloody fire.'

There was a mad scramble and Lennie pushed with all his strength on the brake pedal. The brakes weren't much value at the best of times and it took what seemed like a mile to bring the vehicle to a shuddering stop. The beaming driver of the Chevrolet whizzed by with a cheery wave and a final toot as the men flogged the blaze with the hessian spud bags that served as draught-stopping floor mats. Eventually the fire died and the cricketers resumed their journey. Uncle took a deep swig at his bottle.

'Christ it's been a bloody good day,' he chortled.

'It's all right for you, you bloody idiot,' snorted Lennie. 'Look at me bloody truck! I'm gonna have to rebuild the bastard.'

Dad smiled, sipping from the bottle and dragging deeply on a cigarette. He too felt it had been a bloody good day.

Chapter Four

Eganstown ~ Roy Ellison ~ bush drive ~ the rifleman ~ a new home.

'I'm bloody sick of this.' Uncle announced one morning. 'Why don't we piss off to Blackwood? You hear of blokes finding a bit of bloody gold over there.'

We were pretty settled at Eganstown with Alan, now seven, and Frank, aged five, at school. Nevertheless, Dad and Mum had little hesitation in agreeing with the move. Anything would be better than what we had.

Dad had somehow obtained a pushbike, so next day he rode through the bush, returning late in the afternoon with the news that he'd found an abandoned house at Blackwood that would suit us.

Uncle asked Lennie if he would shift us in his small truck.

'I'll take youse as far as I can, but by Christ I'm not driving on the main road. I ain't got no license and me truck's not registered. We'll have to go by Sullivan's track through the bush.' Lennie was adamant and he received no argument.

Before we left though, my mother had one very important and urgent task. She arranged for me to be baptised at the Methodist Church in Eganstown. The only other church there was Catholic and that was definitely not acceptable. To become a temporary Methodist was moderately acceptable for an Anglican, but never a Catholic. The entire family trooped off to the service and Mum was now happy to know that if I died I would go to Heaven. Amen.

On Saturday morning the truck arrived, chugging and fuming as most Model T Fords did. Lennie sat in the cabin while Uncle and Dad loaded the tray with our scant furniture, odds and ends, six chooks and Mum's pot plants. At 10 o'clock we set off.

The track hadn't been used for donkey's years and Dad and Uncle had to walk ahead clearing the path of large branches, scrub and fallen trees. Alan and Frank walked beside, while Mum nursed her beautiful baby (me) with Maurie wedged into the seat between her and Lennie. After an exhausting two hours we had covered about eight or ten miles and arrived at the edge of the Trentham to Blackwood road.

Lennie drew the truck to a halt. 'This is it,' he announced. 'This is as far as I'm going. Youse can unload here. I ain't goin' no further.'

'What the hell are you on about, you bloody idiot. You can shove that up your arse,' shouted Uncle Roy.

'You can't leave us here Lennie,' yelled a bewildered Dad. 'How will we get our stuff to Blackwood?'

Uncle was not as polite. 'You stupid old bastard!' he roared. 'It's five f...n miles to Blackwood. You'll take us there you ignorant old prick. A man orta belt you, you mangy, fly-blown bastard. Bugger you.' This was getting pretty serious

'Don't swear at me you sawn off little dog,' bellowed Lennie. 'I told you I wouldn't drive on the main roads. No further mate! Not a bloody inch. And I'll have your guts for garters ya mongrel if you keep this up. Unload me f...n truck.'

'Get nicked,' shouted a furious Uncle.

With that, Lennie leapt from the truck, glowing with rage as Mum and we kids cowered in the cabin. He flew at Uncle with his fists flying, but all he hit was the air. Uncle showed the fancy footwork of his years in the boxing ring, ducking, dodging and weaving. This further infuriated Lennie.

'Stand still so I can hit you, you sawn off little bastard.'

Uncle didn't oblige and after a couple of futile minutes, a gasping Lennie gave up the chase, leaping onto the back of the truck. Grunting and heaving he began hurling our possessions onto the ground. There was a hell of a din when the box of six chooks hit the turf, the frantic squawks and frenzied flapping echoed through the bush.

'Cut it out, you stupid maniac,' yelled Uncle. 'You'll kill the bloody chooks and smash every bloody thing.'

With that, Lennie leapt from the truck, threw open the driver's door and emerged with a .22 rifle. He climbed back amongst the load and clutching the rifle in one hand he hurled our goods to the ground with the other.

'Try to stop me and I'll bloody shoot you, you little prick,' Lennie directed his fury at Uncle.

In minutes, all our property littered the roadside. Mum, clutching baby me and a petrified Maurie, scrambled from the cabin as Lennie leapt in, still brandishing the rifle.

'I'll get you for this, you gutless animal,' yelled Uncle.

'Get stuffed, bastard,' retorted Lennie, and with a cough and splutter, the Model T took off through the bush the way we had come.

Everybody was stunned speechless by this sudden turn of events, but we had little time to think of the predicament, as almost immediately, an old tip truck rumbled down the road.

'Looks like you could use a bit of help,' grinned the grey-bearded driver as he surveyed the scene.

There was some quick explanation from Dad, and pretty soon our possessions were loaded into the tipper.

'You know it's funny when you think of it,' grinned Dad, and before long everybody was laughing, even Mum who had been terrified by the events.

Mum and I rode up front with the driver with everyone else in the back with the goods and chattels and we headed for Blackwood. Light rain began to fall, and by the time we arrived at our new home it was bucketing down.

'Everyone out and I'll back up to the road edge,' called our driver and we all complied, standing drenching wet.

The old fashioned tipping body of the truck was raised and lowered by a hand-cranked cable on a drum. It was secured by a ratchet. The man quickly reversed the truck, coming to a jarring halt as the wheels hit the gutter.

Maybe the ratchet wasn't properly secured, but for whatever reason, the sudden stop caused the ratchet to let go. The tipping body rose rapidly, depositing furniture, chooks, pot plants, clothing and food in a soggy heap on the roadside. The rain tumbled down.

Mum sat on an upturned tallboy safe amid the sodden mess and wept.

Chapter Five

STOLEN CHILDREN ~ BALLARAT ORPHANAGE ~ THE DEPRESSION ~ DEATH OF A SON.

We did a lot of moving when I was a kid, so much so that I can't recall half the places. But during the first eight years of my life we rarely moved beyond the Blackwood, Trentham, Daylesford and Ballarat area. Later on we were to move much further afield but I guess it's because I spent my youngest years around Blackwood and Trentham that I always feel as if I belong there.

And there were many things that I didn't know about until I was much older, things that my mother never fully explained to me. For instance, as a child, I wasn't aware that both Mum and Dad had been married before and each had other families.

Mum was married at seventeen, a child of a broken home. Her mother had run off with a man said to be an Indian. Her Dad had abandoned them when he first learned of the affair. He is said to have gone to America, never to return. As a result, Mum and her two sisters and three brothers were placed in children's homes and later 'boarded out' to a foster mother, Ma Scott, of Coburg. She was a good woman who saved the family from an orphanage life, but was as tough as a supermarket steak.

Mum was always defiant and strong-willed and never got along with Ma. She could barely wait to leave home and at fifteen she took a job as housekeeper for a doctor at Sunbury Mental Hospital. There she met a young man named Murphy, and as a lass longing to be loved, she fell pregnant. She tried hard to conceal the fact, but eventually had to confess to her employer.

In shame and disgrace she was returned to care at the Presbyterian Girls' Home in Fitzroy. Her baby, whom she named Ron, was born at the Women's Hospital in May 1923. Her son was taken from her a month after his birth and made a State Ward. The boy's father was charged with carnal knowledge, but the charges were dropped when he persistently denied his role. Probably Veronica was judged by the authorities as just another immoral social welfare supported girl not worthy of any fuss.

In late 1925, Veronica met and married a young man from the Rushworth district and was then given custody of her baby. She soon had another son and she named him Tommy.

The marriage ended when she discovered evidence that caused her to believe that her husband was molesting the children. She was devastated and fled to Melbourne where she was to meet my father, Andrew 'Shoog' Braybrook at Diamond Creek.

Ron and Tommy Collard, my half brothers.

He was seeking a housekeeper and carer for his children, as his wife had died giving birth to their sixth child, Alan. Mum saw his ad in The Argus, eventually found her way to Diamond Creek for an interview, was hired and moved in.

Almost immediately, Andrew lost his job. So soon on top of the loss of his wife and being left with five young children and an infant, this was a devastating blow. Australia was deep in the depression, and he couldn't hope to find another job, especially having a weak heart as he did.

It wasn't long before Veronica and Andrew began to share their lives, no doubt a comfort to one another. By then the family was living in wretched poverty, existing on handouts from the local Church of England, which they devoutly attended.

Soon, acting on information from the church and 'for the good of the children', the Childrens' Welfare people came and took Andrew's and Veronica's children away to the Ballarat Orphanage. The couple was distraught and the children terrified as they were piled into a car with their few belongings and driven off to they knew not where. Were these not 'stolen children'?

Two weeks later, Mum's youngest boy, Tommy, took ill with pneumonia. The police called to notify Mum of Tommy's sickness but she was unable to reach the orphanage before he died, in spite of her desperate effort.

I can only guess what transpired then and later, but I do know the families were broken up forever. Somehow, when he was seven, baby Alan finished up with Andrew's and Veronica's new family of Frank, Maurice and me.

I reckon that Andrew stole him away, which would explain why we never stopped in one place for long; sometimes only a day or two.

We boys didn't know until we were men that our parents weren't married until 1941 when a family friend and Church of England minister, Reverend Mr Alley, organised Mum's divorce. That was when I was four.

My Mum was a real battler, not one of the $1500 a week 'battlers' the P.M. John Howard often spoke of. She had a tough life from go to whoa, even compared to the standard of those days.

She was a good looking woman, a mere five feet tall, always neat and tidy, even in her home-made dresses and hessian aprons, hand-trimmed with brightly coloured material. She had dark hair and brown eyes; eyes that sometimes reflected her bitterly hard life. She remained that way right up until the day she died in 1983, aged 77.

Like Uncle, my Mum was made tough, with the heart of an elephant and the stamina of an olympian. But she was always a lady. Even when cooking over an open fire outdoors or washing in a tub beneath a pepper tree, she displayed the best manners and a true dignity. In spite of the deal fate handed her, she was never one to complain and used to be always singing as she worked around what we called a house; in the earlier days, often draughty humpies with dirt floors, no running water or electricity and outside thunderboxes. A decent bathroom was only a dream and at best the house was lined with hessian and paper pasted on with flour and water. The mice found it quite delicious.

She sang songs like 'The Bluebird of Happiness' and 'Goodnight Sweetheart', songs I still love. God knows she had little to sing about.

Mum was hard on us kids; 'a good clip around the ears' was common, but she loved us and cared for us very well.

Dad was a kind, loving and caring man, as gentle as they come. Everybody called him Shoog but I don't know how he got this childhood nickname. To me he was not Shoog but simply Daddy. He was liked and admired by all he met. My esteemed Uncle Roy once told me he was the best bloke he had ever known. Coming from a man I much admired, it was very meaningful and made me proud of a father I barely remembered.

Dad never showed the pain he must have felt from his bad heart or from the heartbreak and hurt he must have had inside. Life had handed him a pretty rotten deal. He played with us boys, encouraged us and took us for long, educational walks through the bush, the bush that he loved best, next to my mother and his sons. Like Mum he never complained and he sang, joked and laughed a lot.

* * *

Somehow we had found a home at Blackwood, not much different from the rest; a tired old shack that had been nothing more than a miner's humpy even in its heyday. We'd hardly moved in when the owner turned up from somewhere and ordered us to leave.

'What we should do is build our own bloody house,' said Uncle Roy. And they did.

Uncle and Dad spent the next few days scrounging basic items for the venture and pretty soon we had an impressive array of gear stacked at the back of the house. There was canvas, wire, a bag of lime, a 5 gallon drum of dripping, nails and a roll of hessian among a number of other items. Where the two got the stuff nobody knew and nobody asked.

One morning Dad and Uncle set off to find a location for the new home and within a couple of hours they were back.

'We've found a spot just up the hill above the sports ground,' announced Dad, and before we knew it, we had moved there in a horse and wagon Uncle borrowed from a local.

The site was high on the hill, more like on the edge of a cliff, but it was public land and it gave some privacy. The bush all around was thick and a small clearing had first to be made. Dad and Uncle got stuck into it, felling a number of trees with a rather blunt axe.

As they worked at a distance, a stranger rode into the camp on horseback. He looked about quizzically.

'Planning to stay here?' he directed the question to Mum.

'Yes, for a while,' said Mum. 'We've no home and we are building a shelter here for the time being. That's my husband and my brother,' She indicated the two axemen.

'Well I'm Clarrie Spence, the Forest Ranger.' Pushing back his hat he scratched his head thoughtfully as his eyes took in the scene; a woman with four small children, with a few pitiful belongings piled on the open ground.

'Look Missus, you're not allowed to do this, but I don't know anything about it, see? I haven't seen you. Just tell the men not to cut down any big stuff.' He tipped his hat.

'Good day, missus.' He smiled, and turning, rode his horse back the way he had come.

As Mum prepared a meal over a campfire Dad and Uncle erected the new house. The frame of green saplings lashed together with wire; the walls were of hessian and the roof of canvas, secured to the frame by large nails. It was about twenty feet square, divided into two rooms by hanging hessian. There were bunks for us kids that Uncle made from saplings, with hessian spud bags stuffed with leaves for mattresses. Mum and Dad had a real bed.

The entire task was completed in a day and by nightfall we were in occupancy. For us kids it was all very exciting.

All that remained next day was to waterproof the walls with a coating of melted fat mixed with lime, and the building of a stone and mud fireplace and chimney. It wasn't much, but nobody could put us out. Uncle christened it 'The Villa'. Dad called it the 'Blackwood Members' Stand' as we had a perfect, uninterrupted view of the sports ground far below. Dad could sit under a tree and watch his beloved cricket without leaving home. Sheer luxury!

Chapter Six

Black Friday - roof collapse - Ballarat - Bunninyong - Blakeville.

The big bush fire of 1939 almost burnt us out. I don't recall it, as I was so young, but heard the tale from Mum many times.

It was a stinking hot day in January that followed a stinking hot night, and even as we rose from our beds, they knew we were in for it. There could be no mistake; a big fire was heading our way. The roasting wind screeched by, laden with ash that fluttered earthward or swirled wildly through the air. And the smell of burning eucalyptus was unmistakable.

By mid-morning the sky was dark with smoke which totally obscured the fierce sun and cast an eerie, frightening glow as we were evacuated to the public hall in town. Alf, one of the local fire brigade men, came and got us in his truck and we all crammed into the tiny hall, along with every other woman and child in the area.

We were able to take our new dog Darkie, a bit of a cocker spaniel, but in the rush to escape Mum had left her chooks locked up and she fretted about them constantly.

Dad and Uncle went off with the rest of the men to fight the fire which was driven by a rushing, raging north wind. Somehow or other, those valiant, exhausted men held the fire at bay until late afternoon when a wind change turned the fire back on itself. A couple of hours later, it started to rain and we were saved. The town and all its residents survived unscathed but not so fortunate were the 74 people in other parts of the state who tragically and horribly perished in the fires.

Next morning, we all tumbled out of the hall to return to our homes. Our family, with Darkie trotting ahead, plodded wearily up the hill toward The Villa.

It was a depressing scene with the area surrounding the hut blackened and still smouldering. Miraculously, The Villa was still standing, completely undamaged, in a sea of grey and black ash. Even Mum's chook shed, including its ash covered and bewildered occupants, remained intact and so did her tiny garden patch. Our main loss was the small water tank that Dad had bought from a local for five bob. It had sprung a leak when the heat from the fire melted the soldered joints. Much of the water that Dad and Uncle had carried in our homemade kerosene tin buckets from the Lerderderg up the steep bank to The Villa was lost. The group stared in silence at the depressing scene.

'I told you the other day that a fire was coming,' said Uncle. 'Remember when I lit that match and it had a white flame? It's a sure sign of bushfire, any bushman will tell you that.' Nobody argued the point. The two men did their best to clean up the mess but it was pretty hopeless. 'We'll just have to wait for the wind and rain to do the job,' sighed Dad.

Alan had wandered off through the nearby bush to explore the area when he came upon one of the tragic victims of the fire, a badly burnt three foot long black snake. The creature writhed helplessly as Alan approached, doing its utmost to lash out with bared fangs. Alan picked up a stick and began to poke at the snake further tormenting and terrifying it.

Mum, preparing a billy of tea under the big tree spotted him and seizing a big stick ('a bloody log,' Alan later described it), she rushed over and whacked him a beauty around his bare legs. Poor Alan collapsed with pain and lay there in the black ash sobbing as Mum killed the snake with the stick.

'Don't you ever play with a snake again,' shrieked Mum as she hit him again around the back. Alan never forgot that incident. My guess is that she took her frustration out on Alan.

Within a week, things were back to normal. Alan and Frank were attending the Blackwood school, and in February, when holidays were over, they took Maurie along with them. Now, only I remained at home through the day with Mum, Dad and Uncle. Life went on as before with the two men spending most of their day fossicking along the river for gold. They found none.

In March, the first of the Autumn rain began to fall. It was coming down in torrents as we went to bed. 'Pissin' down,' as Uncle described it. As we slept, the flat tarpaulin roof formed puddles of water. The roof sagged and the puddles grew larger and heavier. We slept on soundly.

At about five in the morning, all hell broke loose when the enormous weight of the accumulated water on the canvas roof caused the nails holding it to let go. The leaden, sodden roof collapsed with a rush on the sleeping family. Nobody had any idea what had happened and the rain pelted down through the blackness of the night.

'What the bloody hell's going on?' Uncle roared. It was bedlam, with shouts from Dad, cries from Mum, whimpers from the kids and increasingly loud cursing from Uncle.

'The bloody roofs collapsed,' came a muffled bellow from Uncle as he struggled to free himself and us from beneath the tarpaulin. It was an awful experience, made worse by the rain and the pitch black of the night. We couldn't see a thing until finally Dad managed to strike a match. Eventually, with the light from countless matches, we all struggled free, looking like a bunch of waterlogged rats. Mum herded us kids down the back and into the thunderbox.

'Hop into the lavatory, you boys. At least you'll be dry there,' she ordered and fumbled her way back toward the collapsed Villa. She returned minutes later with our wet blankets.

'Wrap yourselves in these and try to get warm.' This was a tall order under the circumstances.

Have you ever spent three hours on a stormy, black night with three others crammed into a backyard dunny?

Daylight finally came and the adults emerged from their shelter beneath the tarp. We kids bolted from the dunny toward the fire that

Dad had already kindled. The rain had stopped, but the water still dripped from the trees above. Mum made us a warm drink and we toasted damp bread on the fire coals, spreading it with wet dripping. Steam rose from our clothes as we all huddled around the big fire.

'I dunno about you,' announced Uncle, 'but I've had a bloody enough. I'm pissin' off to Melbourne right now.'

Within an hour he had rolled his swag, kissed Mum and us kids, shook Dad's hand and was gone. We didn't see him again for six years.

Dad went into town, found Billy Sullivan and got him to use his truck to move what was left of our possessions. By dinner time we were in Ballarat and Dad had found us a new house, an abandoned and roughly furnished hut in Larter Street, Eureka, owned by a friend of his brother, Sidney. It was a run-down old house with few amenities, but we were used to such things. It was off a lane behind a bakery. The other boys briefly attended the Golden Point primary school which was nearby.

We didn't hang about there long, and three weeks later we moved to Buninyong where Dad was made caretaker of the local gardens in return for rent of a very dilapidated and partly furnished house. It was, however, in a very pleasant location, right in the middle of the botanic gardens.

The three older boys resumed school at Bunninyong, but not for long. For an unknown reason we moved again to yet another old shack adjacent to the Geelong Road. Nearby was the old Buninyong Butter Factory which was being used as a training camp

Ian at Bunninyong, aged about four.

for about a hundred army men. Two months in one spot appeared to be all that Mum and Dad could bear.

In the meantime, Frank had given himself an awful fright. Armed with a box of matches he lit a small fire in the long grass. To his horror it soon became a BIG fire. It was huge and raced away out of control. Luckily, the army men at the butter factory spotted the blaze and managed to extinguish it before it did any real harm.

Frank stood and watched the action, transfixed by his handiwork, still clutching the box of matches. One of the soldiers spotted him. 'Look at that kid. He must have started it, he has a box of matches.'

The Sergeant, a fierce looking bloke, approached poor trembling Frank and gave him a very severe lecture.

'Never ever play with matches, son,' he growled, 'You were lucky we were here or you would have burnt down the town. I won't tell your parents this time. Now go home and put the matches away.'

Frank quickly did as he was told. An angry lecture from a man

The family at Bunninyong. Mum & me (front left), Alan and Frank (wearing caps) and Maurie (front right).

wearing a uniform was enough to cure him of playing with matches for the rest of his life! I'm sure he never played with fire again.

'We're moving back to Blackwood,' Mum told us one morning soon after, and by morning tea time we had our gear loaded onto someone's truck, provided via Dad's brother, and shoved off. Oddly enough, we had more furniture than we arrived with. I know it was sometime in 1940 because Bing Crosby had a hit on the wireless, 'Swinging on a Star'.

We didn't go to Blackwood but to a hut in Blakeville, a settlement of a scattering of old houses and a school. The older boys began school there, but in four weeks we moved again. Mum had found a house in Blackwood.

Back in Blackwood we took up an abandoned shack on the Golden Point road. The yard was overgrown with long grass, blackberries and broom. It was a dreadful place, set in a small bush clearing, three miles from the shop and school and it was on the verge of collapse. It didn't even have a dunny, let alone a bathroom. Dad and Alan's first job was to dig a hole, make a seat of saplings and erect a stringy bark screen around it for a thunderbox.

The roof of the house was missing shingles everywhere and none of the three rooms was lined. There was what remained of a Planet wood stove, and Mum struggled to cook our meals on the monster. Nothing Dad could do would stop it from filling the house with choking smoke whenever it was alight. Gee, it was good to be back in Blackwood!

Chapter Seven

ANOTHER MOVE ~ GOAT'S MILK ~
JOE CALLAGHAN ~ BARRY'S REEF.

We had been in our new residence only two weeks when a man named Billy Gribble came by and offered us rent-free use of a house he owned in the town 'for a while'.

It was a shabby house, but a big step up. Bill Gribble also gave Mum a day of paid work cleaning his house. He was obviously a good man, concerned for the welfare of this poor family. He even gave us a billy can of milk and some homemade butter.

We couldn't pack and move to the house quick enough. Mum got stuck into cleaning the inside, and Dad and the big kids worked hard outside. It wasn't a real flash house but we had a dunny of corrugated iron, a shed, a chook house and a wash-house-cum-bathroom with a copper. The kitchen had a stove and we had a large water tank.

In no time, Dad also had the beginnings of a vegetable garden and Mum, of course, had her flower garden up and running almost instantly. I hoped we'd stay forever and so did my brothers who had started school, which was just up the hill a bit.

One of our neighbours, Mrs Curtis, had a goat which gave milk to spare. She used to regularly send over half a bucket, handing it over the fence to Alan. We were grateful for the kindness and devoured the milk with gusto.

One day Mum was visiting Mrs Curtis, who had a small baby, and as she chatted in the washhouse she noticed a bucket filled with soiled, foul smelling nappies. It was the bucket we received our milk in!

Mum continued to accept the offering but never again did a drop pass our lips!

Dad never gave up looking for gold and one day a month later, as he panned in the Lerderderg, a stranger drove up in a horsedrawn cart and stiffly stepped down.

Dad looked him over; a man perhaps in his fifties, rotund, weather beaten, smiling, clean-shaven and smoking a pipe.

'G'day mate. Any luck?' he said as he approached, dragging one leg stiffly. He extended a hand.

'I'm Joe Callaghan from up at Barry's Reef, been wanting to catch up with you.' And here on the banks of the Lerderderg River began a family friendship that lasted to death. The two sat on the riverbank and yarned for an hour before Dad invited his visitor up to the house.

Mum was out back feeding her chooks with her special food of cooked food scraps mixed with pollard, a rough form of bran. She swore by it, and besides, it meant she didn't waste a thing from the kitchen.

As she saw the men approaching she dashed inside to make herself presentable, and by the time they arrived she was spick and span with a clean hessian apron, hair brushed and a light smear of precious lipstick. It was 12 o'clock and that was always dinnertime in those days, so Joe stayed on for the meal of bread, homemade butter and jam, washed down with a cup of weak tea.

I liked Joe from the start and he seemed to like me, patting my head and actually talking to me. Most grown ups ignored kids like me, and I was impressed. Late in the afternoon, Joe drove off but he returned next morning.

'Look,' he said as he came inside. 'I don't want to interfere but there's a house next to me for sale. It's not too bad and it's only eight pounds. I'd like you to have a gander at it and if you want it I'll help you buy it. I've got a few bob and I can make you a bit of a loan.'

Mum and Dad were delighted. Their own home had always seemed impossible.

Next day we walked up to Barry's Reef to look the house over, Dad pushing me most of the way in my old pusher.

The house turned out to be pretty good for the price. It had four rooms, all lined with hessian and paper, a dunny and a shed way down the back, each overgrown with blackberries, and there was a corrugated iron washhouse with a tin bath and copper. Out front was a thirty-foot deep well which ensured a constant water supply.

There was a gate leading into Joe's place next door, about fifty yards away, and in times to come I was to use that gate at least once a day.

'We'd like to buy it, Joe,' said Dad. 'But we will need you to lend us all the money. We don't have any I'm afraid.'

'You bet I can loan it to you,' beamed Joe obviously delighted to have neighbours.

'I'll pay the eight quid and you can pay me back at five bob a week. Is that alright?'

The deal was struck and in 32 weeks the house was ours. Now that's the way to buy a house! No lawyers, loan agreements, interest, tax or titles. So we moved yet again and in two days we had settled in at Barry's Reef. Maurie, Frank and Alan weren't all that rapt with the move, preferring to stay in town and near the school, but who

Barry's Reef. My first real home. It was in a state of near collapse in 2018 when this photo was taken. We lived there for almost two years, by far our longest stay in one place.

argued with their parents in those days? From then on, my brothers had to walk the four miles to school each way, every day, rain or shine, more often the former.

Barry's Reef was wonderful and gave us some of the best times of our lives. What's more we stayed there for over a year!

There weren't many residents, about six not counting us, and it didn't take long to get to know them. Behind us was Old Jimmy Johnstone, opposite was the widow Mrs Clara Rae, and down a rough bush track that went into the bush behind the mullock heap were Tommy Johnston and Mr and Mrs Murphy who had the Barry's Reef post office. Not one of them was under sixty.

Jimmy, Mrs Rae and Tommy had been there all their lives. The Murphys and Joe were relative newcomers of a decade or so and the Braybrooks were real blow-ins.

At last we had a house we could call home and everybody worked enthusiastically to make it good. After a few months the old place looked great, with weatherboards freshly painted, the garden blooming and the interior spotless. We had a stretch of grass to play on, usually cricket, because Dad loved to join in, but we also played chasey and hidey and cowboys and Indians.

Cricket was nearly the death of me! No wonder I don't like the game. One day I was wicketkeeping and Frank took a mighty swipe at the ball with the bat, an old shovel handle with the metal socket still attached.

Wham! He hit me right between the eyes. Next thing I knew was opening my eyes as my three brothers looked anxiously down on me. The blow had knocked me unconscious. The boys thought they had killed me and were more concerned for their own hides when Mum got hold of them than for how I was. Hence they were very relieved when I came to.

After serious threats about what they would do to me if I told Mum, the game resumed, me none the worse for the experience, but I still carry the scar on my forehead. Mum found out of course and gave the boys the rounds of the kitchen.

On the rise above our house, at the turn-off to the remains of the brewery, sawmill and Jimmy Johnstone's, was a big lightwood tree. Beneath this tree at the roadside was our mail box, an emptied kerosene tin nailed to a sapling. It wasn't really for mail, as there was no roadside delivery then, all the mail went to Murphy's Post Office for collection. It was, however, used by the mail contractor who was our lifeline to Trentham. In the tin he deposited all manner of goods for us; meat, bread, groceries and the occasional package. Later, there was to be change-over wet batteries for our wonderful wireless.

Mr Robson was the contractor, and he would pick up our orders from the tin on his thrice weekly trips from Trentham to Blackwood and deliver on the next trip. He charged threepence a parcel and never let us down.

As a result of the mail box being there, we kids spent a lot of time at the lightwood tree, it became a favourite spot to play. It was shady on sunny days and acted like an umbrella in the wet. We made tracks for our make-believe toy cars beneath it, and when we played chasey, we chased each other around and round it. It was always 'home' when we played hidey and the safe refuge when we called 'barley' as we played chasey.

It was a magnificent tree, our lightwood tree, far larger than any I have seen since. Maybe it was a blackwood tree, but to us it was lightwood, because that's what Mum called it. 'You kids nick up to the lightwood tree and play,' she'd say to us. Or, 'You boys run up to the lightwood tree and get the meat.'

Our make-believe motor cars that drove on our make-believe roads were a treat; usually a block of wood with Nugget tin wheels that Dad nailed on for us. Sometimes we just used old tobacco tins, without wheels. We had no shop or factory toys but we had a lot of fun beneath the lightwood tree.

Chapter Eight

Gold by the ton – an unusual barber – death of a postmaster.

Barry's Reef! Where the gold was mined in tons! Where the gullies and ridges were littered with old shafts and workings, the remains of quartz stampers and several decaying, abandoned houses.

We boys spent our days roaming the bush with Dad and we knew it well. We did a bit of fossicking in the Split Tree Creek about a mile east, where we would find many small garnets and tiny specks of gold. We knew they were valueless, but finding them was a thrill. Usually we would take them home tied in a corner of our hankies and promptly lose and forget them. When I visited Barry's Reef years later to visit my mother, who moved back there in the 1960s, Mrs Rae still lived there, alone in her decaying humble home. She told me stories of her days growing up at The Reef eighty years before. Pointing to the hills and gullies she'd describe the scene as it was back then.

'Over there were the breweries. There were three of them and thirty pubs. There was four hundred of us kids at the school!'

Pointing to the hills all around she'd describe them alive with activity as miners sought their fortune. She would point out the water races that criss-crossed the hills, still clearly visible then and still carrying water when it rained heavily.

Built to carry water for the miners to wash their dirt, the races wound their way for miles, each up to ten feet deep; all dug by hand through stone and gravel with pick and shovel. They were an amazing feat of engineering which appeared to make water run uphill. The men who dug the race sold the water to the gold seekers and thus earned their living. The water was released from hand-dug dams. Shaw's Lake on a hilltop near the Blackwood mineral springs is a surviving example.

Dear Mrs Rae was by then a little eccentric. Several times she told me the story about the pilot who landed his aircraft in her backyard.

'The cheeky devil. I slapped him in the face and told him to nick off.' Presumably the man leapt into his plane and took off to a safer place.

As a girl, Mrs Rae used to dance and roller skate on the parquetry floor of the Mechanics Institute. The building still stood in perfect condition when I was young but was destroyed by fire in the 1960s. A group of young campers was suspected of lighting the fire deliberately, but nobody was charged.

Mrs Rae remembered when Barry's Reef was a bustling, prosperous town with mines like the True Blue, British Lion, Four and Bella, Nalders, The Sultan Co. and The New Sultan Co. that produced between them officially, a massive sixty-five tons of gold, but probably much more.

* * *

Next to Joe, my best friend at Barry's Reef was Tommy Johnston, whose cottage was tucked up a track behind the Old Sultan mine. He was about seventy years old, with thin white hair, a warm cheery face and a magnificent white beard. He had only one leg, having lost one when he was crushed by the wheel of the bakers' cart when he was eleven. He was the town baker's boy and skipped from door to door with a basket full of fresh loaves that were piled in the horsedrawn cart he drove. One day he missed his footing and slipped beneath a moving wheel, his leg was smashed beyond repair. To save his life, the local doctor amputated it in the crude town hospital. Tommy quickly adapted to hopping around on one leg, sometimes aided by a crutch.

When he was eighteen he quit working in the bakery and bought a pub, which he kept for many years until the town was finally deserted. He then retired to his little cottage and his vegetable garden where he grew wonderful vegetables, which he was glad to share with us. The house yard was neat and tidy, and matched the interior of his cottage which was immaculate, with not a thing out of place. The open fireplace in the kitchen was always glistening white from regular coatings of pipe clay. The bare floorboards were scrubbed clean and smooth, as was the old pine kitchen table.

Tommy was my barber, and every couple of weeks I would make my way to his place for a trim. I reckon I had the most unusual barber ever. Tommy would sit me on a chair outside the back door and start snipping with his scissors. With his crutch discarded, he would hop around me on one leg. He had excellent balance and could stay on one leg for ages. Round and round he'd go, snipping all the while to my delighted shouts of 'More, Tommy, more.'

Tommy would get carried away in response to my enthusiasm and I'd finish up with hardly any hair and it was mighty rough around the edges but, as Tommy often said, there's only two weeks difference between a good haircut and a bad one.

He used to get pleasure from spinning yarns to Dad and me about the old days. I'm so glad he did because I realise now that he was living history. He enabled me to appreciate the past of the town.

My barber, Tommy Johnson, celebrates the connection of electricity to Barry's Reef in 1959.

When Tommy worked at the bakery the mines roared night and day, with men on twelve-hour shifts. The population was around seven thousand and by 1880 Barry's Reef (by then officially named Bayup) had surveyed streets, rough made roads, gas lighting and many substantial buildings. The creeks and flats were jammed with tents and men, and thirty hotels and shanties catered to the miners' thirst. There were the three breweries, and Tommy recalled the closure of the last and biggest, The Golden Pass. There were several sawmills, all kept busy supplying timber to the mines. The bushland around was soon stripped almost bare.

By 1890, the mines were not profitable, and underground water kept the pumps going flat out day and night. With that, the town's decline began. By the turn of the century, the water had won and Barry's Reef lay almost deserted. From a population of seven thousand in 1885 to a few hundred in fifteen short years. Enough people stayed on to enable Tommy to keep his pub going for some years, the only 'watering hole' remaining, but as people died or moved on, Barry's Reef became a ghost town. Soon there were only six residents, and that's the way it was when we arrived.

We had a lovely dog named Darkie and we also had a cat called Puss. She was a fluffy, friendly and loveable creature and we all spoiled her. Her breeding was not recorded but she came from a long line of Barry's Reef cats, born and bred there. One of her infuriating habits was killing and eating the birds that Dad encouraged into the garden by feeding them bread crumbs and sugar nectar. When these murders occurred Dad would get pretty angry and throw things at her, accompanied by threats of dire consequences should she re-offend. He never did hurt her of course, he was a real softy.

Other than this, Puss was well behaved. For instance, she never 'did her business' in the house, always digging a hole in Mum's garden for this and carefully covering it.

Puss also had the habit of curling up in the oven where she slept in warmth and comfort. Mum always left the oven door open to help warm the kitchen.

One morning Puss was slumbering in the oven as Mum prepared to do a day's baking. Mum stoked the fire and shut the oven door to pre-heat it. An hour later she opened the door to slide in a tray of biscuits. There was our beloved Puss, roasted alive. We were mortified.

We got to know well Mr and Mrs Murphy who kept the post office. How this aging couple ever handled the rush I'll never know! With six households' mail to attend to three times a week, as well as operating the telephone exchange for two subscribers, it must have been hectic!

One day, Mum walked to the post office to collect the mail and she sensed immediately that something was amiss.

'You're a bit early Vron', said Mrs Murphy. 'I haven't finished sorting yet.'

'That's alright,' said Mum smiling inwardly as she glanced at the bundle of perhaps a dozen letters. 'I'll take a seat.'

'John hasn't woken yet,' said Mrs Murphy. 'I'll just take him a hot water bottle.'

She hurried off to the kitchen and bedroom, returning a few minutes later.

'Excuse me, Vron. I have to get some wood for the fire. It's cold in the bedroom.' She hurried outside, appearing quite agitated.

By now, Mum realised there was something amiss, and she quickly moved behind the counter and ran to the bedroom. At a glance she knew that Mr Murphy was dead. Probably Mrs Murphy realised it too but couldn't accept it.

Mum went to the phone switchboard. She had watched the Murphys use it often and plugged in a lead she hoped would connect her to Trentham exchange. She cranked the handle vigorously. It worked.

'Trentham,' came a female voice.

'Oh, Trentham,' said a relieved Mum. 'I'm at the Reef Post Office and Mr Murphy – I think he's dead. Can you send Doctor Gwen right away?'

She pulled the plug and resumed her seat just as Mrs Murphy appeared with an armful of wood. The old woman moved through the tiny office toward the bedroom. Mum followed her.

Chapter Nine

SUNDAY'S BUTTER – HOBYAHS AND OTHER SCARY THINGS – DR GWEN'S DELICATE SURGERY.

It was Sunday. I know it was Sunday because we had butter on the table for our midday meal. Every other day we had dripping. Sunday dinner was a big event at our place when we had a big roast of beef or mutton and all sorts of vegetables. We also had Thursday's bread, and most memorably, we had butter.

After a good brisk walk into Blackwood and back for church we were always starving by dinnertime.

I had recently learned a brand new word from my friend Joe. He used it quite a lot, especially if things went wrong, like when Dolly wouldn't stand still as he harnessed her to the cart. I was keen to try out my new word and the chance came when I wanted the butter for my slice of bread.

'Pass the fucking butter, please,' I said loudly and with considerable pride to Maurie next to me. There was a stunned silence. For a couple of seconds nobody moved or uttered a sound.

'Uh, oh,' I thought. 'There must be something wrong with that word.' Finally Mum gathered her wits.

'Where did you learn that word?' she cried in a voice that showed disbelief at what she'd heard. There was no way I would dob in my friend Joe and I didn't hesitate.

'From Alan, Mum.'

Mum grabbed a stick from the fireplace and laid into the innocent Alan with all the force she could muster. Poor Alan crashed in a whimpering heap under the onslaught before being pushed headlong into our bedroom, where he was ordered to stay the rest of the day and night without food or drink.

When he finally got around to speaking to me again it was to threaten me with death if I ever did that to him again. I now understand why.

Mum had a ten shilling note in her purse. Frank was impressed by this and noticing that the note was a little grubby he decided to give it a good wash and hang it on the line. It wasn't long before Mum noticed the note was missing and questioning quickly revealed its whereabouts.

Outside, the wind was blowing and she was horrified to see the precious note in soggy pieces scattered over the yard. It was all hands on deck to retrieve the pieces which were dried in the oven.

Fortunately, there was enough left to identify and Mum was able to convert it at the post office. Frank received a serious lecture for what would have been an utter disaster had the note been lost. Ten shillings was a fortune to Mum back then.

I've mentioned that the bush around our place was a sea of abandoned mine shafts, many of them very deep. Mum and Dad lived in constant fear that one of us would stumble into one. To discourage us from going too near they invented creatures of indescribable ugliness and fierceness that lived in these shafts. Anti-wanti-gongs.

Anti-wanti-gongs were, I imagined, a cross between the dreaded Hobyahs and the fearsome trolls of the Second Grade Reader. I was in horror of being grabbed by one. Hobyahs frightened me enough with their 'creeping, creeping through the forest' and trolls with their hiding under bridges and devouring passing goats. God knows what an anti-wanti-gong looked like and would do to me! I therefore avoided mine shafts like the plague.

Modern child psychologists may be aghast at the lasting damage these fears may have caused, but anti-wanti-gongs certainly did the trick for Mum and Dad and I don't think there was any lasting harm. By the way, Hobyahs and trolls have long since been banned from the School Reader.

Pipe clay was in common use in homes in the bush back then. Principally it was used to whiten fireplaces and to paint rooms and shed interiors. We used it regularly for the fireplaces, the envy of visitors who couldn't afford to splash it around. Our advantage lay in the bank of the creek in the gully behind our place where we had our own secret supply. All we had to do was dig it out and put it in a bucket. That was my regular job, along with keeping up the supply of dry sticks for the 'mornings wood'.

Every home in those days had a supply of morning wood at the door, so called because in pre-slow-combustion stove days everybody had to relight the fires each morning. Dry, crisp wood made it so much easier to get a bright blaze going.

We spent a lot of time exploring the bush and developed a love and knowledge of it that comes naturally to most country kids. There was beauty all around and fascinating creatures like echidnas, possums, kangaroos, wallabies and wombats. There was nothing we had any fear of, except snakes, and although we had many encounters with them, we were never harmed. Given the chance, they will invariably scurry away. Bites generally come about when they are trodden on or are threatened or attacked. We always walked with our heads down and eyes wide open. I had more fear of the dreaded spitfires, actually harmless caterpillars that congregated in writhing clumps on gum trees. They were common and, according to my brothers, squirted a death dealing substance at you if you got close to them. I gave them a wide berth.

I still love the bush around Blackwood, especially now that there are no anti-wanti-gongs!

One day, Mum was busy in the kitchen when she observed through the window a black Overland sedan coming to a halt on the roadside. The car door opened and several peculiar, short-legged dogs poured out, six of them. Then, rolling out of the car came a rotund and rough looking figure that Mum took to be a bush worker. The figure wore a knitted hat pulled well down and a heavy woollen overcoat. The person carried a small leather bag and, to Mum's surprise, strode purposefully down the track toward our house.

'Probably looking for directions,' thought Mum as she answered the knock at the door. She was confronted by a round, ruddy and bespectacled face that wore a big smile.

'Hello.' To Mum's surprise it was a cultured female voice.

'I'm Doctor Wisewould the new doctor. I understand that you have a sick husband. Can I see him?'

And so began an association and friendship that we came to value so highly as the years went by. From that day on Dr Gwen attended Dad every few weeks and every family illness. Not once did she ever send an account, rejecting every offer of some payment out of hand. This was the woman who was to become a legend in the Central Highlands, Trentham's famed Gweneth Wisewould – Outpost Doctor.

I had no idea then that I would one day write a popular and successful book about her and see my story being adapted for a possible film screen play[*]. She was a wonderful, talented and caring person, more than a little eccentric in later years. The people of our district came to adore her. My family loved her.

Frank, Alan and Maurie walked to and from school each day, and it was a big effort for skinny young legs and feet, in weather that was often foul. Snow, wind and ice were common. Each Thursday Dr Gwen attended her rooms at Blackwood House guest house, and whenever possible, timed her return journey to Trentham to coincide with school home time. This was so she could pick up our three boys and give them a lift home. How many Doctors would do that?

As it turned out, I was the first patient in our family to be attended to for surgery by Dr Gwen at the tiny Trentham hospital. It was to be a baffling procedure and I squirmed with embarrassment as this woman examined the offending organ.

---

[*] *Alas the film has not yet eventuated – a great pity as it is a remarkable story about a remarkable woman. However, as I write, it is being developed – there is still a chance.*

'Hmm,' she said, turning it this way and that and fiddling with it. I was certainly not too young to understand what she was saying and I cringed with fear at her next words.

'Yes, Mrs Braybrook. It'll have to come off.'

My God! What was this mad woman about to do to me? Was she going to cut it off?

I closed my eyes tight, my future in her hands. I didn't feel anything after that, not until an hour or two later. To my surprise the thing was still there when I took a peek, but it hurt like hell.

The operation was considered a success, but the claim put to me by an aggrieved woman some years later remains: 'Dr Gwen didn't take that operation far enough!'

Chapter Ten

BLACKWOOD MINERAL SPRINGS – RADIO COMES TO BARRY'S REEF.

Some of our walks took us to the mineral water springs at Blackwood. It was a much quieter place in those days, with few visitors. We always took along our Marchants screw-top lemonade bottles for filling from the springs, bottles that were tan coloured from the constant refilling with water rich in minerals.

The Lerderderg River at the springs was crossed by a bridge suspended on thick cables and we boys loved to get in the middle and jump about, causing the bridge to sway alarmingly. The old bridge has been gone for many years, replaced by concrete, taking a lot of fun out of a visit for kids, I'm sure.

We did a lot of walking in pursuit of rabbits, too, and we were pretty good at trapping them. I know now how cruel the traps were, with their serrated steel jaws that sprung shut on the victim's leg, crushing and usually breaking it. Sometimes the delicate front leg was almost severed.

The poor rabbits must have suffered agony, and the terror showed in their eyes as we would approach them to grab them for killing. It was a nasty business but almost essential for our survival. We ate the meat and sold the skins.

Dad was very conscious of the damage the steel jaws did, and instead of using the usual piece of paper to cover the plate that sprung the trap, he taught us to use pieces of soft flannel. This cushioned the jaws a little and helped reduce the steel-to-flesh contact. Dad said it was the humane thing to do. He was a gentle man.

Sometimes we would get to feel a little of the pain the rabbit felt when the trap went off as we were setting it, grabbing our fingers. God it hurt. I quickly learned to be careful, and by the age of seven I was a pretty good rabbit trapper. By that time I knew how to kill the rabbit by stretching its neck with a bone-crunching pull. I thought nothing of it at the time.

Our family ate rabbit almost every day, cooked in one form or another; baked, fried, grilled, broiled or in stews. We even had rabbit sandwiches for school lunches. Like many families in the depression, our basic meat diet was rabbit. The rabbit skin was also a valuable commodity, and we would carefully remove it with a sharp pocket knife and pull it over fencing wire bent to an elongated U-shape. The skins hung in the shed until properly dried, and when we had a hundred, we bundled them with string and sent them by train to Kennon and Co, skin buyers in Melbourne. We got threepence each for them and the cheque for twenty-five shillings was always very welcome.

One day Mum put the cheque on the mantelpiece above the fire, from where it fell and wafted gently into the blaze. It was consumed before her eyes.

We didn't know then, because we had no experience with such things, that we could have got a replacement cheque. It was a total loss.

* * *

It was a memorable day when the mail contractor delivered an item that was to change our lives. It was a second-hand wireless set, a very early model, with three knobs and a round dial set in a rectangular box, with the speaker on top. Dad had already erected an aerial in anticipation of the delivery. It was strung between two freshly cut and planted bush poles with the wire attached to ceramic insulators.

Dad and Mum were just as excited as we boys were as the machine was placed in the sitting room by the fire. Dad connected the aerial and an earth, turned it on and after a minute's warm up we had music! It was wonderful. My life-long love affair with radio began that day way back in 1941. Just about everybody else we knew had a wireless, and we now felt equal.

We had no electricity, so the wireless was powered by two batteries. One was an Eveready 'dry' battery, large and heavy, and the second an acid-filled 'wet' battery. The wet battery was a pest as it kept going flat and had to be sent to town for recharging. When that happened we were without our wireless for two days, which meant we missed our serials, and Dad and Mum missed the vital news from the war front. Soon, Dad managed to buy a second wet battery which was used in rotation. We no longer missed out.

The wireless was a real luxury and was treated as such by Mum. We boys were not allowed to touch the set at all, and it was turned on only for a few hours a day to preserve the batteries. Charging the wet battery cost only one and sixpence, including delivery each way, but the big dry battery was another story. A new one cost almost twelve shillings and one time, when it went flat, we had to wait two weeks for a new one, a real disaster.

The use of the wireless may have been restricted, but it was a boon to us, keeping us informed and entertained and relieving our isolation from the outside world. After tea at five o'clock, we would all sit around the fire and listen. No chatter was allowed and at seven-thirty we kids were sent to bed.

Mum would allow only one kerosene lamp to be lit at a time to save cost, so we usually undressed in the dark and crawled into bed. Mum never wasted a thing; paper bags, pieces of string, paper and cardboard wrapping all found there way into drawers and cupboards, along with the rare butter wrapper, retained for greasing cake trays. She enjoyed baking and when she baked a cake it was a contest to see who got to lick the remaining mixture from the mixing bowl.

Our beds were comfortable enough, and Mum gave us plenty of blankets but, because of the severe climate and the dilapidated state of our houses, the beds were always cold and damp during the long winter months. The climate in the central highlands is as wet and cold as anywhere in Australia. Rain is frequent, the winds bitterly cold and the frosts stark white. Often a blanket of snow covered the landscape.

Chapter Eleven

BLUE MOUNT – A BOY GOES TO WAR – LITTLE BOYS LOST.

I don't know why we moved from Barry's Reef, but in late 1942 we were on our way to Blue Mount, about a mile along the road to Trentham. We boys were unhappy with the move, but we weren't consulted or given a reason.

We moved into an old shack hidden up a bush track that wound its way from near the roadside horse trough below Waterwheel Farm. The horse trough was one of thousands around the state, placed by horse lovers, Annis and George Bills. George, an Englishman, had made his fortune manufacturing wire mattress bases for beds. An animal lover he decided on retirement to distribute some of his wealth in providing for horses. Many hundreds, probably thousands, of councils around the country applied for the free troughs and they were readily provided and installed.

This isolated trough was kept permanently full to overflowing by a natural spring trickling from just above it in the embankment.

We stayed in that shack only a few weeks before moving again. Dad had arranged to rent an old farmhouse about a mile away owned by Kit Trewhella, one of the family who made the famed Trewhella Jack at their Trentham foundry.

Our new place was set behind a protective bank of huge cypress trees about halfway to the summit of Blue Mount*. It was a big house and quite comfortable and the views were spectacular but I found it hard to accept. My heart was still down the road at Barry's Reef with my friend Joe.

---

* *It is now the site of a movie/TV mock-up town set and by coincidence I worked there on a number of occasions in features such as* The Man From Snowy River *TV series,* Ponderosa *and a Ned Kelly documentary.*

We didn't get off to a very good start because, within weeks of moving there, our dog Darkie died after eating a poisoned bait intended for foxes. We all shed a lot of tears.

Somehow, my half sister Mary Braybrook, now working as a housekeeper in Ballarat, heard of our loss and arranged delivery of a new dog for us. Bill Bunt, from down the bottom of the Mount, delivered us our new dog, a beautiful border collie pup, round, fluffy and full of play. Dad named him Colonel, and we all fell in love with him. It helped ease the pain of losing Darkie, but I never forgot him.

It is one of many mysteries of my childhood, how Mary managed to hear the news and send us such a wonderful gift.

We settled in on the western slope of Blue Mount. It was good there, except that I developed a fear of the misty mountain that towered over us. Unwittingly, it was my Dad's fault. He came back from a walk one day carrying a shield-shaped piece of blackened wood.

'This belongs to one of the blackfellers who live up there,' he said in fun, giving me a hug.

I took him seriously, and for all our time there I lived in secret

Mum, Dad, Darkie and me at Blue Mount, c. 1941.

fear of murder or worse by marauding Aborigines! I also believed that an echo lived on the mountain. Dad and I used to stand at the woodheap, face the mountain and call out. Our echo came back as clear as crystal. There was a popular song at the time, 'Little Sir Echo' sung by Vera Lynn and I used to stand at the woodheap for ages singing the chorus as loudly as I could: 'Little Sir Echo, how do you do. Hello, hello.' I would sing and the 'hello' always came back – or so I imagined.

It was a snowy July day that I began school at Garlic's Lead State School. It was so cold that a small dam on the roadside had frozen and I watched in fear as the older boys walked around its edge. I refused to do so and I know now I had more sense than they. The ice must have been quite thin and very dangerous to walk on.

School was a big adventure for me, and I enjoyed it, welcoming the opportunity to play with other kids. Not that there were many, in fact, apart from our family, there were only a handful of others, in six grades. Some of the names I recall are Max, Faye and Pam Glover; Kevin and Shirley Marx; Albert Stevens; Alvin, Ted, Tiger and Ethel Robson; Ted, Neale; Beth and Beryl Leach; Yvonne and Clarence Boyle and another brother and the Emmins family. Only about half of them attended the school at the same time as me. The lone teacher was a youthful Mrs Molly Falls.

We were devils sometimes and loved to throw our ball onto the top of the water tank because Mrs Falls had to climb a ladder to retrieve it. We boys would huddle below her, sniggering as we looked up her dress.

Mrs Falls always boiled the kettle for her dinnertime drink on the open fire in the school's only classroom. One day, one of the boys, a good shot, lobbed potatoes taken from the paddock next door, down the chimney. One hit the kettle and sent it sprawling across the floor. The spilled hot water almost splashed her, closely avoiding scalding the poor woman. She was always called Spud Falls after that, behind her back of course. The culprit was never identified.

That was not the case in another particularly nasty incident. One day, as I studied the questions that Mrs Falls had placed on the blackboard for grade one and I wrote my answers in indecipherable scribble with my slate pencil on my slate, a boy returned from a visit to the dunny.

'Please, Mrs Falls,' he said. 'Somebody has done their business on the boys' lavatory seat.'

A heavy silence descended on the room as this startling claim reverberated from the walls and the pine ceiling. Some students tittered but most were grim faced, finding it difficult to believe that such a dastardly act could occur.

Mrs Falls hastened to leave the room to inspect the crime scene and motioned us all to follow. Sure enough there lay a grade-one-sized turd, right at the back edge of the seat. One by one we all filed past and gazed at the offending object. The evidence was plain and all that remained was to catch the offender.

The kids at Garlics Lead primary school, c. 1942. Maurie is front left and Frank at start of standing row. Teacher is Molly Falls. Alan is second from right. I had not yet started school.

By a process of elimination Mrs Falls reached a verdict and pointed the finger of accusation at the youngest pupil, the one who knew no better. Me!

I cried my innocence to no avail and Alan, the oldest of my brothers, was made to clean up the mess. Alan protested wildly, but his cries also fell on deaf ears.

After school he threatened to kill me, rejecting my claims of innocence. I will always maintain that it wasn't me, and I believe that one day the guilty party will come forward and clear my name.

We played another game with the girls that I enjoyed, a sort of 'show and not tell'. One girl was particularly keen and frequently visited the woodshed with the boys. She would take off her bloomers, dress hoisted high and stand revealed as a line-up of boys queued to show her theirs and to have her fondle it. This day, a new boy joined the queue, and to his eternal humiliation and immeasurable psychological damage, she refused to touch it, except briefly, declaring that it was too cold. Curse my draughty short pants.

I was never aware of it, but from time to time either Mum or Dad would be away for a couple of days visiting the children in the orphanage. I didn't realise that these children existed until one day we had a visit from a young man who was working picking up rocks at Waterwheel Farm just below us on the main road. It was Charlie, one of Dad's other family – my half brother.

He was about nineteen, and we got to like Charlie during his three day stay. He played with us kids and even helped Dad to build a rough shed which they made from saplings lashed together with wire. With the frame erected we went inside to have dinner. When we emerged, the entire structure had collapsed.

'A magpie must have sat on it,' chortled Charlie, and the shed remained forever unfinished.

Charlie also gave us a demonstration of a hanging, placing a rope suspended from a tree around his throat. He hung there by the neck for some time before Alan realised that he was actually choking to death! The big kids managed to hold him aloft until the rope was removed and Charlie was saved. He swore us to secrecy.

Mum, Dad and Charlie spent a lot of time indoors in earnest talk, from which the rest of us were excluded. We listened outside catching bits of the conversation and I know now that they were talking about the reasons for Charlie and the rest being in the orphanage. Before we knew it Charlie was gone and I didn't see him again for 57 years.

Within days we had another young visitor, this one wearing an army uniform. It was Ron, Mum's surviving son from her unhappy marriage. Another half brother! Ron was a fine looking young man in the uniform, aged just seventeen, lightly built and only five feet four inches tall. He was still a child really and remained officially a resident of the Ballarat Orphanage until age eighteen, although he had been working on a farm property near Horsham. It was the practice at the orphanage to assign the male children to farm service and the girls to housekeeping and similar jobs as soon as they were fourteen, some even younger. The orphanage was a good source of cheap labour. The farmer, Captain Oates, and his wife treated Ron quite well. It was often not the case with others.

Ron astounded Mum with the news that having joined the army and completed his training he was about to embark for somewhere overseas and the war.

Mum was distressed and furious. She couldn't understand how he could join the Army without her consent. It turned out that Ron was a ward of the state, and the superintendent of the orphanage was his legal guardian. He had signed the consent forms, even though he knew that Ron had falsified his age.

There was nothing Mum could do, although she tried so hard, visiting the orphanage superintendent seeking intervention, and similarly pestering members of parliament in Ballarat. It was to no avail and Ron was kept in the service. She hated the orphanage superintendent forever after.

Ron stayed only a few hours before leaving to catch a special train leaving from Ballarat next morning. Mum resolved to go with him to see him off. The duo had to walk to Trentham and from there catch the train to Daylesford and then a bus to Ballarat.

Mum would stay for a couple of days with Uncle Syd, my Auntie Mabel and their daughter Clarabelle. We said goodbye and watched the two figures until they disappeared from view far below. Dad had a faraway look on his face.

'Come on boys,' he said. 'Let's get a cup of tea.' And we went indoors. We never saw Ron again.

* * *

I loved the mushroom season and would walk for miles collecting them. We kids had a special way of cooking them, straight on top of the hot wood stove. A light sprinkle of salt and a couple of minutes sizzling and we had a delicious snack. I can still taste those mushies! Any other cooking method is not the same.

Another sometime favourite was turnips eaten raw. One of the local farmers had a big crop of turnips on the roadside just south of the Garlic's Lead school and as we walked to and from school we would crawl through the fence and steal a couple each, munching them as we walked. I can't imagine food much worse but, as kids, we used to love them. Stolen fruit I suppose.

One afternoon, as we straggled home from school we stopped off in Bunt's barn for a spell and a smoke. The weather was cold so we lit a small fire and after thawing out and a having a drag or two on cigarettes of stringy bark rolled in newspaper we headed off home. You could say that I started smoking when I was five.

That night the barn burnt to the ground. The cause was never discovered, although foul play was expected. Frank advanced the theory that it may have been a swagman we had seen on the road, and that seemed to gain some credibility.

High in the mountains, the nights are often clear as crystal and the stars so bright they dazzle. If ever you feel important try a night under the stars in the highlands. You will soon realise how insignificant you really are!

It was on one such night that we were to observe a most astonishing, phenomenal display. I have never before or since seen anything to equal it. It was wartime and at first we thought the sky was lit by searchlights, seeking out a Japanese aeroplane but Dad soon realised it was the Aurora Australis, the Southern Lights. He had read about it.

The entire sky from north to south was crammed with the most dazzling display. There was a moving pattern of spectacular white and coloured lights, in countless groups of what seemed to be many thousands of lights. First one group would blaze and then fade and then another would replace it. The sky from horizon to directly above us was filled with dancing, swerving, bobbing light. It was at once both beautiful and frightening, an absolute wonder to us all.

* * *

I was often sick with a feverish complaint, and it was because of this I was allowed to stay home from school one very bleak winter's day. Mum had sent the other three off after the usual inspection to see that the boots had been polished and that there was no dirt in unwashed ears.

'You'll have spuds growing out your ears if you're not careful.' Mum would say if she found a speck of dirt.

Rugged up in coats, hats and scarves and their dinner of jam sandwiches stuffed in their leather school bags the trio set off on the regular two mile hike to school.

Snow had begun to fall through the night and about two inches covered the ground as the lads plodded off down the mountain slope.

It snowed all day and the wind blew at terrific force. By four o'clock the lads hadn't arrived home and my parents began to worry.

Darkness came swiftly at Blue Mount on such days, and at four-thirty, Dad announced that he was going to look for them. It was already becoming quite dark as he disappeared from sight into the trees at the edge of the cleared paddock below, his kerosene lantern casting a feeble glow. It was hard going in the deep snow. His first call was on Bill Bunt. Bill had seen the boys pass by earlier, about the normal time, a quarter to four. Why, then, were they not home yet? Dad really began to worry now as he paced as fast as his bad heart allowed, back the way he had come.

He called at the top of his voice but the sound was lost in the swirling snow and howling wind.

It was dark now and Dad felt panic. Children lost on the mountain in this weather would surely perish. He pushed on through the blackness, trying desperately to think where his sons may have sought shelter.

He recalled an abandoned shed about five hundred yards down the fence line and headed in that direction. By following the fence he was able to stay on course and eventually made out the obscure outline of the old shed.

He found the boys huddled together inside, so cold that an icicle hung from Maurie's running nose. Dad wept with relief as he hugged them all, and by the flickering light of the hurricane lamp he led them home. They had lost their way in the thick swirling snow where everything looked the same. They had the sense to go to the shed that they knew about from going after rabbits. So, in a way, rabbits saved Braybrooks again!

Pretty soon the boys were none the worse for their experience.

Chapter Twelve

Trentham – ferrets – grape picking – the Yankee Mine explosion.

It wasn't long before we moved again, this time a few more miles along the Trentham road to Newbury. Don't ask me why! We crammed into a small miner's cottage that we rented from the Kaye family. Dad had to walk about twenty kilometres to Musk to see the owners about renting the place. They were sawmillers there.

It wasn't much of a house, drafty, damp and cold and I always seemed to be sick there. Mum had only one cure that she applied to almost everything – lots of cups of homemade barley broth, a tasteless, muddy looking liquid that Mum assured us was 'full of goodness'.

Her other cures were Iodex for aches and pains, and for ant bites and insect stings generous coatings of blue liquid squeezed from her Reckitts Blue bags from the washhouse. It seemed to work alright. Dad really hopped into the Iodex, as he suffered a lot of mysterious aches.

Alan acquired two ferrets while we were at Newbury, they were his pride and joy, although we all referred to them as 'Alan's stinkin' ferrets'. But they were great for flushing rabbits out of their burrows and into the cooking pot, and they were more fun than setting traps.

By God it was cold in those mountains, especially as we walked to and from school. And it wasn't helped by Mum's insistence on sewing up the pockets of our trousers, at least on any store-bought ones we may have had. The ones she made for us on her Singer were pocketless from the start. Mum said it was 'ungentlemanly' to put one's hands in one's pockets. Perhaps she thought we would play pocket billiards if we had pockets. I don't know, but whatever the reason, we suffered for it. The chilblains on our hands were huge and itched, pained and burned like hell, especially at night in bed. Often the skin would break with the scratching and become infected, and this meant a good covering with Iodex. That was painful in itself.

As well as being without pockets, our homemade pants had no button up fly like everyone else. We had penis pop-holes at the front with a flap of material sewn inside for modesty as the pop-hole sometimes gaped open. All the other kids wore proper shirts, too but we had to wear Mum's homemade blouses; real bum and tummy freezers, as they were too short to tuck in. I hated those blouses!

At the back of our home was a huge mullock heap covered with grass and it was a perfect slippery slope for riding the sled that Dad made us. We spent many a happy hour sliding down our imaginary mountainside, but as the youngest, I mostly copped the job of dragging the sled up the hill for the others to ride.

It was wartime and there was a desperate shortage of labour for the fruit harvest at Redcliffs, so Mum and Dad decided that we would go picking to do our bit for the war effort. In the wink of an eye we were on a train to Redcliffs on the Murray River, where we were assigned a ramshackle pickers' hut.

My only clear memories of Redcliffs are paddling in the water races and of having a large snake in the kitchen that caused uproar as Dad chased it about the hut to kill it. There was also an ample supply of luscious figs on a tree outside the hut door. I ate fig after fig and developed the greatest tummy ache and dose of the trots in the history of man. I thought I was going to turn inside out.

Alan and Ian. Note my oversized braces and the odd trouser buttons. Times were hard at Cosmo Road, Trentham, c. 1945.

The harvest ended and we were back at Newbury. We had missed a bit of school, but nobody seemed concerned, least of all me.

Soon after, the opportunity to buy a house nearer Trentham came up, and we were able to buy it because Mum sold the Barry's Reef house. I believe that she got ten pounds for it, enough for a deposit. Land values on the edge of Trentham were not very high in 1943 – or was it 1944?

The new house was in Cosmo Road, about five hundred yards west of the busy sawmill and the adjoining cemetery. It was a lovely little home of four main rooms and a delightful detached kitchen. We loved it and it meant we were a lot closer to school too. It was a mere mile and a half walk away.

The new house had many conveniences, including a bathroom lean-to at the back.

The detached kitchen was a classic. Twenty feet long and ten feet wide, one wall was fitted with a pine bench and the south end wall had a fireplace that was fitted with an almost new Planet wood stove of green enamel. There was a large table and six 'kangaroo' chairs included in the purchase price of fifty pounds. The west wall had a small window and the flag floor was smooth and polished. To top it all there was a water tap over the bench that was connected to a large water tank outside. Rusted red, big and square, its previous life was as part of a steam driven gold battery. For the first time Mum had indoor plumbing. There was even space for a large sofa which Mum and Dad used on occasions for daytime recreation. I know that because I walked in on them one day. I didn't see a lot but there was a hell of a flurry of activity.

The bathroom roof was leaky, so Dad decided to fit a new one of a remarkable new cheap product called Malthoid, a rubbery sheeting. It was great until he stepped back to admire the finished job and fell through, his crutch landing with a jolt on one of the cross timbers. There was a lot of bruising in the region, but nothing that a bit of Iodex wouldn't fix. Alan managed to repair the damaged roof, being a young man of fourteen by then and quite a handyman.

One day, Mum arrived home with a stray dog she had collected in Trentham. It was a scruffy looking terrier of some sort that we named Towser. Colonel, our wonderful border collie accepted Towser without fuss and he soon became one of us, going everywhere that we went in our roaming through the bush.

Things were going really well. We even had our own milking cow, a delightfully friendly and pleasant beast named Bonny. She became one of our family, although Alan frequently cursed having to milk her twice every day. Bonny gave us gallons of lovely milk from which we made butter and fresh scalded cream. Making the butter was one of my jobs and it was hard work whipping the cream until it thickened and eventually turned to butter. I became quite an expert and strong in the wrist too.

If there was one food us kids liked better than cream and butter it was the dark brown stuff that used to accumulate in the bottom of Mum's dripping tin. Heaven knows what it was or how unhealthy it may have been but there were frequent arguments between us boys as to who would get to eat it, spread on their slice of bread. It was probably swarming with bacteria, salmonella bugs and other extreme nasties. We could never buy Vegemite or Marmite but it looked the same, so that's what we called it – and I don't know that it ever made us ill.

Alan with our dog Colonel at Cosmo Road, Trentham shortly after the death of our father. October, 1945.

I don't recall much about my

days at Trentham Primary School except having a fight with one boy, which I won easily when his nose bled all over the place. I landed one of my Sunday punches fair on his snout, and I was a bit of a hero for a couple of days. I'm still famous for my mighty punches.

I also remember sneaking one of my girl classmate admirers into a big hollow area in the cypress pine hedge and being given a good hard look at her private part. It didn't do a lot for me, I'm afraid, and it was with some reluctance I dropped my strides and let her look and touch. I soon got tired of that and after half an hour or so I told her to stop!

Gordon Boyd and one of his mates were involved in a similar event. They offered a girl a penny if she would give them a look. The lass was eager to accept, grabbed their pennies and dropped her pants on the spot. Gordon complained later to anyone who'd listen that the boys wanted their penny back as there was nothing to see!

Under pain of a horrible death we had to attend Sunday school, rain or shine. We hated every moment of it. It was utterly boring, but our teacher did a good job of drumming some things into us. I can still recite the 23rd Psalm and I know the Lord's Prayer backwards. One Summer Sunday we made our way down the dusty track toward Sunday School and, as usual, as soon as we were out of sight, we hid our despised school caps under a roadside bush.

Because we had no pockets, we carried our handkerchiefs with our penny for the plate tied in the corner. Near the sawmill we met up with two other boys, brothers Neil and Max. They were free spirits who didn't have to go to Sunday School and who were making their way out of town to explore the bush. They must have been very persuasive individuals because they convinced us we should wag Sunday School and go with them.

The choice between Sunday School and an hour in the bush was obviously a difficult decision for four boys but we proceeded into the bush, Neil, the oldest wheeling his pushbike.

Our first stop was the rifle butts where we picked up a few discarded

.303 shells before heading toward the abandoned Yankee Mine. There had been a bushfire through only days before and in many areas there were still burning logs and smouldering piles of leaves and sticks. It wasn't long before we came on the mine where we threw a few 'yonnies' down the deep shaft, as was customary.

It was all quite mundane until Neil found a tin in the abandoned shed. The label said in bold letters, 'Danger Detonators'.

None of us had a clue what a detonator was, although Neil felt sure that they went off like a penny bunger.

'We'll try one,' said Max. Everyone agreed, but the problem was there was no wick to light.

'I've got it,' said Neil. 'I'll shove the end over this nail.'

Before him was a still burning piece of timber from which protruded a very hot four inch nail. We all nodded approval and Neil squatted beside the burning timber and reached for the hot nail. He managed to get the open end of the 'penny bunger' over the nail and pushed it home hard. The bang was a lot louder than we had expected, much louder than any penny bunger I'd ever heard.

Neil screamed almost as loud as the explosion as he clutched a shattered hand. There was blood all over the place and his hand was a grisly sight, with blood pumping and spurting onto the ground. It was awful. I could scarcely believe my eyes and began to cry.

'Shut up baby,' yelled Maurie, as panic stricken as the rest of us. I quickly shut off the water works.

Alan took his clean Sunday School hanky and bound Neil's hand as hard as he could, partially stemming the flow of blood. He then placed Neil on the bar of the bike and we all shoved off toward town, as fast as our legs would go. Neil was ashen faced and very quiet as he held his injured hand aloft.

'For Christ's sake,' he managed to say. 'Don't nobody say nothin' about this or we'll get into real strife.'

We all vowed silence, but on reflection, that was pretty futile. How the hell could you keep the biggest event in Trentham since the Vicar's wife ran off with a farmer's daughter quiet? And that's the way it turned out.

We parted company near the sawmill on Cosmo Road where the two town boys made for Doctor Gwen's surgery, with Neil on the pushbike bar and Max pedalling as fast as he could. As usual, Dr. Gwen did a wonderful job in repairing Neil's hand, managing to piece together all the shattered fingers. To their credit, they made no mention to anyone that the Braybrook kids were with them.

We retrieved our caps, at the same time stashing our pennies for future use at Roy McKenzie's milk bar. At home we tried to act normally, with considerable success.

'How was Sunday School?' asked Dad.

'Oh, pretty good,' replied Maurie. 'Same as usual.'

For weeks after I was a nervous wreck. I let the team down. Mum was puzzled by my behaviour because every time anybody lit the kerosene lamp or struck a match I would scream and cry. Dr Gwen couldn't offer any reason either.

It wasn't until several months had passed that Mum heard the story of our adventure at the mine from Mrs Bunt and, as predicted by Alan, we all got a good hiding from Mum.

'No wonder Ian behaved as he has,' said Dr Gwen when she heard the story. 'Poor boy may be scarred for life.'

I think I've recovered but I will never forget that day at the Yankee Mine. Neil made a perfect recovery, too, regaining full use of his hand. Dr. Gweneth Wisewould's reputation as a surgical magician grew further still.

Chapter Thirteen

The War – death of a neighbour – Fitzroy – another school

The war dragged on, touching every family. Some people became rich because of it; the rest of us paid the price.

Dad's oldest sons, Sydney and Arthur, were serving overseas somewhere and he got an occasional letter from them which he read over and over. All of the letters had been dealt with by the censor and large slices of text were missing, cut out by razor blade. Mum received one solitary note from Ron, and that was shortly after he arrived in Suez in late 1941.

In July 1942 she received a letter from the Army advising her that Ron was missing, believed a Japanese prisoner of war in the Pacific. Mum was very distressed and cried a lot. By then we were hearing stories of Japanese atrocities and Mum was forever fearful of his fate.

'I'm sure he'll be alright,' Dad would say. But, of course, Mum worried just the same.

Almost everything was rationed, and although we received ration coupons, we were too poor to use them all, but down in Melbourne Uncle Roy had a good use for our surplus.

He needed lots of sugar. Whatever the reason we did not know or ask, and Mum sold what coupons we didn't use to Uncle for a couple of bob. Uncle was working in an essential service, the Austral Bakery, and missed out on serving in the forces; instead making cakes for dispatch to our overseas servicemen. As a result of his job, we got a package of stale cakes every week, delivered by train to Trentham. A real treat – for a while.

Dad grew hundreds of carrots and in return he would send Uncle and his new wife Sadie a bag of carrots each week. After this had gone on for several months there came a letter from Uncle.

'For Christ's sake don't send any more bloody carrots. We are all looking like bloody rabbits.' We felt similarly about his cakes.

We eventually found out why Uncle need so much sugar. There was severe rationing of beer at the time and a thirsty bloke would kill for a bottle or two. Being a bit of an entrepreneur, Uncle set up his own highly illegal 'brewery' in his backyard. He used an old laundry copper to boil the hops, and with other homemade gear, he churned out dozens of cheap bottles a week for a large clientele, mostly his mates.

He had a fantastic distribution system going. Once each week the old-time recycle man known as the 'bottle-o' would call on each house in the street to collect empty bottles for re-use. The bottles that left Uncle's yard in the horsedrawn cart were far from empty, filled with 'a pretty bloody good drop', to quote Uncle. As he made his calls on his regular round, the bottle-o would also make the deliveries and collect the cash. Uncle didn't make much money out of it, but he got lots of satisfaction. 'A community service', he called it.

Back in Trentham, us kids had a pretty good deal going that also involved bottles. Roy McKenzie would stack the empty soft drink bottles, returned for the penny deposit, in the backyard of his fruit shop where there was usually quite a pile. It would be difficult to tell if any were missing. What sort of crooked kids would jump the fence, grab a sugar bag of bottles, and take them back to the shop to re-collect the deposit?

We didn't have any near neighbours in Cosmo Road, the closest being the Clarke family near the cemetery. There were three brothers, and we used to go bush with them now and then. Harry Watmough's dam was our favourite destination, where we tried unsuccessfully to catch redfin. The Clarke boys were pretty tough and used to illustrate this by getting leeches from the dam and letting them suck their blood. To make the leeches let go they would burn them with their cigarette butts.

Mrs Franzke, a widow, lived with her son Stan just a few hundred yards past Watmough's dam, and we were good friends. Mrs Franzke would always have a couple of jars of jam for us whenever we visited with Mum.

Her son Stan was a eucalyptus distiller and I used to watch as he worked in the nearby bush harvesting the gum leaves and then ride with him on the dray back to his homemade distillery. It was a fascinating experience, and I am privileged to have seen one of the last remaining bush distillers at work. It is all gone now, including the house. All that remains are a few old cypress trees to indicate that anything was ever standing there.

Miss Annie Clarke was our closest neighbour to the south, and she lived alone in a single-roomed hut. Alone, that is, except for Mickey, the most ferocious dog that ever lived! Miss Clarke was a shadowy figure. Nobody knew anything about her, not even her age, but I think she was quite old. Only rarely did we ever catch a glimpse of her as we walked by her hut. As soon as she saw anyone coming she would disappear into her tiny home. Mickey would go bananas and hurl himself against the wire netting fence in his effort to get at us.

Ian, age 12, at Trentham on holiday with Frank at Watmough's dam about 1949–50.

His teeth were bared and his black hair stood straight out from his huge body. We were terrified of him.

The mailman used to deliver all Miss Clarke's requirements once a week, hanging the hessian bag on the fence. One day he noticed that the previous week's sugar bag remained untouched where he had left it. He went to the police who called Dr Gwen, suspecting that something was amiss.

Doctor Gwen was the only person around who could get past Mickey. She had a fearless way with all dogs and made her way indoors without a lot of fuss. She found Miss Clarke dead on the bed, where she had been for almost a week. After her body was taken away, the police shot ferocious Mickey. I suppose poor, lonely Miss Clarke would have been happy that her beloved dog followed her so soon after and was not left to die alone, as she did.

We liked our new home. We were getting set up pretty comfortably. Mum had a lovely flower garden and Dad had the best vegetable patch he had ever been able to grow. We had plenty of water, lots of firewood for the taking all around us, and the house was in good condition. We were as poor as ever, but there was not a lot that we wanted for, as far as I was aware. So we were surprised when Mum told us that we were going to live with Dad's former father-in-law at Fitzroy, a Melbourne inner suburb. Dad had been told of the chance of a job as the caretaker of the Fitzroy Public Baths! I have no idea how this came about, he couldn't even swim, but soon we were packed and on the train to Melbourne. The possessions that we would need in Melbourne were all stashed in the train's guards van, our two dogs and Alan's 'stinking ferrets' included.

It all happened so fast. One day we were at school in Trentham and the next we were booking in to new schools in Melbourne.

The episode was a disaster, and I can't imagine how we came to be guests in the tiny household of Mr and Mrs Champion. For a start, there was longstanding bad feeling between Dad and his late wife's parents, most likely something to do with Dad going off with Mum, and the children being taken to the orphanage.

Mum and Dad called Grandfather Champion 'Rotter', behind his back of course. He was a white-haired, bent over old bloke with a white moustache. Grandmother I can't remember at all.

We lasted less than two weeks, just long enough for us kids to get started at school, Alan and Frank at Collingwood Tech and Maurie and I at George Street State School. None of us went to school very many days of our ten days in Melbourne, mostly we wagged it and hung about the streets, and wagging school was something we never did as a rule. Near the end of our stay, Frank began to feel a bit sick. Mum said it was probably the change of water, and nothing was done for him.

It was a glorious relief when Dad told us we were going home to Cosmo Road. We couldn't pack quick enough. Nobody told us what happened. I can only guess that the job didn't eventuate

When it came time for us to depart in the hire car to the station we were horrified that we couldn't find Towser the dog. We searched frantically until the last second but finally had to leave without him. We were heartbroken.

But gee, it was good to be going home.

George Street Fitzroy primary school, c. 1944.
I'm in the row at the extreme right of the picture.

Back at Cosmo road, two weeks passed and we were back to normal when Alan, who had quit school and got a job at the Trentham Dairy on our return, came home with news that he had seen a dog he was sure was Towser tied up outside Dr Gwen's surgery. We could scarcely believe it and all hastened into town. To our amazement the dog was Towser, a sad and sorry wreck if ever there was one. Thin and sore, he could barely put a foot to the ground. Towser nearly turned himself inside out when we approached. It was a joyous reunion.

Dr Gwen had seen the lost dog wandering the road outside the town, and with her characteristic kindness and love of animals, she picked him up and took him home for adoption. He was ravenous, and Dr Gwen was shocked to find that the pads of his feet were worn red raw.

She treated his injuries and fed him well, and within a few days he was returning to normal. That's when she took him for a walk to her surgery and when Alan spotted him tied up outside.

How did Towser make it from Fitzroy to Trentham? We will never know. He wore no collar or identification, so it's unlikely that anybody carried him to Trentham, nor did he come by train. We checked that with the station master, on the chance that Rotter had found him and dispatched him.

We, including Dr Gwen, were convinced that he somehow had made his way on foot, an almost unbelievable accomplishment.

Ten days later, Towser was dead, crushed beneath the wheels of a horsedrawn wagon on the road outside our home. Dad's face reflected the gloom of us all as he carried the small body to a grave we dug behind the house.

For all this time Frank was not feeling well, but there were no definite indications, so Mum didn't think a doctor was necessary.

Dr Gwen recalled Towser in a letter to me over a quarter of a century later. 'I forget his name but not his dedication.' Human patients she sometimes forgot, but a dog, never!

Chapter Fourteen

THE TIMES ARE CHANGING – DEATH CALLS ON US.

It was now 1945, and Towser's death heralded a dramatic period of change in our lives.

A week after we buried Towser, our precious cow Bonny died and Dad had to call the knackery at Kyneton to have her taken away for whatever they did with dead animals. Then the district was gripped by an epidemic of rheumatic fever and it struck down a dozen local kids.

The first victim in our house was Frank. Maybe it was he who brought the illness to town, having felt ill for so long. He came home from school very ill, vomiting and with chest pain and painful swollen joints. Now alarmed, Mum immediately sent Alan to get Doctor Gwen. In half an hour, she came bustling through the door, her medical bag in hand and stethoscope around her neck.

She kept a close watch on Frank for several days, advising our parents that his condition was extremely serious. He had rheumatic fever which had turned to a much more serious rheumatic heart, and the muscles and valves of his heart were badly damaged. There was no known treatment except complete bed rest, assisted by Mum's prayers.

As it turned out, Frank was confined to his bed for sixteen long months, flat on his back, without even a pillow, and Mum became his full time nurse.[*]

---

[*] *Testimony to the treatment from Dr. Gwen lies in the fact that Frank's heart beat on until, in 2006, he was successfully operated on in Brisbane for replacement of damaged valves, as well as a quadruple by-pass. Sixty-one years had passed in which time he had enjoyed generally good health. Arthritis limited his movements when he was 86.*

Frank accepted his fate with typical quiet equanimity. He read mountains of books and comics, listened to the wireless, and through it all he kept smiling.

A highlight for Frank in those months in bed came when he saw advertised 'a rubber stamp engraved with your own name'. It was two shillings and included the stamp pad. Mum sent away for it and in due course the mailman delivered the exciting package. From that day on almost everything we picked up bore the indelible stamp 'Francis R. Braybrook'.

Our mother had so much to contend with: Frank so ill, Dad's poor health, her own health was not good and the worry of Ron in a Japanese prison camp somewhere. Just what she didn't need was for me to be struck down with the same illness as Frank. But I was.

I came home from school feeling sick but didn't say so at first as I wanted to ride the new billycart that Alan had just made for me. Half way through my ride I had to retire and was sent straight to bed. There I was to remain for several months, flat on my back like Frank. Rheumatic fever! Fortunately, my heart damage was not as severe as his but Mum now had two patients to nurse full time, with help from Dad of course. To allow us to be together and in a room with a fireplace and near the wireless, Frank and I took over the sitting room. Both Mum and Dad were wonderful to us.

Maurie was the only one at school now, as Alan was a working man, rising at 4 am to head off to his job at the dairy. After the morning milking, he would do the milk deliveries around town, dispensing milk into the billy cans that hung at every front gate. After the deliveries, he worked around the farm until the night milking, which didn't finish until almost dark. Alan hated the job, working six days a week and twelve hours a day for miserable wages. He handed all his pay to Mum.

The long months passed, and I improved enough to be allowed one pillow. Dr Gwen called on us at least twice a week, carefully going over Frank and me with her stethoscope. We loved Dr Gwen, with her ready smile and kind ways. She was short and round, always dressed in men's clothing, and she had a Craven A cork-tipped cigarette constantly in her mouth or clamped between tar-stained fingers.

After she finished with us, she always gave Dad the once-over before settling down for a ritual cup of tea with Mum. There will never be another like Dr Gwen. For all her care over all the years, we never once received a bill from her. There was no Medicare then, so she was totally unpaid.

Mum also became ill with some kidney problem, and to ease the burden on her, Maurie was sent off to Melbourne to stay with Uncle Roy and Auntie Sadie for a couple of months. Poor Maurie was very upset at being taken from school and stuck in a strange home and strange school at suburban Preston in the big city.

He was treated very well, but the experience had a lasting effect

Maurie and Ian dressed for Sunday School just prior to Dad's death in 1945. Alan is in the background.

on him, and our family was not the same without him. We were all relieved when he returned and it was not hard to see the joy on his smiling face.

With Frank out of danger and me on the mend, things were slowly getting back to normal at Cosmo Road.

In July, the postmaster knocked on our door with a telegram for Mum. Dad was out the back at his garden and Mum answered the knock. Frank and I listened to the conversation.

'I'm afraid it's bad news, Mrs Braybrook,' said the man. 'It's from the Minister for the Army.' He stood there awkwardly.

Mum nodded. 'Thank you, Mr White. Thank you for coming.' She closed the door and came into the room. Dad had come in from the yard to see who the visitor was. Mum had slumped into a chair, she already knew what the telegram said.

Dad took it from her, opened it and read it to himself. Mum looked up at him with eyes pleading as if to say, 'please tell me it's not so.'

'I'm sorry, girl,' said Dad. 'It's Ron. He won't be coming home. He has died.'

His words struck out at us. I buried my head in my pillow as Mum's heart-rending cries filled the room. I wanted to shut out the whole world.

The telegram read simply. 'We regret to advise you that your son Ronald Leslie Collard VX 502110 has died of cholera whilst held as a Japanese prisoner of war in Thailand.' That was all. I remember that the word 'wounds', handwritten by the postmaster, had been crossed out and replaced with 'cholera'. Probably because he was so used to writing 'died from wounds'. (Ron's death was definitely from cholera.)

Somehow Dr Gwen arrived at our door and she set about comforting Mum and putting her to bed with a sedative, all the while talking quietly.

Ron had actually died in July 1943, two years before the telegram, but no word ever came from his dreadful captors. His body was cremated by his mates on site at the Hintock River Camp on the

Burma Railway. His memorial is in the Kanchanaburi War Cemetery in Thailand. He was just nineteen years old.

A month later, the war ended, and a beaming Dad hung a makeshift Australian flag over our front fence, but Ron's death was still fresh in our minds. It was August 15th 1945. And then it was spring.

The day dawned bright and sunny on September the 21st, a little over a month since the war ended. Frank and I were in our beds reading, and Maurie was at school. Mum was not feeling well and was still in her room. Dad and Alan were preparing our breakfast porridge in the kitchen. I don't know why Alan was not at work this day.

Suddenly, Dad dropped the spoon onto the floor and staggered to the table, leaning on it for support. He clutched his chest.

'Alan. Go quick. Get the doctor. I'm sick.'

Alan needed no second bidding and he bolted through our room shouting to Mum. 'Mum! Mum! Dad's sick. I'm going for the doctor.'

He ran out the door, leaving it open. Mum came from her room half dressed and ran to the kitchen. Dad wasn't there. He had staggered down what we called Gooseberry Lane to the thunderbox. Dad had named it Gooseberry Lane because the path was lined each side with gooseberry bushes. Mum found him there, struggling for breath and with perspiration dripping from his forehead. She clasped Dad in her arms and half carried him inside where she put him on the bed in Maurie and Alan's room, which adjoined where I lay.

Frank and I couldn't see, but from the next room we could hear faintly, and against Doctor Gwen's orders we half sat up in our beds straining to listen. I could make out Dad's gasping voice.

'Vron, I'm going.' There was a pause. 'Oh girl, you've had a hard life.' There was another pause as Dad struggled to speak.

'Oh! Vron. What are you going to do with the boys?'

There was complete silence for a short time, and then I heard a dreadful cry from Mum.

I lay there bewildered, listening to the awful sobs and cries from Mum. I was so confused, guessing but not really comprehending, that my dear Dad had just died. It didn't seem real. It was unbelievable, like a dream. I had never considered death for anyone, let alone my father. Frank and I lay there, unable to look at each other across the room, or to speak

Alan had run as fast as his skinny legs would carry him. As he hurried by the sawmill, one of two men working there, Alex Matheson, called to him.

'Hey Alan. Where are you going in such a hurry?'

Alan gasped out his story. The men urged him to keep running to get the doctor and then ran to our home. They came inside and looked at Dad. There was a bit of discussion and they soon emerged. One stayed in the kitchen trying to comfort Mum while the other went out to the roadside to wait for the doctor.

Dr Gwen arrived soon after, pushing quickly through the door. Her first thought was for Frank and I, and she promptly checked our hearts with her stethoscope. Satisfied there was no damage from shock she went through to Dad. The sawmill man had already told her that Dad was dead. She went to check him, soon coming back into our room gazing at Frank and me.

She didn't speak, but as I looked at her through a misty haze I saw what I am sure were tears on her ruddy cheeks. Swinging into action, she then took control of the situation, sedating Mum and putting her to bed where Alan sat with her, trying his best to be brave through his tears. She then took off in her ute to Trentham to get Maurie from school and to break the news of his father's death. Before long, she led the sobbing boy inside and placed him in the room with Mum and Alan, moving again to where Dad lay.

When she had arrived home, Dr Gwen telephoned the undertaker in Kyneton and around lunchtime he arrived in his ute. A short time later he took Dad away.

I don't know now how I coped with the death of my father. My memory of that is almost blank. My brothers are similar, Frank told me when he was 86 years old that he couldn't properly comprehend it. 'I didn't grasp that it was the end of the line for Dad. I expected him to turn up again.'

Maurie still felt guilt many years later. 'Dad asked me to get him some firewood before I went to school, and I said I didn't have time. I always have wished I had done as he asked.'

I believe our collective poor memory is nature's way of helping us to cope.

The night before he died, Dad came to my bed to kiss me goodnight as he always did.

'Goodnight, Jock.' He sometimes called me Jock. 'See you tomorrow.' He kissed me on the forehead.

'Goodnight, Daddy.' I snuggled down in my blankets to go to sleep.

Chapter Fifteen

A FUNERAL – NEW FRIENDS – SOUTH KINGSVILLE – SPOTSWOOD.

Frank and I, both bedridden, couldn't go to Dad's funeral. My mother was in a terrible state; all things combined were almost too much for her. She said to me when I was a man, 'Your father was the only man I ever really loved. When I lost him, I was not sure what I could or would do.'

There was nothing in the Trentham Gazette except a small notice of the death of Arthur Andrew Braybrook, placed by the undertaker. There was no obituary or any further word. The Braybrook family were relative unknowns and certainly not worthy of any space in the Trentham Gazette. Although we regularly attended church and Sunday School, Mum received no help from that quarter.

Because Dad received monthly copies by mail of the communist newspaper The Guardian, it was thought by some that he was a communist. He wasn't, but was a true Labor supporter. He had become disillusioned during the depression, and for a time, became a member of the Communist Party, as had so many others. News travels fast in small towns.

Most of Dad's friends came to his funeral, as well as Uncle Roy and Auntie Sadie and Mum's sister Phemie from Melbourne. Dad's children from his first marriage couldn't attend; Arthur and Sidney were off in the Army, and Mary, Margaret and Charlie could not be contacted in time. My mate Joe from Barry's Reef came, picking up Bill Bunt from Blue Mount in his spring cart as he passed. There were a number of others, including Alf and Olive Flenley and Stan Franzke, the eucalyptus distiller, and his mother. Phemie made a wreath from native plants.

The big surprise was the arrival from far off Sydney of the Reverend

Mr Alley to conduct the service. Mr Alley was a long-time friend of Dad's from his time in Ballarat, a minister of the Church of England. When contacted by phone by Uncle Roy, Mr Alley insisted on making the long train journey for the funeral, delaying it for a couple of days.

A true friend, Mr Alley had played an important part in our lives several years before, but we boys weren't aware of it at the time. Mum and Dad were always deeply troubled by the fact that they could not marry and confided in Mr Alley. It was he who arranged for a quiet divorce for Mum. Divorces were not usual and were often humiliating public affairs in those days. The divorce became final on September 3rd 1941, and Mr Alley married the couple three days later.

Uncle Roy built a brick surround for Dad's grave before he and Sadie returned to Preston. The bricks remained there until replaced by a proper memorial to Mum and Dad, placed by my brother Ken Rae in 1984.

A week after Dad's funeral, everybody had gone home and we were left to ourselves. It was a sad and empty house.

Then it was Christmas, our first without Dad. I was now fully recovered from my illness and Frank, now aged fourteen and a massive seventeen stone, was allowed out of bed occasionally. Mum took us for a walk to visit Dad's grave and we all wept.

Mum had managed to find a few small things for the pillow cases we optimistically left out for Santa Claus. My favourite was a gift from Alan, a wooden car with Nugget shoe polish tin wheels that he had made himself. It meant a lot to me. We had a great Christmas dinner, too, with all the trimmings – baked spuds, mutton and fresh veggies from Dad's garden. Mum had even managed to find ten threepenny coins for the Christmas pudding, making sure we each got two when she served it.

Dad had always said grace at every meal and today Mum said a special prayer I remember well.

'For what we are about to receive, Lord, we are truly thankful.

Your boys will be alright. Amen.' There was a lengthy silence as we thought of the man we loved so much.

After we boys had washed up, we went outside, making our way to the vegetable garden down the back. Somehow, the garden brought us closer to Dad. We stood in silence until I took my toy car and ran it over the path.

'Brrmm, brrmm.' Alan looked at me tearfully and kicked a tomato stake out of the ground. With Frank and Maurie he walked silently toward the bush. I pushed my car with the Nugget tin wheels over a mound of earth, trying not to think of Dad or anything else.

* * *

George and Lorna Thomas were a young couple with two small daughters and had a holiday shack up the road, about a half-a-mile away. They lived in the city but spent as much time as they could at their retreat. They knew of Mum's situation and one day called in to visit, to see if they could help.

From then on they called on us every time they came to their shack and we became very good friends. Mum told us we were to call them Uncle and Aunty.

Uncle George was young and extremely fit, being what we called a health fanatic. Dark-haired and bright-eyed he was a caring, helpful person and Aunty Lorna was the same. A big lump of a woman with bright blue eyes, she radiated warmth and had a great sense of humour, with an accompanying ready laugh. We looked forward to their visits.

On one such visit they brought a strange man with them, Gilbert Rae, their widowed neighbour from South Kingsville. We liked Mr Rae, and he also became a frequent visitor. Black-haired, wiry looking and about forty years old, he was obviously a man who worked hard with his hands. He paid a lot of attention to Mum, and they seemed to get along well. Mum told us that Mr Rae had three sons at home with him and a daughter who lived with his aging aunts.

Mum wasn't in good health, and on one of the Thomas' visits, it was decided that I should go with them to South Kingsville for a while, to give Mum a break.

I was mortified and cried at the suggestion, but I soon found myself in the back seat of Thomas' old Overland tourer with the girls, blue-eyed blondes, Lorraine and Lesley. Everyone came to the car to see me off while I bawled my eyes out.

'Mum, I don't want to go,' I sobbed. 'I want to stay here with you.' I tried to clamber out of the car, restrained by Aunty Lorna. The girls giggled. I hated girls and especially those two.

'Now you be good for Aunty Lorna, Ian,' said Mum. 'Off you go. It's only for a week or two. Be good. You'll be back soon.'

She patted my hand which was firmly gripping the door sill. The Overland engine roared, and I was whisked away toward Melbourne. I felt shocked, betrayed and bewildered. I hated Melbourne. I loved my home and my brothers, and I was just settling back at school after my long illness. I had never felt so miserable.

Two hours later, I was at South Kingsville, in a strange house with two horrible girls that I despised. I had never had girls around before, and I didn't have any use for them.

I didn't have much time to reflect on my fate because at eight the next morning Aunty Lorna enrolled me at the Spotswood State School. It was awful, and Aunty Lorna had to drag me every step of the way.

'Why do I have to go to school? I'm only here for a week!'

Lorna ignored my protest, and soon I was sitting in the grade three classroom with twenty strange kids who seemed to regard me as some sort of alien.

There were some positive things about city life. For example, I had never lived in a house with electricity before, and I marveled at that. And I saw my first movie ever at The Sun theatre in Yarraville, a short bus ride away from South Kingsville. The big yellow Maple Leaf was the first bus I ever rode in, too, and I loved that.

I got to know the three Rae kids, sons of our regular visitor Mr Rae, the Thomas's neighbour. They were tough street kids, prone to throwing punches and therefore respected by all the kids in the neighbourhood who gave them a wide berth. There was Bill, the quiet one, about fifteen years old and already at work at Henry B. Smith's woollen mill at Williamstown with his father; Gil Junior, eleven, and Murray, who was dark-haired and cheeky looking, aged nine. I got to walk to school with Gil and Murray and to know them well. They were always dirty, with uncombed hair, rough clothes and they rarely wore shoes and socks.

Under the grime I found two good mates. They even gave me a nickname, a real status symbol. 'Brains' they called me; nothing to do with my intelligence, it was probably derived from Braybrook, but I tried hard in third grade to live up to it. 'We'll look after you, Brains,' said Gil one day as we played 'kick the tin' on our walk home from school. 'If any kids give you any strife you tell me, and I'll belt the shit outta them.' The word spread, and no kid ever gave me any strife.

My week or two at the Thomas's had stretched into almost two months when, one Friday morning, George announced that I was going home the very next day. I was thrilled to bits and was beside myself with joy when the Overland finally drew up at our gate at Cosmo Road. I leapt from the car to wrap my arms around Colonel our dog who ran

Gil Rae Junior in uniform at Puckapunyal. National Service, 1956.

to meet us, and I think he was more excited than me. Then Mum appeared, smiling and happy, wiping her hands on her hessian apron. No woman had ever looked so good.

'Oh, Ian love. It's so good to have you home. We've all missed you so much. I'm sorry it was so long.'

She hugged and kissed me, fussing at my unruly hair, trying to slick down my permanent cocky's crest with saliva on her hand. She always did that and I hated it. I cried a little, though.

Leaving Mum with George and Lorna, and with Colonel at my side, I ran off to find my wonderful brothers who were felling trees in the bush behind the house. I was home at last!

Chapter Sixteen

Mum gets a job – leaving Trentham – a surprise wedding.

I wasn't at home at Cosmo Road for long, however, because Mum told us a short time later that she was going to the city about a job, the details of which she spared us. If she accepted it we would be going to live there. Next day she boarded the train and was gone for three days.

Things sometimes change overnight, and so it was while Mum was away that Alan got sacked from his job at the dairy. The owner had decided to pension off his old carthorse, Sam, and replace him with a flighty youngster. Alan loved Sam and hated the idea, especially when the dairyman took Sam out into the bush and shot him. Alan was shocked, angry and very bitter toward the boss.

To break in the new horse the man took control of the deliveries, driving the cart himself as Alan ran to and fro with the milk billies. In Market Street, something spooked the young horse and he bolted, completely out of control, with the driver frantically trying to rein him in. It was no use. The horse hit the next corner at a gallop and the milk cart tipped over, throwing the driver to the roadside in a shower of milk and a clatter of cans. The cart was wrecked, but the boss was unhurt, sitting on the grass among his battered cans and his clothes and face sprayed milk white. The runaway horse careered on at a gallop toward the edge of town, dragging the shattered cart with it.

Alan ran up to the scene shouting, 'I told you, you bugger. You shouldn't have shot Sam.' The boss was livid and sacked Alan on the spot. My brother could scarcely conceal his delight. As he related the story at home, we all fell about laughing, the only dark spot was how he was going to tell Mum when she returned.

As it eventuated, it didn't matter, as when our mother arrived home she announced that she had taken a job as Mr Rae's live-in housekeeper and that we were leaving next week for South Kingsville.

So that's what the job was!

'I'm not going,' stated Alan.

'Me neither,' defied Frank. Maurie and I said nothing but we shared our brothers' sentiments.

'Oh, yes you are. How do you expect us to stay here? I just can't manage on my own and that's that,' growled Mum, and that was the end of the matter. Nobody defied my Mum for long. Looking back, I now understand the impossible situation she was left in when Dad died, although I couldn't at the time.

A furniture van arrived a few days later. We loaded every possession in it, including our dog, Mum's chooks and pot plants and Alan's stinking ferrets, and we were away.

I hated leaving Trentham, but leaving my Dad all alone was the hardest part. Leaving the school also bothered me. I had made some friends there.

Mum left instructions with a real estate agent to sell the house, which he did soon after, for two hundred pounds. It was a windfall, as Mum had been able to pay the house loan off with Ron's deferred pay and back pay from the Army.

It wasn't a big house at Greene Street, South Kingsville, and I'm not sure how we all fitted in. Mum and Mr Rae had their own separate rooms and the seven of us boys slept where there was space.

I finished up amongst a roomful of furniture in the lounge room at the front, and Alan and Bill occupied a sleepout to which was attached Gil's pigeon coop. He was right into pigeons, as were many city working class kids then. Gil, Maurie and Murray shared one room

It's just as well that we all got along together, but somehow we were kindred spirits, with me gravitating to Murray, the one closest to my age. We became good mates. Alan got a job with Bill and

Mr Rae at Smith's woollen mill in Williamstown, Frank got work at Massey's Garage in Yarraville, Maurie went off to the Geelong Road State School in Footscray where they still taught eighth grade, and I went back to Spotswood school with Gil and Murray. We had all settled in pretty well after a couple of months when Mum made a shock announcement. She and Mr Rae were to be married the next weekend!

You could have knocked us over with a feather. The next Saturday they took their vows at the Presbyterian Church in Yarraville. It was November, 1946 and my dad had been dead just over a year. As usual, we kids were left out, with only Uncle Roy, Aunty Sadie and Aunty Phemie attending the wedding. There was a bit of a booze-up party in the afternoon, with beer and whiskey, and some cakes, lemonade and sandwiches sent out for us kids playing in the street, and that was that.

I suddenly had a stepfather and we were told to call him Pop. That was a relief as there was no way I could have called him Dad. I also had three new brothers and soon I was to have a sister, Lillian.

Lillian was Pop's seven-year-old daughter who was raised the past two years by maiden aunts at Carnegie following the death of her mother. The weekend after the wedding, Mum took me on the train to Carnegie to meet Lillian and the aunts, the Misses Winder. There were four of them, all spinsters, Lily, Liza, Lal and Ethel, all perfect ladies, like figures out of a Dickens novel. They were all in their seventies

Ian, Murray and Lillian about 1947 at South Kingsville.

and lived in their spotless home in Jersey Parade, and they doted on their great-niece.

I then met Lillian for the first time, a cute little girl with a red ribbon in her fair hair and a shy, warm smile. We had nothing to say to each other. When we arrived at Jersey Parade it was lunchtime and Aunt Lily had prepared a delicious meal of tripe. I hated tripe. I loathed tripe. It revolted me. There was nothing in the world I abhorred more than tripe and Aunt Lily served me up this whopping great pile of the muck floating in white sauce and green parsley. I poked and prodded at it, forcing some down my throat but at the same time smuggling handfuls into my blazer pocket. Great dollops of white, sodden, squashy tripe, garnished with parsley, soon filled the right pocket. I couldn't reach the left without being detected so I had to eat the rest.

I have no other memories of the visit, but it must have gone well, with the Aunts voting Mum as suitable to take over the rearing of Lillian, and giving Pop the go-ahead.

Lillian, Ian, and Maurie in the saddle. About 1949, possibly at Dixie.

Left to right: Maurie, Gil, Lillian, Murray. Rear: Pop and Frank. About 1946.

While everyone else talked, I sneaked down the yard and emptied my pocket of tripe behind the shed, sponging the vast mass of white sauce from within my pocket with my handkerchief at the gully trap tap. Nobody was any the wiser after I'd finished my remarkable job of cleaning.

It was decided that Mum could collect Lillian next weekend, which she did.

The weary duo arrived at Greene Street the following Sunday afternoon, both lugging suitcases as big as themselves, exhausted from the long walk from the bus stop.

Lillian was assigned to share the front room with me, and we jammed another bed into the already crowded space. We were the shyest pair of kids you'd ever meet and got on well after we overcame the initial strangeness. In later years, Lillian described me as a frightened, scared little boy. I certainly was. It's fair to say that I had been through the mill in my eight years of life. Lillian and I went on to become lifelong friends, probably as close as any true brother and sister. We all called her Lil, but she preferred Lillian. 'I have four names really. I am Lillian, Ethel, Margaret, Rose, Rae.'

I have never been sure if that was truth or her romantic imagination.

In spite of being reasonably happy the Braybrook boys couldn't come to terms with being city dwellers, and we longed to be back near our father.

Unknown to me, Alan and Maurie devised a plan of escape. They also took Gil into the plan as he was one for adventure, besides he had an old bike with wheels that would be handy. Frank was left out because he liked his job, and I was just a kid who would get in the way.

Down in the shed they constructed a large timber trailer, mounted on Gil's wheels, with a drawbar to attach to Alan's recently acquired Malvern Star semi-racer. It was cumbersome and heavy, but it would suffice for the planned getaway. Over the next week they secretly loaded the trailer with necessities for the proposed journey, and on a dark, overcast Saturday morning they ran away, heading for

Trentham and home.

The plan was a dismal failure. It began to rain soon after they departed, and by the time darkness fell, they had made it only as far as the ABC Radio transmission tower at St Albans. They weren't even a quarter of the way, and already, all the food, calculated to last a week, had been eaten, mostly by Maurie and Gil, the water bottle was empty, and the walkers and riders were wet and exhausted. To add to the problem the trailer got a flat tyre and there was no puncture outfit.

The dejected trio abandoned the trailer at the 3AR transmitter site. The engineer in charge told them they could leave their machinery there. 'I don't think the ABC will mind,' he laughed. I wonder if the decaying bike and trailer might still be there, hidden behind the transmitter hut!

After a sleepless night camped on the ground by the roadside, the would-be escapees made their way home. Not a word was said by either Pop or Mum, much to the astonishment of the runaways who expected a thrashing.

We eventually adjusted to life in the city, even got to enjoy it at times, and it seemed we were destined to remain city dwellers. We boys had a meeting and resolved to make the best of it.

Chapter Seventeen

CITY LIFE – BEACH BUMS – LANCE CREEK – A NEW UTE.

Murray became my friend at Greene Street. Mostly we played motor cars with Murray's tiny Bakelite toy car that we called Mandrake's car because it looked like the one Mandrake drove in The Herald comic strip.

Occasionally I played with Lillian, but initially I preferred to ignore her, leaving her to her sissy dolls and things. Gradually, however, I got used to her being a girl and we got to be great playmates.

Riding the see-saw, slide and swings at the nearby, sparsely equipped public playground and seeing who could swing the highest and 'see London' was a popular activity and we played a lot of hopscotch on the pavement, which Lillian always won, and we played cricket on the vacant land opposite with all the kids in the neighbourhood.

Being the youngest, Lillian and I always ended up doing the 'foxing', retrieving the ball, and only rarely were part of a team. When that did happen, the big kids scorned our feeble efforts at batting and bowling, and we were sent back to foxing.

I loved to play marbles with Lillian, Murray and the neighbourhood kids. We'd be down on our haunches or on hands and knees on any flat patch of ground, usually just plain dirt, and we'd play for hours, covered in dust and dirt. We each had our own little rag bag of marbles, beautifully coloured balls of glass. We each had a special marble that had special power for a 'taw' and, if lucky, a tombowler. The taw was the marble the shooter used to fire at his opponents marbles. We would draw a two-foot circle in the dirt, scratch a straight line in the centre on which to place a selected number of our marbles and we had our playing area. The first one to knock all the opponents' marbles out of the ring was the winner. Sometimes we played 'for keeps', meaning you kept all the marbles you knocked from the ring, but mostly it was just pure fun, as marbles were too precious to lose.

The big bonfire on Guy Fawkes night was a highlight. We kids spent a lot of time and energy piling collected timber, rubbish, old car tyres – anything that would burn – on the vacant land opposite our home. It was a fabulous night with huge explosions as the neighbourhood kids (and adults) let off hundreds of crackers and rockets. Some kids had massive penny bungers that made a hell of a noise. It was fabulous fun as the huge bonfire belched thick clouds of choking black smoke, most of it from the car tyres.

Skipping the rope was another favourite pastime and we skipped our little hearts out. As we skipped, we chanted: 'Charlie over the

Murray and Ian show off their new toys. Murray holds his bakelite Mandrake car and Ian holds an unknown toy.

mountain, Charlie over the sea, Charlie came to my house and had a cup of tea.' Or: 'Who you gonna marry? Tinker, tailor, soldier, sailor, rich man, poor man, beggar man, thief'. And things like that, simple games and simple fun, but we enjoyed it so much. We kids talked together and played together, got to know each other well, and were real mates.

We played cowboys and Indians with homemade six-guns made of wood and bows and arrows made of sticks from bushes; we flew homemade kites made from newspaper glued together with paste made from flour and water; we kicked homemade footballs made from tightly rolled newspaper tied with string; we had tug-of-war and tunnel ball and sack races. We made shanghais, officially called catapults, and we set up targets and held shooting contests. Some of our shanghais were works of art and took hours to make, mostly from cut up old bike tubes attached to forked sticks. No wonder kids back then were so much trimmer and fitter – we never stopped still. Obesity was unheard of.

In December, Pop quit his job at Henry B. Smith's and began at McVey's Poultry Farm which was only a stone's throw from home. He was a hard worker, and it seemed natural to him to have his family at work also, so he got Gil and Maurie an after-school job with him. The two lads were not at all impressed, especially as they had to pay most of their earnings to Mum for board.

Our pleasures remained simple – games we made up ourselves, and in the evening, listening to the wireless. My favourite wireless shows were 'Fifty and Over' and 'The search for the Golden Boomerang', a nightly serial proudly sponsored by Hoadley's Violet Crumble Bars.

I made friends with a boy of my age who lived directly behind us. His name was Ray Sargant. Ray and I built a billycart out of an old pram. It wasn't flash but we felt 'just it' as we took turns in pulling each other in rides around the block.

Around the corner from Greene Street lived a rough and ready boy named Georgie Smith, one of the local tough kids. He built himself a racer billycart just to show off and make Ray and I feel bad. We hated it when he and his mate raced past us at high speed with Georgie shouting 'Caltex Oil does this', a well known advertising slogan of the time. Then we found out that his wheels were discarded ball bearings from a truck gearbox. No wonder he went so fast. We thought it was cheating, and Ray and I hated him more after that.

One day, Gil came home with terrible news. My mate Ray had taken ill and been rushed to hospital where he had died. I was absolutely crushed. I could not understand how one so young and healthy could die. I didn't go to visit his parents again because I had no idea what I could say to them. I was never told what caused Ray's death, nor was it discussed at home.

Just near home, a railway spur line led to Borthwicks Abattoirs and Hardies Asbestos Factory, about two miles away. Gil and the others used to go to Borthwicks, 'Bothies' they called it, to watch the slaughtering. They took me along one day, and I'll never forget the spectacle of the horror mixed with fascination I felt as I watched the slaughtermen at work. It was crude and disgusting. The bovine victim would be herded into a crush, unable to move in any direction. Above the animal was a platform on which stood a powerful man with a pointed sledge hammer. He would swing his arms high and bring the hammer down with all his force between the eyes of the animal. The cow fell instantly and within seconds it was hoisted by the rear legs high on a block and tackle where another man slashed its throat with a wicked blade. Blood would gush sickeningly in a huge volume into a large, tub. Another man slit the belly and the guts spilled into a vat on wheels, then it went to a processing plant. It was horror as bad as I could imagine, and I visited only once.

Another time came news that one of Gil's mates was almost killed when he fished a discarded wartime mortar bomb from a culvert along the railway near Borthwicks. He fiddled with it and it exploded. There was a lot of talk about that at home. The boy was badly hurt but fully recovered.

I shudder when I think of the boat rides we used to take in the huge depths of water in the abandoned quarries nearby.

The bigger boys made a boat out of second-hand corrugated iron. It was about eight feet long and there were plenty of nail holes. The folded over ends were sealed with nothing more substantial than mud! Our boat leaked like a sieve, but we managed to keep her afloat by bailing with a couple of five pound jam tins. Two or three of us used to get in the boat and push off, using bits of board for paddles, and it was terrific fun. The water in those old quarries would probably have been very deep. I couldn't swim a stroke and would surely have drowned if anything had gone amiss.

Some stories should not be told, but there are a couple involving Maurie and Gil that deserve to be, in spite of the suspect morality or legality. Let's face it, neither they nor I considered their actions illegal or immoral at the time.

The two haunted the Williamstown beach, and when a group went in to swim they raided their pockets and bags for cash. They got away with heaps of small amounts and had a secret cache for any money not immediately needed to buy lollies, drinks or smokes. One day, Maurie went to the cache for funds and it was empty.

'I never really trusted Gil again after that,' Maurie told me years later. Maybe there is no honour among thieves!

Maurie and Gil were learning boxing at Yarraville, and when walking home one summer evening they carried out a most daring raid.

The two had built a crystal radio set, but couldn't listen to it without a set of headphones. Their need was desperate and when they spotted through a shadeless window an aging man slumped in a lounge chair asleep with headphones attached to his ears, they struck. They crept silently inside through the open door and, as quick as a flash, Gil snatched the headphones from the sleeper's head. The startled man leapt to his feet and the two thieves bolted. The shouting, cursing man gave chase but had no hope of catching the super fit youngsters.

Gil and Maurie explained the headphones to Mum as being found at the tip and she accepted that without question.

I'll bet that the old man who lost his headphones wondered about the attack and theft until his dying day.

The dilapidated old dressing sheds at the Williamstown beach were a popular spot too. We were told that by a difficult climb onto the roof and a bit of contortion that a clear view into the ladies shed was available through an opening. Murray and I went up there once and no such view was available. Alas, we would have to keep wondering what a naked female looked like.

In mid 1947, Pop decided he'd had enough of city life. He was a bushman at heart, having been born and raised at Foster in Gippsland, and later struggled on a Mallee wheat farm where he had stayed until starved out by yet another drought.

He applied for a couple of share farming jobs from the Weekly Times and soon landed a farm at Lance Creek, near Wonthaggi in South Gippsland.

We were to become farmers and therefore needed a suitable motor vehicle, so Pop went out and bought a 1927 Studebaker tourer.

Bringing the car to a halt outside our Greene Street home, where all the kids in the neighbourhood swarmed to get a geek at the new car, Pop announced some changes had to be made to the Studie. 'A tourer is alright for the city but in the bush we'll need a ute. Help me get some tools and we'll cut her down.'

We all trooped into the garden shed, emerging with axes, pinch bars, hammers and saws. Out in the street, Pop got to work, cutting off the canvas top, re-shaping the rear of the body, ripping out the rear seat and putting down a timber floor and fitting a rear tailgate. Within a few hours we had a pretty good looking ute.

Pop took off to the shops at Yarraville and returned with brushes, turps and a gallon tin of bright red enamel. All of us kids got stuck into painting, and in an hour a gleaming red machine sat shimmering at the roadside, the quickest transformation of a car in history.

Pop sent Bill in to get Mum and when she emerged she stared in wonder.

'Oh my God,' she stammered. 'Look at it! It's awful! The colour. It's dreadful. It's like the Red Terror.'

And that's what the Studie was called forever after, the Red Terror.

A week later, we departed number 27 Greene Street for Lance Creek and this bold new adventure.

We helped load our stuff in the furniture van. God knows how the driver crammed it all in. There were nine beds and mattresses alone, almost a load on its own, but finally he squeezed the tailgate closed. The few remaining bits, including Mum's pot plants, six chooks, Colonel, and Lillian's scooter went in the ute with all of us kids. It was pretty crowded, with Mum and Pop up front and Maurie, Bill, Alan Frank, Murray, Gil, Lillian and me in the back. We must have looked like the prototype for Ma and Pa Kettle, whose first movie appearance came in the same year.

We could scarcely move, and the overloaded Red Terror lurched and swayed alarmingly as we followed the furniture van down the

The 'Red Terror' loaded for Lance Creek. L to R: Gil, Maurie, Frank, Pop at the wheel, Lesley Thomas, Lillian, Colonel the dog and Ian.

Princes Highway. Pop had a hell of a job keeping the old car upright, let alone in a straight line, and we passengers clung on for dear life to whatever solid piece we could find.

Ten miles from Wonthaggi, the constant sway of the ute caught up with me, and I was hit by a rush of nausea, vomiting profusely over the ute's side. The rush of wind hurled my vomit backwards and those behind me were sprayed voluminously with fresh vomit.

It was pandemonium, and the outraged cries and shouts eventually reached Pop who slowed the old ute to a steaming stop. There was a lot of abuse, muttering and mopping from my fellow passengers, most of whom copped a spray.

It was a welcome stop and boys lined up on one side of the road and girls squatted on the other.

After half an hour, with tempers and Studebaker cooled, and during which Lillian rode her scooter up and down the dusty road, I felt better and we resumed the journey. At four o'clock we arrived at our new home and a new way of life, Dave Atkinson's dairy farm at Lance Creek.

Chapter Eighteen

ANOTHER SCHOOL ~ SNAKES ALIVE ~ THE PIG ~ CUDGEE CALLS.

It was almost dark by the time we unloaded the furniture, and after a 'throw together tea', as Mum called it, we were all ready for bed.

It was all hands on deck at 5.30 next morning for the first milking. Dave Atkinson came along to familiarise Pop and the boys with the procedures.

Dave was a typical cow cocky, a bit rough and ready, tight as a fish's arsehole, but a nice enough bloke. He was about forty-five, craggy-faced, tall and thin and lived with his wife on his other farm about two miles away.

He also had timber interests and offered Bill and Alan a job felling trees nearby, which they were glad to accept. Neither were too keen on being cow cockies, in hindsight a prudent outlook.

Even by our standards the farmhouse was run down. Inside and out hadn't seen paint for years, the rusted roof was lifting in places and the verandah sagged sadly with decayed boards, joists and stumps. It was filthy too, and Lillian, Mum and I spent our first week cleaning it and placing the furniture. It didn't look too bad after that. I reckon it had been home to rats, possums and snakes for a few years. Cows had roamed the garden and it was a mess, but Mum soon got that looking pretty good. The main garden feature was an aged mulberry tree that hung over the back verandah and we feasted on its fruit that summer. Right then it was early winter, however, and a relatively quiet time on the farm. Many of the cows were 'dried off' and only eighty were lined up for milking. By September we would be milking two hundred, with eight machines, so it was a good time to start to learn the ropes. Fortunately, Pop was a natural farmer and picked up 'cow cockying' in no time.

It was evident that the farm couldn't support us all, so Maurie got a job on the next door farm of Mr Bolling. Most of his thirty shillings a week he handed to Mum for board, and Alan and Bill both chipped in. Often it was the only money Mum had.

Maurie got Saturday afternoons off, so he joined the Glen Elvie footy team and played for a while with them. They rarely won a match and Maurie said the best feature of their game was playing at home where the oval had a steep downhill slope to one end. They had a better chance to win then as kicking downhill was an advantage. If he won the toss the captain always chose the downhill end for the opening quarter hoping to build a demoralizing big lead by quarter time. Sometimes it worked and they won.

My biggest dread was starting another school. I was nine and about to make my seventh start, counting twice at Trentham and Spotswood, but as it turned out, it wasn't too bad. There were only about twenty kids and they were all quite friendly.

Mr Vague, the lone teacher, was pleasant enough and as fit as a scrub bull. He rode his bicycle to and from Wonthaggi each day.

Mr Vague wanted to instil a bit of fitness into his pupils, so we had regular periods of physical training – running, jumping, handstands, skipping, tunnel ball and footy were played every day. I liked the

All that remains of the Lance Creek primary school, 2005.

handstands we did every day as I had to hold a grade five girl's legs up by the ankles to balance her. She wore very loose-legged pants and I always got an eyeful. Many of the boys' pants were loose-legged too and few wore underpants, so it wasn't uncommon for an appendage to be revealed, to the delighted giggles of the girls.

I sometimes wonder how one of us kids didn't die from walking to school. It was only a mile, but the hazards were many. In winter, we crossed the creek by walking across a fallen tree which straddled it. The stream was often flooded, and sometimes the water rushed with great power, covering the log with a foot of water. How we didn't slip and get swept away I don't know.

Sometimes the water was several feet above our log and then we had to walk the long way by road, about two miles. Whenever there was any chance of crossing the log we used it rather than walking the extra distance.

One particularly wet day, even the road bridge was well below water. None of us, including Mr Vague, could cross it, so there was no school that day. We kids were pretty pleased.

In that first (and last) summer at Lance Creek we had an even worse hazard than flooded creeks. The path to school, especially around the creek, was moving with potentially deadly snakes. We all came so close to standing on them it's a marvel that we weren't bitten. They slithered in all directions. I have never before or since seen so many, and often our feet missed one by inches as

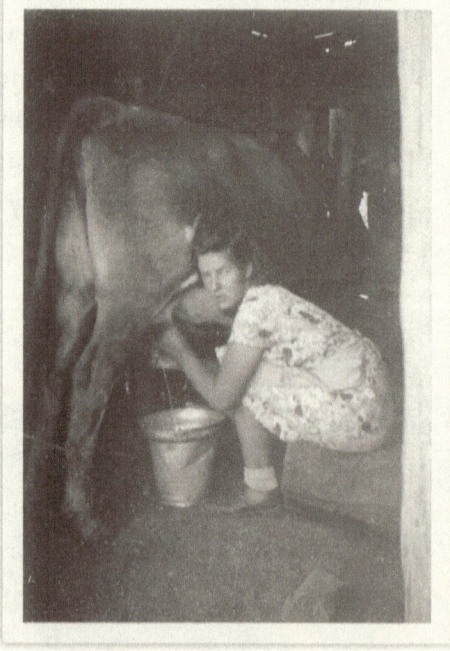

Lillian milking a cow. As you can see, she was not posed.

the disgruntled Joe Blake slipped speedily away. Maurie's boss, Mr Bolling, capitalised on the bountiful snake population and had a lucrative sideline catching the things by the tail and slipping them into hessian bags. He took them to Melbourne to sell to the Commonwealth Serum Laboratories where they were used for making anti-venom, using horses as factories.

I've not a lot of unhappy memories of school at Lance Creek, so I must have enjoyed it, but one incident sticks in my memory.

Mum used to make bread when we ran short of money and it had a very yeasty smell about it. It was more like a large scone, and it didn't taste too flash either. One day, I sat on a stump beside Billy Millikins to eat our lunches. When I unwrapped my newspaper package of plum jam sangers Billy sniffed audibly. 'Struth,' he said grimacing. 'I can smell dead ants.' I shifted my package down wind.

There were other hazards too. Once, in October, a swooping magpie dive-bombed poor Lillian and gashed her skull. There was blood everywhere and I thought she was killed, but it wasn't a serious injury. There was more damage done to her red, hand-knitted Pixie hat that she wore everywhere. The Pixie hat and a brown overcoat. The older boys used to tease her calling, 'Red Pixie! Brown coat!' which embarrassed poor Lillian.

Mum insisted she wear that gear, so she had no choice, even if she had another outfit, which she didn't. What a life for a little, gentle girl among all of us boys, but she coped well.

I turned ten when we were at Lance Creek. It was no big occasion, but Mum made me a cake with candles and I got a shy peck on the cheek from Lillian as we washed the dishes on the verandah that evening. Lillian and I did all the washing up, no easy task for a big family of farmers. We always washed up on the verandah at night, by the light of a kerosene lamp, as there was no electricity at the farm, using a tin dish and a tin tray for draining. We took it turn about washing and drying. The hot water came from the big cast-iron boiler always bubbling on the stove, and we used Preservene bar soap enclosed in a metal soap-saver for suds. Preservene was cheaper than Velvet.

Every day, Mum boiled the copper in the lean-to washhouse for the mountain of washing she had. It was my job to get the wood and light the copper after school. Except for work-wear, she also had to iron most things, using three cast-iron flat irons heated on top of the wood stove. The housework was hard and constant, and Lillian and I helped as soon as we got home from school. We were good at preparing food, polishing, ironing and making beds and experts at washing dishes and making school sandwiches.

My brother Frank proved to be allergic to cows and developed maddening dermatitis on hands and arms. There was no real cure, so he suffered quite badly for all our time there.

Murray loved to ride his pony, which bolted on him one day as he rounded up the cows. It threw him into a gatepost with terrific force and he ended up in Wonthaggi Hospital with bruised kidneys. He soon recovered and was back riding his beloved pony.

I thought I'd killed Lillian one Saturday as we were polishing the vast expanses of Wundawaxed linoleum floors. To make a game of it I sat Lillian on a blanket and whisked her round and round at great speed. It polished very well but alas, it came to an end when Lillian toppled backwards and belted her head a beauty on the hard floor. It laid her right out for a minute but she finally opened her eyes, dazed and hurt. That frightened the shit out of me. She didn't tell Mum, however, and suffered in silence, but we gave that game away after that.

We once attended the local sports day held in a cow cocky's paddock near the school. Dairy farmers and their families came from miles around. It was great fun, with lots of events like egg and spoon races, sack races and climbing a heavily greased pole. Most of the males had a go at that, the object being to find who could climb the highest. Young Gil represented our mob, but he didn't win.

The most exciting event was catching the greasy pig. A young porker was placed in a smallish yard and smothered in grease. Contestants took turns to see who could grab and hold the unfortunate and terrified creature. Again, although he struggled valiantly, Gil Junior didn't win, but he came a close second. How the RSPCA would love to see such an event today!

We loved to play cowboys and Indians. Our six shooters, bows and arrows were all made from sticks. Gil was the expert at this and sat on the fence one day giving elaborate, lengthy instructions. Dangling from the leg of his shorts was his penis. He was completely oblivious to this and Lillian nearly choked with laughter. It was one of those memorable scenes that stay in the mind.

Early summer was harvest time and everybody pitched in to cut, rake and stack the grass hay. It was hot, hard work on top of all the regular farm chores. Lillian and I had our job to do keeping the billy cans of hot tea and rough cut sandwiches up to the workers, carrying them on foot a half mile or more through the paddocks.

One hot day, Dave Atkinson was raking the fresh cut grass into windrows perched proudly at the wheel of his new Fordson kerosene tractor. Stopping for smoko, he leapt back up onto the hessian bag-covered cast iron seat to restart when he let out a God-almighty yell.

'Jesus Christ!' he roared. 'What the bloody hell!'

Maurie, Frank and Gil doubled up with mirth. They had killed a large black snake as they crossed the paddock and carefully placed it beneath Dave's hessian seat cover while he had his smoko. When Dave plonked his bum on the seat he felt something strangely soft and wobbly. He pulled aside the bag to investigate, and when

Pop, the happy pig farmer at Lance Creek.

he saw the snake, the poor bloke nearly had a heart attack. He saw no humour whatsoever in the prank and threatened to 'murder the bastards' who did it if he ever found them.

Sometimes, Pop would shout us all to the flicks at Wonthaggi where the local Coal Miners' Union ran a modern and comfortable picture theatre. Lillian and I would get a penny to spend and we always bought eight black aniseed balls, the best value we could find.

We loved those outings, even if we all had to ride half frozen in the back of the Red Terror. Frank, Murray, Lillian, Gil, Maurie and I squeezed in tightly, as close to the rear of the front cabin as we could in an effort to cut the wind. Mum and Pop rode up front in relative warmth and style.

I remember seeing the movie (we called them pictures then) 'The Egg and I' at Wonthaggi and we laughed over it for days after. We could relate to farm life as depicted in the movie, particularly Ma and Pa Kettle who debuted in that show. It starred Fred McMurray, but the limelight fell on Percy Kilbride and Marjorie Main, with their tribe of kids.

We also saw Graeme Bell's Jazz Band perform at the theatre one time and loved it, too, the first live band I had ever seen.

Mum and Pop may have ridden in style in the cabin of the Red Terror, but Pop and Maurie had a most un-stylish passenger once when Pop ventured into pig raising.

Our Butter Factory contract called only for cream, and every day we used to tip hundreds of gallons of separated milk down the drain. Pop rightly decided it was a waste and would be good for raising porkers.

He got busy and built new sties, and he and Maurie headed for the market to buy a pregnant Large White sow to begin the dynasty.

He bought a huge, fat beauty and loaded her bulk into the back of the ute for the trip home. As they wheeled happily along, Pop was pretty pleased with himself, with a skinful of beer, his new sow and the prospect of profit.

As they wobbled down a hill Pop stood on the brakes to slow down. The sow lost her balance and came crashing through the canvas and wood cabin wall, head first onto the driver's seat. Pop bellowed and swore, Maurie shrieked and swore and the enraged pig squealed, struggled, grunted and sprayed cabin and occupants with hot excrement as she struggled to find a way out.

Pop wrestled with the steering wheel as the Red Terror lurched this way and that. Finally he brought it to a halt, and the foul smelling duo managed to guide the pig back whence she'd come. Pop secured her with a neck rope to the tray of the vehicle and they got home without further incident, apart from the stains and the smell, none the worse for their experience.

Not long after we arrived at Lance Creek, we received our first visitors, George and Lorna Thomas and their two daughters. I think they really came to show off their brand new vehicle, a Bradford two cylinder panel van. It was a beauty, and a big step up from the Overland. There weren't many who could afford a new car in those times, and we felt really proud and important to have them visit.

George and Lorna brought with them a large sack of oranges and we fruit-starved kids really hopped into them, made complete pigs of ourselves. The effect was disastrous and for two days there was a constant queue at the thunderbox, with some kids having to bolt for the scrub with a strange, waddling gait.

A year passed, and we weren't doing very well at Lance Creek, in spite of Pop's 'pig industry' and he started scanning the pages of The Weekly Times once more.

Before long, he landed a job at Watson's farm at a place we'd never heard of, Cudgee. which was two hundred and fifty miles away in the Western District of Victoria, near Warrnambool.

We said goodbye to our schoolmates and were soon in residence at Cudgee. Maurie quit his job and came along, too and somehow or other Alan finished up with us there as well. There were seven of us plus Mum and Pop. Soon there'd be one more!

Chapter Nineteen

PANMURE – POP VERSUS MUM – MELBOURNE BY TAXI.

Kenneth Victor Rae was born on April 5th, 1948 at the Warrnambool hospital. I had another brother!

Pop had started drinking a lot more while we were at Lance Creek, and while Mum was in hospital having Ken, he hit the pubs in town every day. Gil, Maurie, Murray, Frank and Alan were often left to do the milking and, as Pop couldn't pay them, they got pretty angry.

Alan was the first to go after arguing with Pop. Mounting his 1937 Sunbeam motorbike, he took off to a farm job at nearby Allansford. A week later Maurie had got a job at Mailor's Flat, and he too left Cudgee.

By the time Ken was three months old only Murray and Frank were left of the older boys. Gil had a job at Sheeans farm just up the road, and soon after, Frank returned to Melbourne to live with Uncle Roy Ellison at Preston. He got a job with Uncle, who managed a branch of Servex Industries there. Later, when he turned eighteen and got a driver's license he moved to South Kingsville, boarding with Reg and Vera Bower and working as a delivery driver for the local co-op store. He drove a 1949 Standard panel van!

When Murray turned fourteen, he left school to help Pop full-time at a promised four pounds a week, which he rarely received.

Pop's drinking continued and life became a constant battleground between him and Mum. If only Mum had been more tolerant, it may have been different, but she simply hated 'the drink' as she called it. The lives of Lillian and I were affected by this continual arguing, not knowing what to do except lie low until things quietened down.

Lillian and I would amuse ourselves in simple ways – hopscotch and hidey mostly. We often sat at the roadside waving to passing motorists, there were not many in 1948. Those that didn't return our waves we dubbed 'city slickers' and those that did 'country bumpkins'.

We also collected lots of bottles around the tiny Cudgee township, on the roadside and a few on the farm. There was a refundable penny deposit on each. Mum's birthday was coming around so we went to the local store to buy a gift for her. I had been looking at a pair of yellow bakelite salt and pepper shakers in the showcase for a long time. They were not cheap at two and sixpence, but Lillian agreed that we should cash our bottles and spend our hard-earned money on them. Mum was delighted when we presented her with them on the big day.

Pop was not happy working for wages and soon found a share farm just five miles from Cudgee. It was named Rollo's Farm. I presume that Mr Rollo was the owner. The deal was that Pop would get two-fifths of the profit from the milk. Located a mile and a half east of the township of Panmure down a winding dirt road, the farm was run down. The fences were poor, the cows old and poor producers, the cow yard a sea of mud and cow shit. As for the house, it was in a disgraceful condition, the worst so far. There was no electricity connected. We tidied up the house as best we could, and Pop convinced Maurie to

Lillian, Pop, Mum and me at Cudgee with baby Ken.

leave his job and come home to help. Maurie was secretly glad, as his boss was a boozer who helped with the morning milking and then disappeared for the rest of the day to the pub or the races. Maurie virtually ran the farm for two pounds a week.

Lillian and I used to walk the two miles to Panmure School, a long trek, especially in wet weather. We would rise to the shouted wake up call from Pop at 6 am. After breakfast, we washed and dried the dishes and stocked up the firewood for Mum and leave for school at eight. By the time we got home it was half past four, and we would help prepare tea and get in more wood. I'd cut and Lillian would cart it to the back verandah.

Spuds, silver beet and pumpkin always seemed to be on the menu, as we used to grow our own. One of my jobs was to look after the chooks. We had lots of chooks, and one used to be on the table at least once a week. It was my job to kill, pluck and clean the selected victim, a job I hated. Sometimes Lillian helped me. I'd lay the bird's head on a block and cut it off with swipe of Pop's razor-sharp axe. Blood would spurt everywhere and I'd hang the poor chook with a string around the legs from the branch of a tree to bleed. This produced whiter meat. Sometimes, when I severed the head I'd let the chook

Cudgee primary school. Lillian and I went there in 1948. It had one teacher and it was a happy school for us – for a while.

go and it would rush about headless till it collapsed. Lillian used to scream in terror, and I loved that.

I'd gut the bird, then plunge it in an old galvanised tub of hot water to make the feather plucking easier. The rest of the family enjoyed their meal of chook, but I hated it.

The new farm didn't improve relations between Mum and Pop. Pop seemed to drink more, and they never stopped fighting.

One day Pop came home full as a boot carrying a half dozen bottles of beer. Mum went berserk, and seizing the axe on the verandah, she smashed every bottle. Pop was furious and grabbed the axe from her and threatened to take to her with it. It was awful and Lillian and I were terrified. Instead of striking Mum, Pop hurled the axe into the yard and stormed off to the cowshed, swearing and yelling.

Mum wasted no time. 'Come on you two. We're not staying here with that madman. We're going to Melbourne. Come on and pack and help get Ken ready.'

We hastened to comply, fearing that at any moment Pop would come back. Lugging our bulging suitcases and pushing Ken's pram, we almost ran all the way to Panmure. Mum rang a taxi from the phone box at the post office, and in ten minutes we were on our way to North Melbourne and my Auntie Phemie. Mum somehow convinced the taxi driver to send the bill to Pop and we alighted at Auntie's. It must have been a huge bill for a taxi trip of over 150 miles each way!

We spent two weeks at Aunty Phemie's, and just as suddenly as we had left, we returned to Panmure. This time we got the train and Pop collected us at the station. He seemed pleased to have us back. Lillian and I resumed school at Panmure, more than a little embarrassed by our sudden unexplained absence. From then on, things were never quite the same. Over the next few years, Lillian and I were frequently uprooted from home and school as Mum packed and left Pop on a number of occasions. Usually we would go to Aunty Phemie's at North Melbourne.

Chapter Twenty

THE CITY AGAIN - FOOTSCRAY TECH - A FARM IN DIXIE - BACK TO BASALT.

Not long after we returned to Panmure, Pop announced that we were leaving the farm and returning to South Kingsville. Gil and Maurie decided to accompany us.

Maurie landed a job as a porter on Newport railway station, regarded at the time as a secure 'job for life' with the government, and Gil at a tannery in Yarraville.

Murray and Pop went to work at Henry B. Smith's wool scouring works at Williamstown (in Osborne Street, demolished around 1999 and occupied by jammed-tight townhouses). Lillian and I returned to the Spotswood state school.

I was now in grade six, and at school year's end I won a scholarship, free books and stuff, to the Footscray Technical School, awarded by the local council. I was invited to accept the award at the Footscray Town Hall, and there was a dinner with all the trimmings.

It was my first ever formal occasion and I was terrified as I was called to the stage to accept the award. I couldn't get out of the place quick enough.

I took up my scholarship in February 1949. In April 1949, I left! Pop had decided to take on another share farm, this time at Dixie, a locality about eight miles south of Terang in the western district. Gil junior decided to stay on at the tannery, and Maurie elected to toss in his 'job for life' and go along to Dixie. The family now consisted of Maurie, Murray, Lillian and me.

This farm was only marginally better than the others we had lived at and was part of the large Keayang station, owned by A.J. Staughton and Managed by George Rendell. We never saw the wealthy Mr Staughton.

The effort of the trip to Dixie was too much for the Studebaker and she never turned a wooden-spoked wheel again. The Red Terror was buggered. Our only transport now was a horse and gig, which went with the farm.

Life was little different to the previous farms. The house was old and run-down, a faded red weatherboard with a wild privet hedge facing onto a dirt road. The milking shed was dilapidated and the equipment old, driven by an old Lister diesel engine, a bastard of a thing to start, but once going it ran alright. We milked 150 cows twice a day, hard and constant work alone, without all the other farm work.

Maurie soon tired of the unpaid work and found a job on a nearby sheep station owned by Coy Pastoral Company, coming home at weekends. Five quid a week and keep. Murray, always loyal to Pop, stayed on. He and Maurie bought two horses which they hoped to train as trotters. The venture failed, of course!

I managed to earn some pocket money by collecting the wool from dead sheep on Keayang station. There always seemed to be an abundance of carcasses spread over the property, dead from I know not what cause. I'd drive around in the gig, sometimes with Murray, and pluck the wool from the rotting bodies. The stench was awful but the money smelled sweet. God knows what diseases I exposed myself to. Wool was bringing a massive one pound per pound, and 'dead wool', one shilling.

Mum was pregnant again and suffered morning sickness that lasted all day! Lillian and I had to do most of the housework after school to help her. Pop and Mum were still fighting, and several times Mum cleared off to Melbourne for spells at Auntie Phemie's. Pop was drinking a lot

Ian, aged about 12, at Dixie. Our skewbald pony was a great entertainment for Lillian and me.

and almost every day went to Terang and came home half-pissed. Life was one long argument. There were so many fights and moves away for Lillian and me with Mum, that I cannot recall events and moves too clearly.

On one particular occasion Mum ran away and took me with her. Lillian was not with us for some reason and I can't recall baby Ken being with us, but I guess he was. We lobbed at an abandoned two-roomed shack on the Basalt road at Eganstown, near Daylesford. I was just thirteen, but I did not go to school there. We had no money, so Mum went to Daylesford and got a permit for me to cut wood in the forest across the road. With a very blunt axe I felled a lot of trees and cut them into six foot lengths, stacking them in cord lots for sale.

The hut had no chimney, so Mum had nowhere to cook. She made do with a campfire until we built a chimney and fireplace, made from stone we collected in the bush. It was hard work, but it rose from nothing and managed to stay upright. Maybe it's still there.

I fell ill for a time, feverish, and the glands in my neck swelled to alarming proportions. Mum said it was the mumps and I was mortified when she drew back my blankets, pulled down my pyjama pants and checked my balls for swelling. I was thirteen and growing a hint of fluffy hair, as well as developing a quite large* adult penis.

I'd been at the wood cutting for two weeks when Mum found me a job, serving petrol and general hand at Martyn's Garage in Daylesford. The pay was one pound a week. Each day I would walk the four miles to town, and at day's end walk home again. But it didn't last long.

One day, ten days after I started, I was serving petrol and somehow the petrol pump wouldn't shut off as I filled a car. As a result, gallons of petrol gushed into the gutter and ran down the street. I admit I panicked.

Mr Martyn went bananas and sacked me on the spot. 'You bloody idiot. You've just pumped a week's profit down the drain. I can't

---

* *Just kidding!*

afford you. Go home.'

I was distraught. What would Mum say? She was depending on my wages, but she took it well. By lunch time I was back felling trees.

I needn't have worried. A week later, Pop turned up, reconciled with Mum, and we returned to Dixie.

I still wonder if the person who found my unsold wood ever blessed me. Maybe it is still there!

Chapter Twenty-One

A baby brother ~ Austin car ~ Terang hospital ~ twins for Mum.

About a week after we returned to Dixie I got a good belting from Pop. I was sitting in the kitchen listening to the wireless when he came home drunk. He saw red when he caught me idle, called me a lazy, useless bastard and proceeded to whip me with an electrical cord. It was terrifying. The bakelite plug on the end cut into me and I cried like a baby. Pop finally stopped and stomped off to the cow yard where Murray had started the milking. Lillian was helpless to stop the belting and cried with me.

Mum had heard all the noise and emerged from the bedroom shouting at the departing Pop. 'You could have killed him. Why do you hate Ian?'

From that day on I was scared of Pop and nervous when he was around. The incident did nothing to improve things between Mum and Pop either. She may have left him again then but wasn't well and was expecting the baby at any time.

We must have prospered a little, because one day Pop had arrived home with a motor car, a 1926 Austin tourer. It proved to be an awful lemon and we pushed it almost as far as we drove it. It had a thermometer built into the radiator cap and gate gears; the only gate gear shift car I can recall seeing.

On weekends, when Maurie came home, he would take driving lessons in the Austin, and he eventually obtained a driving license at Terang police station. Until then, he and Murray used to drive the horse and gig to the pictures at Terang on Saturday nights. Now they went by car, which they did with great pride, parking in front of the theatre – they had previously hidden the horse and gig around the back.

It was a Thursday, and I had just arrived home from school. The bus used to drop me off about a mile away on the main road, and I'd walk home. I was now attending the Terang Higher Elementary School, which I hated.

As usual, I went to the woodheap to cut the wood for the day. Pop had just sharpened the axe and it was like a razor. I put the axe down on a log, blade upwards, to grab another length to cut. I stepped over the upturned blade and felt a sharp pain in my bare leg. I looked down and was horrified to see a gaping slash down my shin, wide open, shin bone exposed and blood pouring from a ghastly wound. I was still in my school short pants.

Lillian was with me, and she screamed with horror and ran to the cowshed to fetch Pop. I was clutching my leg and trying to hold the gash closed. Mum arrived on the scene, ran indoors and grabbed a bunch of rags which she wound tightly around my leg. She was shocked and shaking.

Pop arrived on the scene, took one look and ran to get the Austin. It wouldn't start, in spite of his frantic swinging on the crank handle.

'I'll have to hitch up the gig,' he called. Just then we heard the

Maurie and Bill (Splinter) at Dixie, about 1950.
In the shed is the 1926 Austin.

sound of a motor, coming our way. Chugging over the rise came the familiar sight of Charlie, the rabbit dealer.

Charlie made a living buying and selling rabbits caught on the farms. His old Chevrolet truck was laden with hundreds of rabbits swinging by their back legs on rails that criss-crossed the tray. Pop ran to the road and waved Charlie down, and in a few minutes I was in the truck cabin with Mum on my way to the doctor at Terang.

The doctor took one look and ordered me to hospital where he promptly stretched me out and inserted a heap of stitches. I was kept in hospital for three weeks as it was a serious wound, chipping the bone. In addition, I had another two weeks off from school, which I greatly appreciated.

Mum was close to confinement, and on August 4th 1949, her birthday, she gave birth to twins, a boy and a girl. Sadly the boy lived only a few minutes, but Marion, weak and tiny, managed to survive. I had another sister.

I went with Pop to the Warrnambool cemetery for the funeral of the boy. I do not know if he was named. I really had no idea what was happening, as Pop told me absolutely nothing. I didn't even know whose funeral I was going to, but I recall the tiny white coffin and a preacher being present. That's all.

Mum brought Marion home after a couple of weeks, and she was not at all well. Shortly after, she went for medical tests. I didn't have a clue what her problem was at the time. Those things were not discussed with children.

I was unhappy at the Terang Higher Elementary School. I was not a dill and really tried, but I think I was affected by my home life. I was constantly embarrassed by my shabby school books and equally shabby clothes. I always looked untidy, and teachers seemed to resent me. I certainly wasn't cheeky; I was a shy kid who wouldn't say boo, with an inferiority complex as long as your arm.

Whatever the reason the teachers had little time for me, or so I thought then. The kids didn't pick on me, because I was best mate with

Jimmy Baird, one of the tougher kids at the school. He protected me at all times from the kids, but was unable to do so from the teachers.

I recall with horror the time I tore my 'good' trousers while cutting the wood at home after school. We had a strict rule that we changed out of our school clothes on arriving home. On this day I hadn't changed my clothes and I got caught in a stick at the woodheap, and rip went my pants. As punishment Mum and Pop made me wear a pair of Pop's cow yard trousers to school for a week. They were far too large and hung like bags. The material was rough cotton and they were grey with lighter vertical stripes. I was so embarrassed I almost died from humiliation. The teachers delighted in pointing out to each class that I was out of uniform, to the amusement of everyone present.

I was in music class when the teacher spotted me talking to my mate, Jimmy. He called me to the front of the class.

'Bring your book with you, Braybrook', he smirked.

I cringed, expecting humiliation. I wasn't wrong.

'Look at you!' the teacher cried. 'Out of uniform, and look at this dog-eared book'. He threw my book in the air and it fluttered in pieces to the floor. The kids in class roared with laughter.

'Braybrook, I am sick of you and your inattention. Get out of here, and take yourself to the principal's office. Take this note.' He scribbled something on a piece of paper.

'Take this mess with you,' he

Ian, Mum Veronica, Ken and Marion Rae. Ken's first day at kinder.

pointed to my dismembered book. I hastily gathered up the pieces and went outdoors, the laughter of the kids following me.

The principal was a man about forty years old, round and fat, with small spectacles perched on his nose. He read the note I timidly handed him.

'Braybrook, eh? I've had complaints about you.' He looked me up and down.

'Out of uniform, Braybrook?'

'Yes, sir,' I stammered.

Headmaster glared. 'My teachers are always talking about you. Out of uniform. Not paying attention. Books like these.' He threw my book to the floor and yelled at me.

'Answer me, Braybrook, you cheeky little bugger.'

I was too scared to speak.

'You insolent boy.' He pushed me hard on the chest and I raised my hands in defense.

'Raise your fists to me will you,' he roared. He let fly with a hard push to my chest that threw me backwards into his filing cabinet. I fell to the floor.

'Get up. Get out of here before I lose my temper. Get out'.

I grabbed my book from the floor and fled in tears, and turned inside out. Why did these teachers do that to me?

From then on I hated school all the more and longed for the day I could leave. It wasn't long before my chance came.

Chapter Twenty-Two

THE 1937 CHEV – NORTH MELBOURNE – I GET A JOB – CHILDHOOD ENDS.

Through the hard work of Pop and Murray the farm prospered, and one exciting day, Pop arrived home with a beautiful 1937 Chevrolet Master sedan. It was fantastic. You wouldn't call the king your uncle in a car like this. In those days it was quite a luxurious vehicle. At seven hundred pounds, it cost the same as a brand new Holden. Pop wanted a Holden, but there was a two year waiting list on 'Australia's own car'.

As far as I was concerned, the Chev was the ultimate anyway. It was in superb condition, traded by a farmer on his new Holden. It was a cream colour, with a narrow green stripe down the sides, with leather seats and lush carpets.

To cap it off, the Chev had a wireless, the aerial of which was concealed beneath the running board. I wasn't happy about that, as nobody could actually see that we had a wireless in our car, a rarity in that era and quite a status symbol! If we had a visible aerial everybody would know!

The new car did nothing to improve relations between Mum and Pop, and the arguments continued.

Ken was toddling by now and a happy little bloke with a big smile always on his face. Lillian and I thought the sun shone from him. We bathed him, dressed him and even changed his nappies. We loved to take him for walks in his pusher.

Below our house, the road went into a steep fifty yard incline to a bridge over the small creek. I would take Ken in the pusher to the top, give it a shove and let it go full steam down the hill. Lillian waited at the bottom, near the bridge to catch the flying pusher. Sometimes she missed and Ken and pusher crashed.

Ken would scream with delight as he hurtled downhill, although sometimes that would turn to screams of pain as he crashed into gutter or embankment. He was well strapped in and never came to serious harm. Thank God.

It was around this time that Mum went off to hospital for a hysterectomy. I think she had cancer of the cervix, but we were never told those things. We kids were not permitted to visit her in hospital. I think they were hospital rules back in those days.

It fell on Lillian and me to look after the little ones. Pop had hired a lady named Mrs Orr to housekeep and nanny, but she quit after three days. Pop didn't worry Mum by telling her, and Lillian and I did everything, including child care for many weeks. Pop kept Lillian home from school. Before long, Mum was back home, and the arguments resumed.

In December 1950, Mum left Pop again, taking Lillian, Marion, Ken and me with her. It was Christmas holiday time, so it didn't effect our schooling.

As usual, we lobbed at Auntie Phemie's house at North Melbourne. Mum decided I was old enough to get a job, so she found me one. The new year of 1951 began with me employed as a telegram boy at Footscray post office, a short journey by train from North Melbourne. I started my job on a Monday, and the next weekend Pop arrived on the scene. He managed to convince Mum that he was a changed man, and she decided to go back with him. With little delay she had loaded all her gear, along with Lillian, in the Chev.

'You'll be alright with Aunty Phemie. You've got a good job and she'll look out for you,' said Mum as she kissed me goodbye.

I stood on the footpath with Auntie Phemie and waved them an unhappy goodbye. They were quickly out of site, and with them went what was left of my childhood. From now on I was a working man.

PART TWO

PART TWO

Chapter Twenty-Three

A WORKING MAN

'What do you mean you've been sacked?' My Aunty Phemie stood at the doorway of her tiny single-fronted cottage in Rosslyn Street, West Melbourne, a look of disbelief on her weary face.

'How did you get the sack? Whatever did you do? It was a good job, a government job, a job for life. What happened?' She was very annoyed with me.

Her real name was Euphemia but everybody called her Phemie. She was warm and friendly unless provoked, when she became as tough as a boarding house steak. From age nine she had been brought up as a state ward in child welfare homes and foster care, along with her siblings, and she'd learned she had to be tough to survive.

I had just finished my sixth week as a telegram boy at the Footscray post office, delivering messages to homes all around the area. Telegram boys were a common sight on the streets of cities and towns. It was 1951 and telegrams were a popular means of sending messages in a hurry; very few homes had a telephone then, especially in the working class area of Footscray.

If a person wanted to send a message quickly they called into a post office and wrote their message, plus the receiver's address, on a special form. There was a twelve word limit and any extra words cost a few pence more. The operator would telephone the receiving office and dictate the message over the phone. At the other end, the operator would transcribe the message onto another form, place it in a sealed envelope, and hand it to the delivery boy. The boy would speed off as fast as his legs could push the red bicycle provided, which carried a 'PMG' plate, giving it some official standing as the property of the postmaster-general. We also wore a navy coloured peaked cap embossed with PMG, and around our waists a small leather bag in which we placed the telegrams.

Sometimes the telegram bore very bad news; on other occasions, good news. One time a telegram boy at another office delivered the great news of a ten thousand pounds lottery win and he was given ten pounds by the winner. We all dreamed that it might happen to us.

There were four telegram boys at Footscray, I was the youngest at thirteen and a half; the others were fifteen. During our half-hour lunch break we boys twice went beneath the city in the huge storm water drains. These carried all the waste water from the centre of town to God knows where. They were huge, we were easily able to stand up and even ride our bikes on the ledge beside the main gutter. We gained entry at a point about a quarter mile below the post office – easy. If a sudden cloudburst had occurred we would have been swept away as these drains quickly became a raging torrent. One day, during a lunch break, I witnessed something in the drain that fascinated me. The three boys, older than me, had a contest to see who could ejaculate the furthest. As a non-participant, being incapable, I was appointed the judge.

One of the boys was bludging on the job. If the ride was some distance he would throw those messages he judged unimportant into a drain near the post office. A passer-by discovered a number of them and took a shabby bundle to Mr Atkins, the manager of the post office.

All hell broke loose, and Mr Atkins lined us four boys up in his office. He was most displeased and we were left in no doubt about it.

His face glowed red. 'Who did this?' he shouted, waving the bunch of papers in the air. 'This is an important job. People are relying on you, and it is a serious offence to tamper with His Majesty's mail. You can go to jail! Come on, who is responsible?'

We waited. We boys suspected it was Barry and expected him to confess. He didn't move or open his mouth.

'All right,' thundered Mr Atkins, 'If none of you admit this I will sack the lot of you.' He waited for a response, but none came.

'Very well, I've given the guilty one the chance to speak up and nobody has. That means you are all sacked. Sacked, do you hear! Go to Mrs Woods and collect your pay. Now!'

It wasn't too late for the guilty one to confess – but he didn't.

I was totally bewildered as Mrs Woods, the senior clerk, handed me my near empty pay envelope fifteen minutes later. My mind was racing from one question to another. Why did Barry sneak away without confessing and saving us our jobs? Where would I get another job? What would Auntie Phemie say? Now that really frightened me!

Most of all I was angry with Barry and thought of dobbing him in. However, none of us knew for sure that it was him, and anyway, the working class rule was: 'You don't dob anyone in'.

This was to be the first of many disappointments and disillusionments with people in my future.

Standing on the footpath on Rosslyn Street with Auntie glaring at me I began to cry. 'It isn't fair, Auntie Phemie. Barry did it and we got the sack.' I bawled even louder.

Auntie softened. 'Oh stop your blubbering and come inside. We'll have a cup of tea and you can tell me all about it.'

Auntie Phemie was about forty-five years old, a largish woman, but not fat. Big breasted, she was five foot six inches tall and stood straight-backed. Her hair was straight and jet black. Her brown eyes were framed by thick rimmed spectacles. She was quite good looking, albeit a little fierce when aroused.

She didn't own her tiny home, it was rented; one of a row of a dozen small homes, all identical, all a bit shabby, although the occupants did their best to keep them nice. The front door opened onto a small patch of garden, with a concrete path midway that led to a gate which opened onto the footpath.

Across the road stood the three storey factory of Symington's Liberty Corsets, which looked down on the surrounding homes. Aunty had a part-time cleaning job there.

The house had a thin passageway that ran on the left for its entire length. Three rooms adjoined it, the front room (reserved for entertaining the rare visitors), Auntie's bedroom and the spare room where I had slept for the month I had lived there. The kitchen occupied the full width at the back; from there a door led into the tiny backyard with its washhouse and the dilapidated lavatory that was flushable. It was my first experience with this wonderful thing, new to me as we always had a pan or the big drop into a large hole in the ground.

My Aunt had divorced and lived alone, although she had a boyfriend who called regularly and sometimes stayed all night. George Murray owned a 1934 Ford truck with a small tray with which he eked out a living.

One night, the day after Aunty and George had had an argument, he came to call, drunk. Aunty saw him coming and locked the door. George bashed at the door with his big fists as he shouted vile abuse at her, which she ignored. With that, George went to his truck and returned carrying a small axe. He proceeded to hack at the door, all the while hurling curses at Aunty. Unsuccessful, he went to his truck and sped off, his wheels spinning in the loose gravel near the edge of the road. Aunty was a little shaken by this, but calm, perhaps the experience wasn't new to her. I was terrified. Aunty soon regained her composure. We had a cup of tea and went to bed.

My Aunty had a son, Bill, who was away somewhere in the Air Force, and a daughter, Thelma, who lived with her husband Douglas and their five-year-old daughter in a flat above a shop across the road from the historic Queen Victoria Market. As with thousands of other people, Aunty did most of her shopping at the Market, a two block walk away. Sometimes I accompanied her, filled with wonder at the number of stalls and the masses of people. Being a country boy I was a little fearful of the big crowd that jammed the walkways between the stalls.

Auntie's kitchen was sparsely furnished; a table covered with chipped and faded linoleum which had been glued to its timber surface, and four 'kangaroo' timber chairs. There was a tallboy, a sideboard, a meat safe and little else. The wood stove, fuelled with coke, was always lit. On its top was an always hot black cast-iron kettle.

Aunty made a small pot of tea in a china pot, poured the steaming brew into two tea-stained cups, added a splash of milk and a spoon of sugar. Now we were able to sit and talk.

After I had tearfully told her my story, she reached out to touch my hand. 'Don't worry, Ian. Tomorrow I'll take you to Excell's Employment Agency. I know Mr Excel, he'll find you a job'.

The next morning we went to see Mr Excell. I was about to learn just how tough it was to be a boy alone in the big, wide world.

Chapter Twenty-Four

Excell's Employment Agency – Drouin – two quid a week

Excell's Employment Agency was located downstairs in a crumbling two storey building in Hardware Street in the city. These days it has been reduced in status to Hardware Lane, which is appropriate, for it was just a short and narrow alleyway. It ran from Lonsdale Street to Little Bourke Street between Elizabeth and William Streets. It was therefore within easy walking distance of Aunt's home on Rosslyn Street.

The business was conducted by Mr Excell, who greeted us with a welcoming smile as he ushered us into his small office.

'Now what can I do for you Mrs Brown?' He spoke in a quiet, confidential sort of voice.

He was about forty years old and badly crippled and moved about on crutches, one leg noticeably swinging free. He was, however, as agile as most people with two good legs. I guessed he may have been a victim of the dreaded polio which was far too common in those days. It had claimed thousands of victims, many of whom died.

Aunt explained that she was looking for a job for her nephew who had just come down from his parent's farm in the country, near Warrnambool. She didn't mention that I had been sacked from the Footscray post office!

'What sort of work would best suit you, Ian?' He didn't wait for an answer. 'I imagine if you are a country farm boy, a farm job would best suit you. What do you think?'

'I suppose so, Mr Excell.' I really had no idea what I wanted to do. I was still only thirteen and didn't have a clue what I wanted or expected from life. I imagine that most boys were happy to accept anything offered to them back then, as was I.

'I have a Mr Bill Johnston who has a dairy farm near Drouin who is looking for a good boy. I think you may be just the lad he is looking for. If you wait a few minutes I will phone him and see what he thinks'.

Mr Excell swung quickly on his crutches up a short set of steps into an adjoining office.

'I'll be back in a minute,' he called over his shoulder as he disappeared into the next room, closing the door behind him

'Fingers crossed,' said Aunty Phemie with a quick smile.

In a few minutes Mr Excell re-emerged with a broad smile on his thin, clean-shaven face. 'Good news, Ian. Mr Johnston says he will be happy to give you a go.' He was obviously pleased with the result of his talk with my future employer.

'You'll find that Mr Johnston is a good man. He has hired lads from me before and I have had no complaints.'

So that was it. My future had been decided, and I was all set for a career as a farm hand in South Gippsland.

We thanked Mr Excell for his good work and made our way home.

He had advised us that I would get the train to Drouin the next morning and that Mr Johnston would met me at the Drouin train station for the ride, about five miles, to his farm at Drouin South. 'Look out for Mr Johnston in a Yellow Cab.'

We headed for home. 'Gee, Aunty Phemie, he must be rich or something, 'cos he is taking me home in a taxi.' I was a bit puzzled. Maybe he didn't have a car, not everyone had one in those days.

'Yes,' said Aunt, smiling. 'I suppose he must be.'

Next morning we had a brisk walk to Spencer Street Station, which was not far away. I struggled a bit, lugging the over-large suitcase that I had brought with me to Aunties when my mother and stepfather had left me there a month or so before. It was rather battered and badly worn, with one of the catches broken. As security, Aunt tied a piece of cord around it.

It didn't contain a lot; a few pairs of socks, a pair of underpants, a woollen jumper, two shirts and a pair of old, badly worn trousers.

That was about it, apart from what I was wearing, a plain blue shirt under a khaki wool jumper, heavy black boots and an ex-army jacket slung over my arm. Only a month before, Mum had presented me with my very first pair of long trousers! They were nothing flash, navy blue and made from rough cotton, but they were long trousers! It was a big occasion, when I was a boy, to graduate to longuns; it was something all boys looked forward to. Long trousers were a signal to the world that you were now a man.

The appearance of my sad looking suitcase embarrassed me as I waited with Aunty on the station platform. I thought everybody was looking at me and talking about me. Probably some were.

I didn't have long to wait, however, as within a few minutes the hissing, puffing steam locomotive monster drew up towing a string of carriages, some labelled First Class, some Smoking and others Second Class. Obviously I was going Second Class, especially as Aunty had purchased my ticket. I never aspired to be First Class – ever – then or now.

Aunty gave last minute instructions. 'Now, Ian, you get off at Drouin station. Keep an eye out and don't miss the stop. Don't go to sleep or anything. And don't forget Mr Johnston will meet you there. He'll be expecting you.'

She gave me a quick hug, at the same time slipping a ten shilling note into my hand.

'Gee thanks, Aunty Phemie. Ten shillings! That's a lot,' I said.

It really was quite a lot, as it represented more than what would soon be a day's pay to me. Mr Excell had told me I would get two pounds five shillings a week for my work at Johnston's farm. Plus my 'keep' included of course, as was the practice. I was relieved, as I had only a couple of pennies in my pocket and was worried that I couldn't buy any lunch, or anything else, until payday. My mother's sister was really very kind to me.

With a final hug and a kiss on the cheek from Aunty I stepped onto the train and made my way to a seat about midway. I was lucky to get a window seat which enabled me to wave goodbye to Aunt as she stood on the platform. I'm sure she was concerned for me, alone as I would be.

With a blast of the whistle and a great hiss of steam the train drew away from the platform and I was headed on a journey that signalled a definite end to my childhood.

* * *

It was seventy miles to Drouin, and I sat quietly in my green upholstered seat where I fretted for most of the way. I was one of six people in the compartment. There was an old man and a woman with three children ranging in age from three to about eight. The kids laughed and had fun, the old man pretended to be asleep, the mother read a book that she produced from a bag, and I didn't say a word.

I know Aunty believed she was doing the right thing, and I guess she was. I wasn't wanted at home – my stepfather had made it clear to me that he couldn't afford to keep me. What else could my aunty do but help me find a job, and one with accommodation provided – I suppose I was on the way to being homeless if I continued as I was. How else was a boy of thirteen, going on fourteen, to survive?

I felt dreadfully lonely and abandoned. I was confused and was fearful of the unknown that lay ahead.

Chapter Twenty-Five

A TAXI? ~ MONEY BAG ~ BAD LANGUAGE ~ SACKED

It was eleven o'clock when the train hissed to a halt in a cloud of steam at the Drouin railway station. Dragging my battered suitcase, I stepped onto the platform and made my way to the exit. There were several cars lined up near the building's front, but there was not a sign of a Yellow Cab. I figured that Mr Johnston had been delayed, so I settled on the footpath, my suitcase as a seat. Perhaps five minutes went by, during which time all except one of the cars had departed. I started to worry that I had been forgotten when I was approached by a man who had alighted from an old ute. He bore all the hallmarks of a farmer, dirty grey trousers, a checked shirt with sleeves rolled up, a battered felt hat and a pair of grubby rubber boots. What really struck me was the canvas money bag he had attached to his belt. It was very dirty, once white, and had a fair sort of bulge in it. He was a big man, maybe six feet four inches tall, ruddy faced, with a three or four day growth and, I guessed, was about fifty years old. His was an unfriendly face.

'Are you Ian Braybrook?' He gave me a questioning look.

'Yes I am,' I gave a nervous reply.

'Well, I'm Bill Johnston, and I've been waiting for you for half a bloody hour.' He didn't seem pleased.

'What are you sittin' there for? Why didn't you come to me ute? Didn't you see it? Didn't they tell you to look for me in me Yeller Cab?'

How was I to know that Yellow Cab was the make of a car? I'd never heard of it before. I later learned that they were American made especially for the Yellow Cab Company. I don't know the maker, but probably one of the majors.

'I'm sorry, Mr Johnston,' I stuttered nervously. 'I thought you were in a taxi.'

'A bloody taxi! What do you reckon I am, a bloody millionaire? Christ, a bloody taxi! What would I be doin' in a bloody taxi? For Christ's sake! What has Excell sent me this time?' This last sentence he muttered just audibly under his breath.

I hadn't got off to a very good start with my new boss. He already thought I was an idiot. And I should have realised by his last sentence, that I wasn't the first idiot boy he had engaged to work his farm.

'Alright, get in the ute. We're late for dinner. The missus would have had it ready a f…n hour ago. Chuck your swag in the back.'

'I wonder if he goes to sleep with that bag of money,' I thought.

It was about three miles to the Johnston farm, a run-down looking place, with sheds that looked ready to collapse and a rough, weatherboard house that had last been painted when it was new – probably fifty years before. He led the way into the house where a grey-haired, thin, tired looking woman, probably around his age, worked over a blackened wood stove. She wore a plain apron that had once been white.

'Marj, this is the new boy. His name is Ian. He'll probably be hungry.'

Mrs Johnston glanced my way. 'Hello, Ian. Put your case in your

Drouin, as it was during the war.
(Jim Fitzpatrick photographer. National Library of Australia, Canberra)

room and come and have dinner. Bill, you show Ian where his room is.' My boss led me along a darkened passageway.

'Here it is boy. Drop yer case here and come on out to the kitchen. Yer can unpack later'.

I looked quickly around the room. It contained a single bed with grey blankets, a tiny wardrobe, a chair and a small table at the bedside. Some faded floral curtains hung listlessly at the cobwebbed window. There was a green bedspread at the base of the bed and a pillow with a yellowish case. That was all. No radio set, of course, and my light was a kerosene lamp which sat on the rickety table. A voice came from down the passage.

'Where are yer boy? Get a wriggle on.' I hastened to obey.

My dinner was on the table. It was a meal that I was to see regularly during my time at Johnston's farm: stale bread, boiled mutton, pumpkin and spuds. We sat and ate in silence. Mrs Johnston didn't say anything and Mr Johnston chomped his way through a pile of tucker a horse couldn't jump over.

So this was to be my home and way of life from now on? I felt pretty miserable.

After dinner, Mr Johnston took me for a walk around the farmhouse paddock. The focal point was the milking shed.

'We are milking a hundred or so cows at the moment. You know what it's like, I s'pose, being a farmin' family's kid. We do the mornin' milkin' at six and the night-time milkin' at four. We've got new Baltic Simplex machines, which makes it pretty easy these days.'

He took me into the various sheds, one of which was the saddle shed where the assorted gear was hung on racks.

'We still use the horses for some jobs, but I got a new tractor a few months ago. Use that for a lot of the work now, but the horses are still good.'

The next shed held a shiny, near-new, David Brown tractor.

'It's a bloody beauty,' beamed Mr Johnston. 'Cost me a few bloody quid, but it's worth it in the long run, I s'pose.'

My days from then on didn't vary. Out of bed at five o'clock for a cup of tea, bring in the cows from the paddocks for milking at six. After the milking was finished, at about eight, we hosed down the cow yard and washed the vats and other equipment.

The machines were driven by a Lister engine, which banged away happily with one heavy clunk and hiss for every fourth rotation. When the milking was done, I would harness the horse and load the cans of milk onto a wagon and drive the rig to a depot about half a mile up the road. The depot was where all the local farmers placed their full cans for pick up by the butter factory truck. Each can was clearly marked with the owner's brand. The truck driver would first unload the factory-cleaned empty cans, collected the day before, and then roll the heavy full cans on their bottom edge onto the truck tray for transfer to the factory.

After this, I would join the boss for breakfast, usually porridge and a slice or two of toast with butter. The butter was always in generous supply, as it was cheap. Mrs Johnston made it herself from the rich cream which I separated from the milk in the dairy. Washing the separator was another of my many jobs.

After our breakfast it was time for the other jobs around the farm. Cutting thistles with a big hoe, digging rabbits out of burrows, mending fences, cleaning stables, weeding the house garden. Most days we worked at felling trees for a couple of hours, and cutting them into manageable lengths and stacking them for firewood. We used a large crosscut saw and axes for the felling and the cutting. It was bloody hard work, especially for a boy just turned fourteen.

Then there was me digging a hole once a week to empty the thunderbox shit can. That was a job I really hated; foul, disgusting, overpowering in its stench. Sometimes the contents splashed the ghastly mess onto me as I tipped the can toward the hole. It was bloody awful burying somebody else's shit!

At night, after the seven o'clock ABC news on the wireless, I went to my room. I sat alone reading my Zane Grey western novels, in my mind living the life of a cowboy riding the purple sage out west of Laredo. I was terribly lonely and ached for the company of my disjointed family, especially my mother. I missed her terribly. I was so damned miserable – smiles were hard to come by.

By late October I had been on the job for several weeks and it was harvest time, time to cut the long grass in a paddock reserved for growing hay. This grass, sun-dried, was to tide the farm over the times when feed for the cows was scarce.

I had been getting on okay with the Johnston's, even though I was not the least bit happy with my job. I quietly did as I was told and worked as hard as my boss, who often toiled alongside me. It was nothing but work. Even on the one day a week that the couple went shopping in Drouin, I was left at home with a list of jobs to do. But it was a job, and I had no idea how to go about getting a better one, or maybe one closer to home. I would have killed for a wireless in my room. Fat chance of that!

To my joy, on the first day of the harvest, Mr Johnston said I could drive his pride and joy, the David Brown tractor, towing the grass mower. I was delighted, probably the first time I had felt any happiness since my arrival at the farm.

The grass mower had previously been horsedrawn and, as was common back in the early days of tractors, the machine had been fitted with a timber draw bar. It worked very well and made the job so much easier and quicker. I was given a quick lesson and soon headed off to cut the grass.

It was a balmy, sunny day and I thoroughly enjoyed what I was doing. I was inclined to daydream, usually about girls and what it may be like to be with one, a most unlikely prospect. The tall grass fell before the chattering blades of the mower and I was at peace with the world.

As I approached the end of the row for my tenth time around I looked up and there, less than ten feet in front, was the barbed wire fence. I wrenched savagely on the steering wheel. I missed the fence but behind me was a loud crack. I had snapped the timber tow bar. It dangled miserably in half.

Mr Johnston had been preparing the old hay rake for the next step in the harvest, about 300 yards away. He leapt into action immediately he heard the sound of the drawbar snapping in two. He rushed to the scene, staring in pained disbelief at the shattered piece of wood.

'Look what you've done! Look at me f...n draw bar! You've smashed the f...n thing to smithereens. It's f...d.'

He turned to me. 'You useless little prick. Get your f...n gear and get going before I f...n kill you, you useless little bastard.'

Well! I nearly shit myself under this fierce attack. I had never heard such bad language before, and I was terrified. I thought the man was going to kill me. I leapt from the tractor seat and bolted to the house and into my room. Mrs Johnston, as always, was at the stove cooking our dinner. I don't know what she thought was happening as I rushed past, but I didn't stop to explain. In my room I changed my clothes, chucked everything I owned into my old suitcase and ran from the house, down the steps, out the gate and onto the road. I went as fast as my short legs would carry me, expecting at any minute that Mr Johnston would be behind me in his Yellow Cab.

After maybe a mile I slowed to a walk. Nobody was following me as I made my way into Drouin down the dusty road. I guessed that my boss had no desire to catch up with me, not even to beat me up, as he never appeared. I assume that he was glad to be rid of me.

In my fear and haste, I hadn't stopped to ask for my pay. It was hardly worth collecting anyway. Luckily, I had been paid a week before and I had almost ten pounds in my pocket. That was more than enough to buy a good feed of fish and chips and a ticket on the afternoon train to Melbourne.

I was really quite pleased to escape from Johnson's farm, for escape it was, but I was worried about what I would do now. Where would I go?

Chapter Twenty-Six

Back to Excell's ~ Doctor's Flat ~ Swifts Creek ~ Omeo.

As I journeyed back to Melbourne, I knew I had nowhere else to go but to Auntie Phemie's. I walked from the Spencer Street station to Rosslyn Street; it was not very far. As I walked, I wondered and worried about the reception Aunt might give me. I needn't have worried, because when she opened the door to my timid knock, she smiled and gave me a hug.

'What are you doing here? Don't tell me you got the sack again?' She gave me a look through narrowed eyes.

'No, Auntie Phemie. He didn't like me, so I ran away.'

She didn't bat an eyelid, 'Come on in and tell me the story. I'll make a pot of tea.'

It seems to me now that in those days a pot of tea was the remedy for all things – at least in Aunt's house. As I told my tale of woe, Aunty showed real sympathy and sadness for me. I know she felt that I was young to be out in the world alone, but there was nothing she could do but help me.

'Let's have a couple of days to think about things, and then we will see about another job for you,' she said. This we did, and I spent the next week hanging about the house.

Early one morning a friend of Aunt's called in with her eleven-year-old daughter in tow.

'I wonder if I could leave Alice here with you for the day. I have been called into work and I have nobody to look after her? The lady was obviously under a lot of pressure. 'I can't afford to say no to a day's work and I don't want to get off-side with my boss.'

'Of course she can stay. I have to go to visit my sister today and will be away most of the day, but she can stay here with Ian.' The arrangement was sealed.

Alice was a pretty, blonde-haired, blue-eyed girl, not very tall and quite slim. I couldn't help notice that she sported two bumps in her woollen jumper.

Aunt went at about nine o'clock to catch the tram to Moonee Ponds to visit her sister Dulcie. I was all at sea, being left alone with a girl, as I had nothing in common with females. I had never had anything to do with them and avoided them like the plague.

Alice and I sat around not saying much. 'Can we play a game of Fish?' I suggested. 'Okay,' she smiled.

I took a pack of cards that resided permanently on the kitchen shelf and set about playing the game. After an hour or so we were getting pretty bored, when Alice said. 'Would you like to play with me in the washhouse?'

Play with me? Why the washhouse? I was puzzled, but readily agreed. We went out the back into the corrugated iron shed that was the bathroom and laundry. To my astonishment she took off a certain garment, exposing something I had only ever briefly glimpsed before.

Alice gazed at me with sparkling blue eyes, a big smile on her pretty face as I felt a violent stirring in my baggy trousers. Before you could say 'Jack Robinson', I was engaged in a totally new experience.

I won't go into detail except to say that, when it ended I felt pretty good, although a troublesome worry began to seep into my brain. I had heard about girls getting pregnant. What if I had done that? All the things I had heard about the subject came rushing back in an avalanche. Was Alice now in the 'in the family way'? I had often heard it called that. Oh God help me!

'You shouldn't have done that. I didn't want you to do that,' said Alice, as she stepped into her homemade blue denim knickers, a small frown on her face. 'Let's go back inside. I'm sure it'll be alright, but you should have stopped.' I am convinced that she actually did want me to 'do that'.

With her assurance calming my fears, we went back inside and resumed our game of Fish. I was still more than a bit bewildered by what had happened and wondered about my new-found prowess.

Alice didn't seem at all perturbed as she shuffled the cards for our next round of Fish, so I felt better about my mistake.

This was obviously my first sexual experience. It was pretty good, and I resolved to do it more often in future! Alas, from then on girls were scarce, so – well, you know.

My experience may have been a disaster, but I realise now that it obviously was not Alice's first go at it. I have sometimes wondered since that day how an eleven-year-old gained her experience, and with whom.

* * *

Aunty Phemie and I sat in Mr Excell's office. I was a bundle of nerves, I really thought that Mr Excell would growl at me. I shouldn't have worried, as he had met us with a big smile and seemed pleased to see us. Perhaps he was thinking of the fee he would get from any new employer of yours truly.

'Don't worry your head about this, Ian. I have actually sent two boys to Johnston's over the past year and neither of them have stayed. I am thinking there is something amiss there, and I won't send any more to him.'

He went on, 'I have a very nice couple at Doctors Flat who need a boy to help on the farm. I have met them here in the office and they are good family people. They have two little girls and run a sheep and cattle farm up there. I am sure you will get on well if they decide to take you on.'

Mr Excell then said he would send them a telegram about me. 'It's no use trying to phone them as the telephone exchange there is only open at limited hours, and it's almost impossible to get them on the line. With that, Aunt and I were ushered out of the office.

'I'll send you a telegram when I hear back from them. Oh, by the way, their name is Stephens and the place is Doctors Flat. It's in East Gippsland. Goodbye for now.'

When we got home I asked Aunt if she knew where Doctors Flat was.

'No,' she replied, 'but I reckon George may know. I'll ask him tonight.'

George came around for tea that night, lugging two bottles of Melbourne Bitter with him. He placed them carefully on top of the block of ice in the ice chest which was just outside the back door.

'Precious cargo,' he winked and grinned at me. George wasn't a bad bloke when he was sober; totally unlike the bloke he was when he got drunk. Sober, he was a gentleman and very polite and caring. Drunk, he was a maniac.

'That farmin' bastard gave you a hard time I hear,' he said. 'The world's full of mongrels like that. Pick on kids and women, haven't got the guts to take on a bloke.'

He went to the ice chest and took out a bottle, which he opened and poured a beer into a large pot. He took a swig.

'Now this joint, Doctors Flat, is a fair way away. It's near Swifts Creek, which is near Omeo in East Gippsland. Here, I'll show yer on the map.' He unfolded a concertina-folded map of Victoria and spread it on the table.

'See, that's it there.' He pointed to a fly speck to the far right of the map. It looked a long, long way.

'I reckon you would go to Bairnsdale by train and then probably get a bus up to Omeo. I dunno, I've never been up that way, but I reckon no trains could get through those mountains.'

'Oh well,' I said. 'I haven't got the job yet, but it looks a long way away. Maybe they won't want me.' I said this more in hope than anything else.

I wasn't so lucky. A week later a telegram came from Mr Excell. It said simply: 'Call at the office. The Stevens will take Ian on. Excell.' It seemed that telegrams were never kind to me.

George wasn't kidding. It turned out that Doctors Flat was almost three hundred miles from Melbourne!

Mr Excell gave me the price of a train ticket to Bairnsdale, with the compliments of my new employer. My Aunt walked with me to the station on Spencer Street, me again lugging the old suitcase.

'Do you have enough money, Ian?' questioned Aunty.

I assured her that I had. I had a little over a pound in my pocket; all that remained of my pay from Johnston's farm.

My aunt planted a big kiss on my cheek, and I stepped on board the train. I was lucky enough to get a window seat again and placed my suitcase on a rack above my seat. Waving an unhappy goodbye to my Aunty Phemie on the platform, I settled in for the journey. The train moved slowly from the platform in a cloud of steam, heading east.

My compartment was otherwise empty, so I rode the entire journey alone. That didn't bother me as I was a shy boy and found it embarrassing to talk to strangers. I would usually turn bright red whenever someone I didn't know spoke to me, especially if they asked me a question. My coat pocket carried an almost new paperback western novel so I was happy enough with reading that. The only person to disturb me was the train conductor when he popped in a half hour up the track to check and clip my ticket.

It was over two hundred miles to Bairnsdale, a very long, slow trip in the steam powered train, but eventually I alighted at the Bairnsdale railway station. Outside stood the waiting Omeo bus, an almost new and beautiful White, painted red and cream. I was delighted to ride in such a machine, having a fascination with them since my first ever bus ride experience as a nine-year-old back at South Kingsville. That bus was also a White. White trucks and buses were made in the USA and were a top seller for many years. The company prospered during WW2 making military vehicles. I loved them because they were American. To me, America and all things American, were simply the ultimate.

The bus was licensed to seat thirty people but only perhaps a dozen of us went on board. The fare for under-sixteens was four shillings, which left me with almost twelve shillings to jingle in my pocket.

The driver was a pleasant man in his sixties who greeted us with a big smile. 'It's almost afternoon teatime, so we'll stop off at the general store and pub at Bruthen. They serve a good afternoon tea there, and it's not too dear. We should be there in half an hour.' He thrust the bus into gear and we moved slowly away toward Bruthen.

The trip to Doctors Flat took me through some beautiful Australian country. Much of it reminded me of Blackwood and Barry's Reef; huge gum trees, blackwood and lightwood trees, with massive tree ferns in the deep gullies. We went through the small settlement of Ensay, and as darkness closed in, the bus came to a halt – journey's end. Doctors Flat proved to be little more than a roadside sign.

'This is where you get out young feller,' called the bus driver.' See that light up the hill a bit? That's the Stevens place. Are they expecting you? It's a wonder they weren't down here to meet you. Anyway, if you follow the track you'll be there in no time. Say hello to Malcolm and Jenny for me. Hooroo.'

The bus moved slowly away toward Omeo in the quickly falling blackness of the mountain and forest night.

I struggled up the hill to the house, mounted the veranda steps to the front door and knocked. I heard voices and sounds from inside and pretty soon the door opened and a man appeared.

The hall at Swifts Creek I went to a dance there and sat at the wall all night. (Mattinbgn, 2011, Creative Commons License)

'Yes, who is it?' The speaker was a man in his mid-thirties clad in slippers and dressing gown. I don't think they were expecting a visitor, especially at night.

'Mr Stevens? I'm Ian Braybrook.'

'What? The new boy? They told me you would be here tomorrow. Oh, goodness me. Please come in, Ian. Sorry not to be expecting you.'

He ushered me inside and to the kitchen-living room. Seated at the table were a woman and two girls.

'Jenny, this is Ian. He's the lad Excell found us to help us around the farm. Sorry again, Ian, that we didn't meet you at the gate. Jenny, didn't they say Ian would be here tomorrow?'

Mrs Stevens nodded. She was a very pleasant looking person, light-haired and quite attractive. She also wore a dressing gown, as did the two fair-haired children seated at the table. Like her husband, Mrs Stevens was in her mid-thirties.

'These are our two girls, Ian – Edith and Jean.' Mrs Stevens indicated the two youngsters, the biggest I guessed to be about seven or eight and her sister about six. They smiled shyly and said a quiet hello.

'My goodness, Ian, you must be tired and hungry. Did you come all the way from Melbourne today?' Mrs Stevens went to the stove. 'I'll make you a sandwich and a cup of tea. You poor boy, I'm so sorry we didn't expect you.'

I was not good at conversation but managed to answer the many questions thrust at me. After I had finished my meal, Mr Stevens said, 'Come on, Ian. I'll show you to your room. We can learn all about you in the morning. You must be tired. Come this way.'

He took me through the back door and down a short path that led to an outbuilding made of corrugated iron. One half comprised the washhouse, bathroom and flushable toilet and the other half my small bedroom.

Mr Stevens led the way, carrying a powerful flashlight. 'Here you are, Ian.' He went to the bedside table and lit the kerosene lamp.

'I'll leave you to it and I'll give you a call at about seven in the morning. We have breakfast about that time as the girls have to get on the bus to school at Swifts Creek pretty early. I think you'll find everything you need alright. Goodnight, Ian, and I'm sorry again about tonight.' He closed the door.

I was impressed with what I had seen and heard so far. They appeared to be a good family, certainly much more welcoming than my previous employer. And that's the way it proved to be.

I gazed about my new home. It had a comfortable looking single bed, a dressing table, a wardrobe, a small table with a matching chair and a picture of a horse on one wall. There was a small fixed window covered with nice lace curtains and linoleum on the floor. There was a small bookshelf with a handful of paperback books on it. Alas, there was no wireless, but it was sheer luxury after what I'd had at the Johnstons.

I settled in quite well at the Stevens farm and I was treated as one of the family. I never did use the given names of the Stevens, it was always Mister or Missus. I also became quite friendly with the two girls, who were inclined to follow me around quite a bit, which I didn't mind. I enjoyed their company. Sometimes they would walk with me as I did my rounds about the property, me always carrying a small pea rifle with which I shot hundreds of rabbits. It was one of my regular jobs and I enjoyed it. The property was alive with the pests and they could be seen almost anywhere I looked. I had no compunction over killing rabbits, which I knew were vermin in a farmer's eyes. My young female companions seemed to be thrilled whenever I managed to score a hit and laughed happily, telling me what a good shot I was. This made me feel pretty proud of myself.

However, I preferred to do this job alone. I loved the freedom of roaming the thousand acre farm, shooting rabbits, inhaling the smells of the bush, watching the kangaroos feeding and listening to the singing of a million birds.

When the girls were with me, except for the shooting, there was none of that, they were too noisy and talked and giggled non-stop.

Helping Mr Stevens put up new fences and repair old ones was on the list of standard jobs. There was always something to be done.

Another regular job was felling trees and cutting them up into fence posts or firewood. Again, it was very hard work, but it didn't bother me. I was quite strong for a fourteen-year-old.

Mr Stevens had a new swing saw, which cut through the fallen tree trunks and its branches with ease. I had never seen one before and was fascinated by it. But, by God, it was a terribly dangerous machine. It is best described as a circular saw at the end of a pole, mounted on wheels. At one end was the engine, mounted over two rubber wheels. There was then a long shaft and at the end of the shaft, the internal mechanism drove the unguarded, rapidly spinning circular blade. It was moved about with handles that resembled those of a large wheelbarrow.

We treated it with utmost caution and Mr Stevens would not ask me, nor permit me, to operate it. After we felled the trees with axe and crosscut saw, and trimmed the branches from the trunk with our axes, Mr Stevens would cut up the trunk and larger limbs with the swing saw. It sure made the job a lot easier, and I enjoyed this work too.

At crutching time, I helped bring the sheep in from the paddocks, assisted by two wonderful kelpie dogs, and kept up a regular supply of sheep for the shearers on the shed board. There were about five thousand sheep on the property.

Whenever the Stevens went to town shopping, either to nearby Swifts Creek or the mountain town of Omeo, they took me along. When they went to the local footy match at Swifts Creek they took me too. I felt 'just it' being driven in their near-new MG Saloon motor car. It had bright, shiny dark red paint and real leather seats. Beautiful! The Stevens were really very good to me.

Although I liked the work and got on well with the family, I felt very miserable at night. If only I had a wireless!

I had been at the Stevens farm maybe six weeks when, one moonlit night, I packed my suitcase and ran away!

On that night, a spell of unhappiness descended on me, a spell that I could not control. I felt so lonely and miserable that I could bear it no longer. I was compelled by a force within me to go back to my Aunty Phemie.

I didn't have the courage to tell the Stevens that I was leaving. I also thought that if I did that they would talk me out of it. I was determined to leave there. Immediately! Without delay!

I packed my suitcase and wrote a long note to the Stevens in which I told them some story of why I had to leave. I have no idea now what I wrote. I pinned it to the outside of the door and I slunk away, like a thief in the night. I know now it was a cowardly thing to do, but I was overcome with a massive loneliness and a dreadful fear that I cannot explain.

It was about ten o'clock as I made my way down the track to the main road. I hastened in the direction of Bairnsdale as quickly as my legs could carry me, all the while expecting a car to come behind me and perhaps take me back to the Stevens farm. I didn't stop walking all night. I don't know how many miles I covered, but it was a considerable distance, driven by fear.

Shortly after daybreak I heard the sound of a motor car behind me. Was it the Stevens coming to look for me? I was afraid that if it was them they would take me back.

To my relief a dark coloured Mercedes Benz rounded a bend a half a mile back from the way I had come. What a relief. It was not the Stevens car! I signalled for the driver to stop, holding a thumb up, just as I had seen them do in the pictures.

The driver came to a halt, opening the passenger side door for me. Before me was a middle-aged man in a suit, a cigarette clamped firmly in his mouth.

'G'day, young feller. You're out early. Put your case on the back seat and climb in. I suppose you are going to Bairnsdale. That's where I'm heading. What's your name? I'm Bob Morrow.'

He said all that without taking a breath. I climbed happily in beside him.

Bob proved to be a happy, entertaining man; a salesman for a water pump company who had been to Omeo.

He talked incessantly, asked me no questions, which suited me, and for most of the journey spoke of little else but his job, his sales record and the delight and love of his brand new 1951 model Mercedes Benz.

Before I knew it he dropped me off in the main street of Bairnsdale, speeding off with a cheery wave.

I soon found my way to the train station where I waited about three hours for the train to leave for Melbourne. The delay didn't bother me. I had plenty of money for food, drinks and lollies and I bought two cheap paperback western novels as well.

* * *

Back at Aunty Phemie's, she was astonished to see me when she answered my knock on her door.

'What are you doing here? I didn't expect to see you again for a while. What happened this time? Goodness gracious me. What am I going to do with you, Ian? Come on in.'

I had no alternative but to confess to my Aunt what I had done.

'For heavens sake!' She pushed a small writing pad in front of me. 'You write to those poor people right now and tell them that you are alright and say you are sorry. I can't believe that you did that. You should be ashamed of yourself. You running away like that. Now start writing.'

I was ashamed of myself, but also relieved. I felt safe at Aunty Phemie's

I did as she told me, writing the letter as she watched over my shoulder. I don't recall what I wrote.

'Alright, now put it in this envelope and we'll post it when we go to see Mr Excell in the morning. And you can explain yourself to him'

I addressed the envelope: 'Mr and Mrs Stevens, Doctors Flat, via

Bairnsdale.' Aunty went to the mantelpiece and took a twopenny postage stamp from a small glass container. She licked it and stuck it on the envelope.

'After we have a cup of tea I'll hear your story.' Aunty smiled at me a little now.

I did my best to explain my behaviour to her, and I am sure that Aunty accepted what I said, even as garbled and unlikely as it was. I know that my Aunt understood the fear and loneliness within me.

Chapter Twenty-Seven

Excell's again – Whittlesea.

So, next morning, it was back to Mr Excell's for the third time. He had already heard from the Stevens by telephone and they had told him about my midnight departure and the note I had left. To my relief he was not at all angry or upset with me. On the contrary, he was very much warmer and more friendly toward me than in the past.

'Look, Ian, it's probably my fault for sending you so far away from your Aunty and your other family. I wasn't thinking of that, and I am sorry. I'll find you another job and this time a lot closer to the city. I'll be in touch as soon as I have something for you.'

True to his word, he sent me a telegram two days later asking me to call and see him. Again, my Aunty Phemie accompanied me to Hardware Street.

Mr Excell greeted us at the front counter. 'Come on in, Mrs Brown.' He looked at me and gave a grin. 'I think I have found just the job for you this time, Ian.'

He sat himself at his large desk. Aunty and I sat opposite him as he looked at me over spectacles perched on the bridge of his nose.

'This job is on a cattle and horse property near Whittlesea. It's only about thirty miles away and there is a bus and train to the city every day which means you can come home to your Aunty's some weekends. It is one of the best properties in the Plenty River district and I am sure you will be happy there. You'll be helping with the horses and doing odd jobs around the property. All your meals are provided, as well as a nice room, and your pay will start at two pounds a week. Is that alright?'

I nodded. 'Yes, Mr Excell. It sounds very good.'

It did sound good to me, even though the pay was small. But the place seemed to be alright and I liked the idea of working with horses.

I was collected at the bus stop in the main street of Whittlesea. It was a Sunday and the street was very quiet. I cannot recall the name of my new boss. I know he wasn't very friendly and his face showed no warmth as he introduced himself. He was a real toff, which showed immediately he opened his mouth to speak. He was dressed in a smart tweed jacket, off-white moleskin trousers and highly polished riding boots. I recognised it as the 'squatter's uniform', worn by almost all of the landed gentry of the time. He was about sixty years old, with grey hair and a neat, almost white, moustache.

'Place your case in the trunk lad and you make yourself comfortable in the back.' The bastard put me in the back seat, probably to make me feel even smaller than I was. His tone and style of voice indicated that he had an upbringing far different from mine.

He was driving a magnificent, black 1940s Lincoln sedan. It was huge and I was completely lost in the vast rear seat area. I had never even seen such a car before, much less get to ride in one.

I may have been very impressed by the car, but I was not by my new boss!

Very soon we drew up in the long, winding driveway that led to a large brick and tile home, prominent atop a green, lush hillside. It was surrounded by a vast flower garden, surrounded on each side by a well trimmed hedge. To the north side was a well treed orchard. The entire place shouted 'wealth'.

The Lincoln came to a halt outside a huge timber and corrugated iron shed, about 200 yards short of the home.

'This is where you will be accommodated, Ian. Bring your case and I shall show you to your quarters.'

I hastened to obey. My boss led me to the rear of the building. Scattered about were pieces of farm machinery. There was a neatly stacked pile of hay bales and bags of chaff on one wall, and opposite were several horse stalls, without horses. Saddles and bridles adorned the walls. In the farthest corner was a small area partitioned by a ten foot wall, painted green. It had one doorway and a small window.

'Here is your room, Ian. There is a toilet and shower next to the first stall. There are towels and the things you will need in there. My daughter Nancy will call and see you soon. She will tell you what she wants done.'

He moved to leave. 'Oh, and she will bring you your lunch and dinner each day. Breakfast things you will find in the cupboard outside the doorway. I will see you around the place I suppose, Ian. My daughter will bring your meal soon.' He left me in the room – my new home. I actually never saw him again, not even from a distance.

Obviously, I was not being invited to eat in the house. I was relieved with that, as I would have been so uncomfortable eating with such elegant and refined people. Not my style, I was just a simple country boy with no familiarity with formality – airs and graces.

I looked around my room. It wasn't too bad, in fact it was sheer luxury to me. I had a stretcher type bed with pillows, blankets and a quilt, a small table with matching chair, and a bedside table complete with an electric lamp. There was a small wardrobe with a built-in set of drawers, and to my absolute delight, a wireless set. From then on, the wireless was my constant companion.

I unpacked and stretched out on the bed and waited for the daughter to come and give me my orders. She soon arrived, bearing my lunch on a tray. I paid little attention to the contents of my meal, I was far more interested in the person carrying it.

Wow! She is pretty good looking, I thought, and she really was. I guessed her to be about fourteen. She wore riding gear and riding boots. Her dark hair was tied up in a bun under a black riding helmet, she had a pretty smiling face and her figure had the lumps and bumps in all the right places.

This was a small slice of heaven. I had a job with a good room and a wireless, and the girl who was to bring my meals and give me my instructions was, well, beautiful. What more could a young lad want?

Despite my interest in Nancy I felt uncomfortable in her presence, as I did with all girls; I had no idea what to say or talk about.

'My name is Nancy.' She deposited a tray of sandwiches on the table. 'Here is your lunch, and after you finish I'll come and show you what I want you to do.'

She gave me a blank look and turned and left my room. She didn't seem to be very impressed or interested in me.

My job for the rest of the day, and indeed for most days, was cleaning out the horse stalls, feeding the horses and generally cleaning and sweeping. I was more a stable hand than a farmhand. There were six horses in all, riding hacks I think they were called. Both Nancy and her mother, who I was never introduced to, in spite of me having to help her with her saddling, went riding every day. It was as if I didn't exist, but I didn't care about that. I wouldn't be able to speak to such an illustrious person anyway. The mother was aged in her forties and quite attractive with blonde hair and a well preserved face and figure.

This was my routine almost every day. Once or twice I was asked to split firewood for the house from a stack of sawn wood in the backyard. That was as close as I got to the homestead.

Nancy and I got on very well and she became quite friendly towards me. For my part, I soon began to feel relaxed with her, and she used to sit and talk with me for hours on end.

I know it sounds like the dream of some wretched pubescent boy, but Nancy and I became a little more than friends. It didn't extend to the actual act but it came mighty close. What's more it was on regular repeat.

I could scarcely believe that this was happening to me. In my many wild, erotic imaginings about her, I never thought that Nancy, or any girl for that matter, would engage in this stuff with me. Think of it, the daughter of a wealthy family fraternising to this extent with their very ordinary stable hand! A sort of Lady Chatterley's Lover!

Thank God we never went any further than we did. Neither of us had a clue about birth control. Nancy almost certainly would have become pregnant and the result of that would have been unimaginable horror. However, I still wonder at the self control I exercised on occasions – most likely fear, I guess!

Apart from the regular delivery of my meals and my times with Nancy, my days were spent working alone and my nights reading western novels and listening to the wireless. This firmed in me my desire to become a radio announcer. These smooth-voiced men, for it was almost exclusively men, were my idols. I knew the words of every song on the hit parade and every popular country song. We called them cowboy or hillbilly songs back then. My favourites were Guy Mitchell's 'The Roving Kind' and Tex Morton's 'Whipstick', a song about his horse – of course.

I fitted the bill, as I fancied myself as both a rover and a cowboy. My big fantasy was to go to Queensland droving, and I had even chosen a new name for myself for when I went north. I would be known as Kid Larsen, a name taken from a character in a Western book I had read. I never did go to Queensland droving or adopt my new name, but gee it was a beauty!

Chapter Twenty-Eight

Yarraville – a brush with the law – camping out – jobs, cars and a flying sausage

I didn't stay very long at my job at Whittlesea. The only thing I enjoyed about it was Nancy, but even that was not strong enough to hold me there. I wanted to be in Melbourne with my brother Frank. This time I didn't run away from the job. I had copped enough from Aunty Phemie to know it was not the right thing to do. So I delivered my decision to Nancy to relay to her father.

'Oh why do you have to go?' Nancy was very unhappy. 'Please stay here. I will miss you I don't have any friends really, only you.'

Of course I was tempted to stay for Nancy's sake, but my longing to be with at least part of my family, Frank, was too strong. So, a week later, I said goodbye to a sad-eyed Nancy at our last rendezvous in my room. I felt very unhappy about leaving her as I walked the two miles into town. I hesitated, in agonised thought, before boarding the bus back to the city.

This time I did not go to my Aunty Phemie's, but to South Kingsville to find my brother, Frank. There was no way I was going to let my Aunty take me back to Mr Excell's Employment Agency!

* * *

Frank was five years older than me. He was a bit overweight, heritage of his long spell in bed from when he was thirteen through to fourteen years old. He was not tall, about five foot seven, and always of a happy disposition.

He was now nineteen years old and had a car and a driver's licence to go with it. A driver's licence was not unusual, I suppose, but not everybody bothered with one in those days!

We had stayed in contact with the occasional letter, so I knew he was staying at Jack Pottage's place in South Kingsville. He and Jack had been mates since the days when we first moved from Trentham to our new home a few doors away, five years before.

When I knocked at the Greene Street door, Jack's mother informed me that he had recently married Olive Durdin, a lass from Yarraville, and he was living there. Frank had gone with him.

Yarraville was a poor working-class suburb at the time, shunned by the well-to-do across the river.

Mrs Pottage gave me the address, and after a short bus ride to Yarraville, I knocked on the door at number ten Globe Street. It was answered by Olive's mother, Sylvia. When I explained who I was, she immediately invited me in. Hers was a happy, time-worn face, framed by white hair which hung over her shoulders which topped a rather plump figure. I judged her to be about sixty.

'Come in and have a cuppa. You must be very tired after your long journey.' She motioned me to a chair at the kitchen table.

I wasn't a bit tired and compared to other trips I had made it was not a long journey, but when she placed a cup of tea and a slice of fruitcake before me I hopped right into it. I was very hungry.

'Now eat up and enjoy it,' Mrs Durdin smiled and went to the kitchen sink to resume preparing the evening meal. I quickly devoured the piece of cake and almost immediately another slice was on my plate.

Most Yarraville people were like the Durdin family, poor, hard-working and warm-hearted. I felt quite at home. These were my people.

Pretty soon, Frank and Jack arrived home, ending their search for work for the day.

Frank was really pleased to see me and gave me a brotherly hug.

'It's good to see you. It'll be good to have some company. It gets a bit lonely when I'm camped out the Geelong Road or Blackshaws Road. We can look for work together too.' He shook his head. 'Jack has scored a job at the Willy dockyard as a welder, but I can't get a bloody thing. I haven't got a skill like Jack. I don't reckon most people realise how hard it is to find work these days.'

Jack was a tall man, about six foot and he was slim and athletic looking. His dark, wavy hair framed a round and smiling face. He was a little older than Frank, about twenty-two. He greeted me with a strong handshake. 'Good to see you, Ian. It's been a bloody long time. Come into my joint and meet the missus.'

He led me into the tiny fibro-sheet and corrugated iron outbuilding where his wife was busy at the kitchen sink. The home was one room. The furniture was sparse, a small table and four chairs, a double bed and an alcove at one end, which I presumed contained a shower.

'This is my wife Olive, Ian.' I shook her hand. She gave me a big hug. 'Lovely to meet you at last, Ian. Frank talks about you a lot.'

Olive was about twenty years old, a little on the plump side, and was wearing a floral dress and apron. She also had an obviously happy disposition.

'I am so pleased that Jack has got a job at last. I just hope that Frank gets one soon, as well. And you too, I suppose?'

She was correct. I had no idea where I would get work and had only a couple of pounds in my pocket, so I needed a job very soon.

Frank spoke up. 'We had better get cracking, Ian. It'll be dark in a couple of hours and we gotta cook our tucker, then go out the road and set up a camp. I've got some snags and spuds for tonight. I do me cooking here in the yard mostly.'

He produced a four gallon drum with several holes punched into its bottom half. With a few sticks from the woodheap, he kindled a small fire, which quickly grew into a fierce blaze. He placed a heavy wire mesh over the top and put in place a small saucepan containing two large potatoes in water.

'They should cook in half an hour, and I'll put the snags on as well. Then we can eat. It's not much, but it'll fill the space,' said Frank as he put some more sticks on the fire.

This was another new experience for me. Eating outdoors from a tin plate set on an old soap box, in someone's backyard in the city! I'd done a few unusual things since I left home but had never done that before.

The meal turned out pretty well, and after we washed our saucepans, plates and cutlery at the gully trap's tap it was time to go.

At that time, Frank was the proud owner of a 1928 Studebaker panel van, in very good condition. In a previous life it had been a McAlpine's Flour delivery van, and the original sign writing showed vaguely through the newish yellow repaint. It was a great vehicle, with plenty of power and lots of space for sleeping in the back. It was ideal for Frank's needs, and even had room for a guest sleeper!

After our meal, it was starting to get dark and Frank put out the fire. 'We had better go. It'll be dark soon. Because we are so late, I'll just go out to Blackshaws Road for tonight and camp there. It's only a couple of miles. There's a bit of wood lying about so we can have a fire.'

On the way, we stopped at a small grocery shop-milk bar on Francis Street, where I bought a tin of baked beans, some butter and a loaf of bread. 'That'll do for breakfast, Frank,' I said, climbing into the front seat. 'We can have a billy of tea if you have any.' He agreed.

Frank parked the 'Studie' on the grassed edge of the deserted road. There was a large peppercorn tree nearby, so we set up our fire beneath it in a rough fireplace built of stone. The nearest house was at least 500 yards away.

'We won't disturb anyone here. I sometimes camp here so I built a fireplace for safety.' My brother broke twigs to kindle a fire.

Soon a cheery blaze was going, casting a warming glow around the perimeter. Reaching into the van, Frank produced a large can of water and filled his blackened billy can. We sat and talked about my experiences as we waited for the billy to boil.

After a while we ran out of conversation and retired to our bed in the back of the van. There was no mattress, just a blanket on the timber floor, and only one pillow, an unsavoury looking item that

I didn't want to share, even if offered. I'm afraid that hygiene and personal cleanliness wasn't a luxury we could afford at the time.

We slept quite soundly only to be awakened at daylight by the sound of voices outside the van. They were obviously female.

'It wasn't here when I came home on the bus yesterday,' said one.

'Maybe it's been stolen,' said another.

'Do you think we should tell the police?' said voice number one.

There was a sharp rattling at the rear door.

'Shit,' whispered Frank. 'They're trying to get in.'

Thankfully the door wasn't easy to open, requiring a very hard tug to shift it.

Frank and I looked at each other with worried expressions. If the women managed to get the door open and peer inside, they would be confronted by two half-naked males cringing in the half-dark interior. We couldn't allow that!

'It's alright,' called Frank. 'It's only us two blokes in here. We camped here for the night. We're okay, thank you.'

There was silence from outside for a few seconds.

'Oh! Sorry to disturb you. Marj and I thought it was a stolen car or something.'

Frank assured the lady that it was not stolen and the two voices went on their way, speaking in hushed tones with a giggle now and then.

'Bloody hell,' said Frank. 'That was a bit of a worry.'

We headed back to Globe Street cruising down Williamstown Road, near where it now joins the freeway. Just ahead of us a rectangular can fell from the tray of a truck, bounced a couple of times and came to a halt. Frank stopped to inspect the object which turned out to be a full four gallon can of Kerosene. 'I reckon the old Studie will run on this,' said Frank. I agreed. 'They run tractors on kero on the farms, so why not.' Frank found a funnel under the seat and tipped the kero into the tank.

At that moment a black and white Ford V8 drew alongside. It bore a prominent sign that read 'Police'. The cop on the passenger's side wound down the window. 'We've been watching you two. Do you realise what you did is stealing? Most likely worth a jail sentence.'

Shit!

The second cop emerged and stood before us. 'Do you reckon the old girl will run on it?' He had a trace of a grin on his face. He had obviously observed our dress and general appearance and figured that we were a couple down on our luck. Frank muttered something about, 'hoping so, but not sure'.

'Look we won't take any action here. We really just want to see if it actually works. Give her a try.'

The cops returned to their car. With window down, cop number one gave a cheery wave.

'Good luck with it, boys. Hope she runs okay,' said the cop from his window, grinning from ear to ear as they sped off.

And blow me down the engine did run okay, albeit belching a bit of black smoke from the exhaust, but the Studie didn't seem to mind a shandy of petrol and kerosene.

Back at Globe Street, Frank heated some baked beans and made us some toast and a billy of tea for breakfast.

It was then time to head off and see if we could find a job. At our first call at the Baltic Simplex machinery factory at Spotswood, I was fortunate.

'Yes,' said the man in the office. 'We do need a young feller to help around the place. Can you start tomorrow?'

I assured him that I certainly could.

He turned to Frank. 'Sorry mate. I haven't anything for you. Just the boy. See you at seven tomorrow morning, lad'

Well at least one of had a job to bring in some money. We proceeded on our way in search of work for Frank, calling at several factories in the West Footscray-Tottenham area. At the front office at the Wiltshire File factory we were directed to talk to the foreman, a Mr Ashford, who was at work deep inside the building. The noise was eardrum bursting. I don't think I've ever heard worse. Finally we found Mr Ashford and spent two minutes shouting at each other, only to be told: 'Sorry, no work here for you, mate'.

We gave it away for the day after that. There are only so many knockbacks you can take in a day. Frank was getting to the end of his tether in his fruitless search. He hadn't worked for four weeks and was increasingly desperate. It was fortunate that I had that couple of pounds in my pocket to keep us afloat.

We were not politically savvy and had no understanding that Australia was going through a recession at the time. Money was tight, and demand had dropped to a very low point; hence, no demand for labour.

Next day, after another night in the Studebaker, off I went to work. Frank dropped me at the factory entrance and he continued on his way to see if the day might prove better in work hunting than it had to date. It wasn't any better, as it turned out. Nor was the next day, or the next half dozen after that. It was pointless really, calling back at the same factories over and over.

At that time, neither Frank nor I had any idea that there was a small, Federal Government funded unemployment benefit available via the Commonwealth Employment Service. It appears that the Menzies Government really didn't want to have too many know about it, as it was never given publicity. If only we had known, it would have made life a lot easier for us – and many others no doubt.

Chapter Twenty-Nine

Street dwellers ~ jobs ~ the Gypsy woman ~ the brown cliffs of Darley.

I hated my job at Baltic Simplex. All day long I pushed a broom between machines over the vast expanse of floor, picking up the sweepings and depositing them in a large bin. I was bored silly.

A week after I started, I collected my first pay of two pounds five shillings and never went back. Instead, the next day, I went with Frank looking for a better job. Again, I was lucky (if you can call it that!) On our second call, I was hired as a general hand at Kinnears Rope Works in Footscray.

Guess what? My job was to sweep the floors, collect the rubbish and place it in a bloody bin! Again, I was bored senseless, but I stuck at it. Without my two pounds and seven shillings pay we would have been in deep trouble.

Frank's bad run continued, so it was just me earning any money, and meanwhile, for some unfathomable reason, Jack had quit his

Kinnears Ropeworks in Footscray where I had a brief career as a floorsweeper in 1952. (Copyright unknown.)

job at the Dockyards. A week later I was given a week's notice at Kinnears, I do not know why, because I did the job well. Maybe they couldn't afford to keep me on!

So there we were, the three of us out of work, Jack by his choice. I don't think he liked work very much. He much preferred to be working on old cars, like his 1920s Model T Ford. It was a beauty – a single seater roadster with a dickie seat at the back. Jack called it 'The Flying Sausage' and had neatly painted the name on both sides of the bonnet.

Frank was forced to sell his beloved Studebaker and buy a cheaper car to get some cash. The replacement car indeed was cheap – and so it should have been. A Falcon Knight was the rarest of rare motor cars, even in 1951. The new car was a 1926 tourer. It turned out to be a monster. The Falcon Knight brand was short-lived, manufactured in 1926 and 1927 by the Willys Company from Ohio, USA, makers of the famed Jeep of WW2. It briefly sold well in America, but few were sold in Australia. Thank God.

Frank collected it from the car dealer in Footscray and drove it the mile or so to Globe Street, where his new machine groaned to a stop, enveloped in a cloud of blue smoke and steam. Frank emerged from the machine red-faced and swearing in the most violent manner. Normally a very quiet person he was quick to anger when roused, and then, everybody duck!

A Falcon Knight tourer. Frank and I made our home in one like this. Not very comfortable. (Lars-Göran Lindgren Sweden Creative Commons License.)

'What a heap of shit that bastard sold me. I swapped my f...n good Studie for this pile of rubbish and fifty bloody quid. A man should have his head read! I should go back and punch the bastard in the nose – I would, but this pile of junk wouldn't get there.' Poor Frank. I loved my brother and he was a sorry sight to see, and it hurt me.

'Don't worry, Frank,' said Jack, ever the motor mechanic, 'I reckon I can fix it. I think these things have wet sleeves and they can be replaced pretty easily.' He went on to explain in detail the intricacies of wet sleeves and how they replaced the conventional valves, or something like that. This sort of talk was far over my head.

Jack sped off to the car wreckers in West Footscray and in no time returned wearing a big smile and clutching a bag full of the mysterious wet sleeves. 'I've got them. They look in good nick and cost only three quid. Pretty good, I reckon. I'll whack them in tomorrow.'

The next morning, whack them in he did, and the Falcon fired up the first try. It belched a fair bit of blue smoke, but Jack assured us that the sleeves would soon 'bed in', and she'd be as good as gold.

Frank was pretty happy with this outcome. 'Come on,' he said to Jack, Olive and me. 'Let's go for a drive and run the sleeves in a bit.'

He headed out the Ballarat Road and proceeded right through Deer Park and all the way to Bacchus Marsh. It was a much longer journey than he had planned but, he said, it was good for running in the new engine bits.

From Bacchus Marsh he headed further out to Darley. The Falcon ground its way up a rather steep hill until we turned off the road, made our way down a steep slope, and sat perched near the cliff that plunged hundreds of feet down the Lerderderg Gorge to the river below. We wandered about for a while, peering over the cliff edge, then sprawling on the grass, relaxed and at peace with the world.

'We had better go,' said Frank, and we all piled into the car. The engine roared into life and Frank engaged first gear, ready to tackle a steep rise that led us back to the roadway.

Suddenly there was a huge burst of blue smoke that poured from under the bonnet. With that, the Falcon refused to budge another inch and jerked to a halt. Steam rose from the radiator as the engine rattled noisily, but it could not compare to the steam from Frank's ears! He was furious. He cursed the car dealer roundly, his face apoplectic with fury.

We passengers wondered what would happen next. Frank crunched the gears into reverse.

'I'll fix this bastard of a thing for all time,' he cried and the vehicle proceeded at a rapid pace backwards toward the cliff. Doors were thrown open and three terrified passengers leapt from the car.

Jack yelled at the top of his voice: 'For Christ's sake, Frank. Stop the car! You'll kill yourself and wreck the bloody car too.' Olive and I just stood and watched, mouths agape. Finally, with only a few yards to go, Frank came to his senses and swung the wheel, avoiding the massive drop by a few feet.

'Shit, Frank,' said Jack. 'You frightened the shit out of us. Bloody hell!'

Frank, still clutching the steering wheel with white knuckles, suddenly burst into laughter. 'Yeah, that was a bit close. But I hate this bastard of a thing. Why did I ever buy such a shit heap?'

'Take it easy, Frank,' said Jack.' We'll get her home and fix her up alright. Just drive real slow and careful and she'll make it home, I reckon. I'll fix it tomorrow.'

We crawled back towards Bacchus Marsh. Then, in low gear and belching smoke, we undertook the very steep climb up Anthony's Cutting. To our amazement it made it to the top, and without further incident, we eventually arrived at Globe Street. Jack immediately lifted the smoking bonnet, a determined look on his face. He fiddled with the motor for a while and then pronounced it cured. 'She won't give much more trouble, I reckon,' he grinned.

'Okay,' said Jack next morning, 'how about we go out to Cobbledicks Ford for a burn. I was out there a while back and there are some old car engines dumped there. Maybe they are alright. We can sell them for scrap anyway, even if they are buggered.'

Cobbledick's Ford was just that, a ford over the Kororoit Creek, about ten miles to the west – out in the sticks. By lunchtime, travelling separately, we arrived at Cobbledicks Ford. Sure enough, thrown down an embankment were two almost complete car engines. 'They're buggered, of course,' said Jack after a quick examination. With a mighty effort, we rolled the two very heavy engines up the embankment. We lifted one into the back seat of the Falcon Knight and the other into the dickie seat of the Model T Ford, 'The Flying Sausage'. We drove directly to Simms Metal in West Footscray where we were handed four pounds for the buggered engines.

'Money for jam,' said Jack with a big grin, as he pocketed his half of the cash.

It wasn't much, but enough to keep Frank and I going for a few days.

Sometimes we didn't drive out of the built-up areas to camp. Instead we camped in the Falcon Knight in the street outside the Durdin's home. It was a way to save a bit of petrol and a bit of money. Two mornings in a row we woke to see a group of four or five workers from the State Electricity Commission (SEC) sub-station across the road peering in at us, faces close to the glass. Huge smiles filled the leering faces. They obviously found our presence highly unusual and quite amusing. It was pretty embarrassing for Frank and me.

Sleeping in the old motor car was not very comfortable, especially for me. As the owner, Frank had first choice of beds, and naturally he chose the fairly roomy back seat. Up front, it wasn't so good, and I found myself on a very narrow and very short bed. Not only that, I had to contend with the steering wheel, the gear lever and the handbrake handle. But somehow we managed to get some sleep.

Frank coined a phrase that has stayed with me ever since: 'A sleepless night in a Falcon Knight'.

Soon I had reached the stage of desperation. My only pair of shoes had worn so badly that the sole of one completely parted company with the upper. I was a cause of considerable amusement at number 10 Globe Street when I demonstrated how I could pull my shoe up to my knee, a most hilarious sight they said.

Frank contributed the few shillings for the cost of a new and very cheap pair of canvas sandshoes. I could hardly seek work wearing my sadly dilapidated pair of brogues.

To avoid any further embarrassment from peering SEC eyes,

Frank decided that we would, from now on, camp on the banks of Koorroit Creek, a few miles out on the road to Geelong. It was actually quite a pleasant spot, lightly treed, with the gently gurgling, unpolluted creek a stone's throw down the slightly sloping bank a few yards away. We built a good stone fireplace for our cooking and hot water. Wood was plentifully scattered beneath the trees and we had a comforting camp fire.

We parked the Falcon Knight beneath a large gum tree, and it was as good as home! However, the beds in the car were no more comfortable.

On the second night at the creek site, two ancient caravans, drawn by equally ancient cars, took up residence a couple of hundred yards north of our camp. A number of men, women and children, perhaps fifteen of them, got out and started to set up camp and light a campfire.

'Bloody Gypsies, I reckon,' said Frank. 'We'd better keep an eye on them as I've heard that Gypsies are bloody tea leaves. We can't afford to lose anything.'

Seated around our cheery fire, we ate our meagre meal and drank our black billy tea. The camp was well lit by a large globe Frank fixed into the car's tail-light socket. It cast a glow of about twenty feet around our fireplace. Compared to the conditions at Globe Street, it was sheer luxury! And no Gypsy could approach us without being seen.

The next day, we met up with Jack and Olive again and in the course of conversation told them about the Gypsy camp near our site. Jack told us that we should beware. 'In Europe and England I hear they are run out of just about every town for thieving and stuff.'

Frank and I spent a few hours in a half-hearted search for jobs, calling on the same factories that we had already tried. Same result of course.

Times were tough – we were in an economic recession and factories were cutting back, not hiring. If only we knew about the dole being available.

That night we sat around our campfire, one eye on the Gypsy

camp up the hill. After our tea, which consisted of toast made on a homemade wire fork at the campfire, a can of baked beans shared equally, and a billy of tea, we were pretty well content. The lamp in the tail-light socket lit the camp quite well and we chatted on about the events of the day, and planned for tomorrow. We had no plan really, all we could do was the rounds of the western suburb factories once more.

As we sat, half asleep, we were startled by the approach of a female figure from down toward the creek. It was obviously a person from the Gypsy camp, but what did she want? We were more than a little apprehensive as she approached within ten feet of our camp. She was lit by the light from the taillight and we could see that she wore a scarf over her head and an ankle length, brightly coloured floral dress. Our apprehension turned to plain fear as she began to emit the most horrible sounds, screeching like a banshee – awful groaning and pathetic wailing. She came closer, all the while screeching and screaming.

It was plain to us that the woman was demented, but what did she want? Was she crazy enough to attack us? Produce a long bladed knife perhaps? She was now only six feet away, clawing at the air and shrieking in a terrifying manner.

Kororoit Creek. Frank and I camped there in his car, and we encountered a lunatic Gypsy woman.
(Reinthal, 2013 Creative Commons License.)

'Owee! Eoww! Ahhhh! Waaaaarah! – at the same clutching at her belly, pulling at her hair and rolling on the ground. It was horrible.

'Go away! Leave us alone' cried Frank.

'Go away, go away. Please.' I echoed, by now petrified with fear. The figure retreated back down the hill to the edge of the lit area. She was going!

To our horror she turned and came back toward us, shrieking and wailing even louder as she waved her arms about and cried out in some garbled foreign language.

'Go away. Leave us alone!' cried Frank. The figure fell to the ground, apparently writhing about in agony.

'Are you alright? What's the matter?' shouted Frank.

I was too scared to speak, almost pissing my pants.

The wailing and groans then turned to insane laughter as the woman rose to her feet, peeling away her head scarf and stepping out of her dress. Standing before us was Jack Pottage, convulsing with laughter.

'You bastard, Jack. You frightened the shit out of us,' said Frank. 'What the hell were you doing?

Jack could barely contain himself. 'I had this great idea. I borrowed one of Olive's dresses and stuff, to dress up like a Gypsy woman and put the hard word on you for a quid – you know payment for services. I just couldn't do it. I saw how bloody frightened you were and I started laughing. The more I saw you – it made me laugh even more. I was just about busting. I couldn't talk – all I could do was try and stifle my laughter. That was all the bloody weird noises I made. Shit, I'm sorry I scared you so much.'

Although we could cheerfully have murdered Jack, we soon calmed down and saw the humour of the situation. Frank made a billy of tea and we sat around the fire, talking about the event for ages before Jack made his way home.

I don't believe I was ever more frightened than that night on the banks of Kororoit Creek.

Chapter Thirty

Homeless – peach picking – goodbye city life – police – Purnim West.

After that frightening experience, we were happy to accept an offer from Mrs Durdin to utilise her absent son's ancient Fiat tray truck which was kept in the garage. Frank and I were pleased to stretch out in the comparative luxury, comfort and shelter of the truck's tray. It was as good as home – well almost.

Frank was in a desperate situation by then and was forced to downgrade his car from the Falcon Knight to a 1926 Bean tourer. Did I say downgrade from the Falcon Knight? Yes it was possible! If the Falcon had been a disaster, the Bean was an absolute horror. It barely turned a wheel until Jack finally managed to get it to run – sort of. The Bean was an English make that was sold from 1919 until 1929. For a short time it outsold Austin and Morris in the UK. But not for long.

Frank and I decided to try the Commonwealth Employment Service (CES) in Footscray to see if they could find us a job. There was a queue of maybe twenty other men of all ages and most looking pretty miserable. The unhappy looking man behind the counter looked up from a pile of papers and nodded.

'They want fruit pickers at Shepparton. Do you want that?' Did we ever! We were happy to sign on the dotted line. The man handed us a name and location on a scrap of paper.'

'Good luck with that, boys,' he said as we made our way to the door.

At home at 10 Globe Street we were pleased when Jack said he would go with us. 'I'll have a go at it. We can go in The Sausage,' he grinned.

Frank was pretty pleased to hear this, as he hadn't relished the drive in the tired old Bean. Nor had I.

Next day, about mid-day, we packed a few belongings in the dickie seat of the Flying Sausage, with me squeezed in amongst it, and set off on this mammoth journey to Shepparton.

By nightfall, we had made it to the other side of Seymour and camped for the night. Jack had spotted a private looking, tree-clad spot alongside the road.

'This'll do us,' announced Jack, pulling the car to a halt. 'Let's get a fire going and cook some tucker before it gets pitch black.'

Frank soon had a nice blaze going, and following our usual camp tucker of fried snags and billy tea, we rolled out our swags.

'Let us sleep the beautiful sleep of the good and innocent,' quipped brother Frank in his poshest British voice. 'The good and innocent!' Bloody rubbish! He must have been thinking of some other blokes. No doubt about it, Frank had a good sense of humour and a good feel for the ridiculous.

'We are just like the three musketeers,' suggested Jack. Nobody disagreed; after all, there were three of us embarking on a big adventure into the unknown.

Huddled around the fire in our blankets, we talked on for a time until we became tired and bored and eventually fell asleep. The hard ground didn't bother us. Ah! To be young again!

About one o'clock in the morning, the sky opened up, thunder crashed and lightning split the air. The rain bucketed down. We three soggy musketeers crawled into the tiny front seat of the Model T Ford and spent a very cramped, sleepless and miserable night. Daylight could not come quick enough and was never more welcome. Frank somehow got a fire going, boiled the billy and fried some more snags; our wet clothes and blankets hung over the bonnet of the car, which Jack parked as close to the fire as he dared. By seven o'clock we set off to our destination.

At the CES in Shepparton, we were directed to an orchard about ten miles west of the town, I cannot recall the exact location. Suffice to say it was a large orchard, similar to a hundred more in the district.

The principal fruit grown there were yellow cling peaches – the sort most used for canning.

The orchard appeared to be alive with pickers – a hub of much activity. We watched as an assortment of men ran up and down stepladders with canvas bags slung around their necks. They sure moved fast.

'We need to get the hang of this,' said Jack. 'Best we watch the others for a while so we know what to do.'

The pickers went up their ladders at high speed and quickly filled the canvas neck bag. They then rushed down the ladder and deposited the contents of the bag in wooden boxes, each about two feet high and maybe a foot wide. The air was filled with the sound of voices and a rowdy old Fordson Major tractor which towed a large trailer laden with full and empty fruit cases. The driver picked up the full cases and deposited the empty ones for refilling, making note of the names and numbers of the pickers' full cases.

'Doesn't look too bad,' said Frank, 'I reckon we can do it alright.'

Jack and I nodded in agreement.

'Yeah. It looks easy enough,' I said, a little uncertainly.

At that stage our new boss appeared on the scene and greeted us briefly, but certainly not warmly.

'Youse the blokes from the CES I suppose?' He demanded with a scowl. We agreed that we were indeed the ones in question.

'Okay, grab a ladder and a bag and get started. You get one and sixpence a case. We're behind to buggery, so get stuck into it. And don't miss any fruit, and be careful not to pull it from the stems.'

He indicated a pile of six or seven stepladders nearby. They were made of solid timber and as heavy as a bag of lead to move around. There were no light-weight ladders in those days.

We had never picked more than a stolen apple from a neighbour's apple tree before, but we soon got the idea by watching the other pickers.

With a canvas bag slung around our neck it was up the ladder, picking the peaches from the highest spot first before gradually descending. The full bags were pretty heavy, and when it was full we'd scamper down the ladder and tip the contents into the timber cases provided. It took a couple of bags to fill a case. Often, when reaching for the furthest peach, we had to teeter on the rung second from the top – a practice fraught with danger.

As we watched the experienced workers, we soon learned that speed was essential. They were quite amazing to see, and good pickers made pretty good money. I doubted that we would ever be in that category. At afternoon smoko, we all knocked off and squatted around to drink the cups of black tea that the boss provided. The large pot, with enamel pannikins, was delivered on the same tractor-drawn trailer that took away our filled fruit cases and deposited the empties for us to refill. The driver was a tall, thin man in his fifties. He was called Spud and was a happy sort of bloke who wore a perpetual big grin.

The break gave us a chance to check our tally. Spud provided the details. 'You blokes together have picked eleven cases to date. Not a bad effort for learners I suppose.' He didn't seem impressed,

'What!' exploded Jack. 'Eleven bloody cases. Shit! What's that? That's about sixteen bloody bob between three of us in three bloody hours.'

This revelation made me just a little bit unhappy, but I figured we would do better as we got more experience.

'I reckon we should be able to do fifty a day,' offered Frank. I hoped he was right, but even at that we wouldn't get rich.

Soon after we had returned to our work following the break, I heard the sound of what I guessed was a falling ladder in the next row. It was accompanied by loud cries and curses. I peered through the branches. One of the pickers, an English migrant about thirty years old, had toppled from his ladder and lay spread-eagled on the ground.

'I've bloody well had enough of this,' he groaned. 'I am getting out of here. I've made fifteen bob in two damned days. It's slave labour I tell you and I have had enough. I am leaving, thank you very much. I am going to collect my pay. Good bye to you all and jolly good luck.' He picked himself up and headed off to find the boss.

We resumed our picking, determined to make more than the few miserable shillings we had to date. Two canvas bags later, in the row behind me, there were further crashing noises and the sound of breaking branches. There were muffled curses, and I recognised the voice of Frank.

Reaching for a distant peach, he had copied the Englishman and crashed through the foliage to the ground, taking several small branches with him. He wasn't hurt, but was badly shaken by the experience. Next thing the bastard boss, as we had named him, appeared, attracted by the noise.

'For Christ's sake! Another bloody idiot! What the bloody hell are you trying to do? Between you all you'll wreck me bloody orchard.' He stood there as if he could not believe what he was seeing. 'You've wrecked me bloody tree. You've wrecked me f…n tree! His face turned red and his body shook with the rage that mounted within him. He turned on the hapless Frank as his anger violently erupted. 'You stupid useless bastard, you've wrecked me f…n tree. Get your gear and get out of here! Piss off. You useless bastards from the city are all the same. Bloody useless. Go to the house and get your pay and f… off. The air had turned blue. I hadn't heard such profanity since Mr Johnston.

'If he goes, Jack and me'll have to go too,' I ventured meekly.

'Please yer f…n self. Youse won't be any f…n loss.'

He stomped off muttering about useless bastards from the city.

At the house, we collected our pay of nineteen shillings and f…d off back to Yarraville in the Flying F…n Sausage.

Chapter Thirty-One

BACK TO THE BUSH ~ RAILWAY COPS ~ WARRNAMBOOL ~ WELCOME HOME

Back at Globe Street, our accommodation had gone from a half star to a three quarter star due to the ancient Fiat tray truck. (Yes, it was a Fiat truck! How come we so often ran into such rare makes and models?)

Mrs Durdin was very concerned for our welfare following the Gypsy incident. 'I can't see you two boys stuck out there on that creek bank with Gypsies and all sorts of things that may be around you. You'll be safer here in the shed.' Mrs Durdin dragged out an old double bed mattress from somewhere and it fitted perfectly into the tray of the Fiat.

The shed sure was a lot more comfortable than sleeping on the ground, or in the cramped confines of a Bean. (That's a car remember – not edible.)

Within a week of our return from Shepparton, Frank finally landed a job as a truck driver for a city delivery company. He was so pleased he couldn't stop smiling. 'Maybe we can now afford to find a boarding house.'

That sounded good, but before we could do so, I decided that I would have to give up and see if Pop would have me at home on the farm at Purnim.

'It's no good, Frank, I just cannot stay like this and I cannot live off your money. I'll have to go home – if they'll have me.'

There was no telephone at the farm so I wrote a letter to Mum asking her to see if Pop had room for me.

A couple of weeks later I received the reply I had hoped for. 'Yes Gil will have you as there are lots of jobs here and he and Murray can't keep up. Let me know what train you'll be on and we will meet you at the Warrnambool station. That's the closest.'

I had mixed feelings about this deal as I wasn't too sure that Pop really wanted me. Maybe he was just doing it to please Mum.

Anyway, it was good news in that I would have somewhere to live and some sort of job. I was at rock bottom, my clothes were dilapidated and grubby and my hair needed cutting. I probably smelt a bit too, but I wasn't aware of that.

It was May 1952 when I struggled with my old suitcase onto the platform of the Spencer Street railway station (now Southern Cross Station) for my journey to Warrnambool. Frank had paid for my ticket; it was cut price because I was under fifteen. I will always be in debt to Frank – a good brother.

Pop had taken on a share farm at Purnim, about eight miles east of Warrnambool. I was looking forward to seeing the new farm and was champing at the bit – I even had a bit of a spring in my step as I handed my ticket to the youthful porter on the gate.

'Stop right there!' the porter ordered in a loud voice that attracted the attention of some passers-by. He took my arm.

'Mate, you can't tell me you're under fifteen. Trying to cadge a ride at half fare, eh?'

I was embarrassed by the attention I was attracting as people queued behind me.

'No, I am only fourteen. I'll be fifteen in July. Please let me go.'

My appeal was to no avail. He checked the tickets of those waiting behind me and shut the gate.

'You had better come with me, and we'll see what the cops say.'

The cops! I was scared now.

'Why the cops? I haven't done anything wrong.'

'They are railway detectives. Just down here in this room.' He stopped at a doorway at the end of the platform. 'Come on. In you go'

He ushered me into a small office where two surly looking men, dressed in suits, sat at desks.

'This bloke says he is under fifteen and trying to get on the

Warrnambool train with a half fare ticket,' said my captor. 'I don't believe he is only fourteen. Do you?'

The policemen ignored me for a full minute as I stood in a miserable state of fear. It was a deliberate tactic, designed to make me more fearful.

Finally one man spoke: 'Do you know who we are? We are railway police and our job is to catch bludgers like you who try to cheat us.'

I protested my innocence and repeated my age.

'Tell it to someone who may be silly enough to believe you,' chimed in the second cop. 'We get people like you all the time. Tell us where you live and where you have just come from. Do you have any parents?'

I explained my position and answered his questions as well as I could, still protesting that I was only fourteen. I am certain that I didn't look any older than that. I was a fresh-complexioned boy from the bush, and I doubt if I even looked fourteen. I may as well have spoken to the office wall.

'Don't give us that bullshit,' said cop number one. He took me roughly by the shoulders and pushed me down onto a chair.

Warrnambool as I knew it in the early 1950s This is Liebig Street. (Corangamite Regional Library.)

'Tell us the truth and we might let you go. No more bullshit son. Tell the truth now, lad. How old are you really?'

I was terrified. I was being bullied by two men twice my size and in the most scary circumstances. What's more I was telling the truth. What else could I do? My eyes filled with tears.

'Please, I really am fourteen and I'm going home to my Mum and Pop. I have to get on the train. If I don't hurry it'll go without me and I don't know what I'll do.'

I was a very frightened boy, with an inferiority complex a mile wide, who had little to say at the best of times. Police and authority put the fear of God into me.

My mind was in turmoil. My heart was pounding. What if they didn't let me go? What if I was put in jail? I wanted to have Frank with me, but he wasn't there.

Finally, the first detective said, 'I know you are lying but we'll let you go this time. Give me the address of your parents and we will write them a letter. Now piss off or you'll miss the train.'

I scribbled out the names and the address. I couldn't get out of the office quickly enough and I hurried to get my train. I fought hard to hold back tears as I stepped into the carriage that would take me to Warrnambool.

I have never forgotten my treatment at the hands of those railway cop bullies.

Chapter Thirty-Two

Lillian and me – my 15th birthday party – Warrnambool Hospital.

The share farm at Purnim, which was named 'Gowrie', was the best that Pop had yet found. It was the best deal he'd had, too, a two-fifth share of the gross milk proceeds. The usual deal was a one-third share The owner was Jim Phillips, a bagpipe playing, sixty-year-old man of Scottish descent. As well as being a very decent and fair man, he was progressive and welcomed Pop implementing the innovative ideas. He had so far been denied the chance of putting his ideas into practice by others. Pop was a very good farmer who thrived on hard work.

To my relief, Pop had welcomed me warmly when he collected me from the train at Warrnambool. I hadn't any idea how I would be received.

'It's good to see you, Ian. There's more work than we can handle at the farm. I suppose you know that Murray is the only one left – Maurie has gone shearing. You can give us a hand with the milking and help your mother around the house. I'll sling you a couple of quid a week.'

So I really was happy to be home with Mum and Lillian. I had a job and a proper roof over my head.

Mum gave me a big hug and planted a kiss on my cheek when I stepped from the car.

'We love to have you home again, and you will be a big help to Gil.'

And so I was, as it turned out.

Milking was pretty quiet at the time, as many of the cows had been dried off in preparation for the anticipated calving in the spring. Nevertheless, there was plenty to do. To start with, Pop had me digging up, with a hoe, the thousands of thistles that plagued the farm. It wasn't hard work, and I enjoyed being alone in the open paddocks. I also helped a bit in the milking shed, but Murray and Pop were well able to deal with that. My job was doing the washing up; cleaning the vats and coolers and sweeping the floors as they hosed and swept the cow yard and shed after the milking. Life was pretty good again.

Murray, three years my senior, was now just eighteen. He was handsome, with a ready smile and a mop of almost black hair. He was almost six feet tall; big and strong for his age and could work alongside Pop with ease. I liked Murray, always had. We were good friends and shared a love of hillbilly music. We spent many happy hours playing his 78s, always hillbilly, on his ancient wind-up gramophone.

He also drove his recently acquired car in spite of having no licence. He took me with him to the pictures in Warrnambool most Saturday nights. We also knocked around the farm together, sharing a variety of jobs.

One afternoon, Murray and I were cleaning up around the milking shed when a stray cattle dog wandered into the yard. It was a blue heeler and very friendly, tail wagging furiously. We were both taken with it, and as far as we were concerned, it was welcome to stay.

'I reckon we should keep it,' said Murray. 'We don't have a dog, and a cattle dog would be pretty handy.' I agreed enthusiastically, giving the dog a bit of a hug, convinced that we could give it a home. Then Pop came along.

'What's that f...n dog doing here. Get rid of it. Shoot the bastard.'

Murray never questioned Pop, so he went to the house and returned with the .22 rifle. The dog stood watching as Murray took aim at its head and pulled the trigger. The shot missed the target, instead striking the animal's left back leg. It yelped in pain and staggered around as Murray aimed again. The second shot also missed and struck its rear end, causing more pathetic yelping from the unfortunate dog. It then sought shelter, cowering in terror beneath the nearby tank stand. It was a dreadful experience, and my heart went out to the dog. Murray took another shot, this time hitting the dog in the head. It collapsed silently, dead before it hit the ground.

I was absolutely mortified at this treatment, but Murray seemed to think nothing of it. The incident changed my attitude to Murray quite a bit. He had a cruel streak, and I will always remember his murderous action with disgust.

At the house, Lillian and I shared much of the housework, just as we had done years before at Greene Street and on other farms. We would wash and polish the linoleum floors, help with the laundry, hang out the washing and wash the dishes.

The dish washing was done in the porch that led into the kitchen. We had a tin dish to wash in and a tin tray for the draining. These were placed on a small table tucked into a corner. The hot water we carried from the big black cast-iron kettle that was forever heating on the hob. We made a game of it, taking it in turns to wash and dry. We would race to see if the drier could stay ahead of the washer. The result was often a pretty rough sort of wash up!

Lillian was a pretty, almost fourteen-year-old, and still going to Warrnambool High School. Therefore she missed doing the breakfast dishes, except on weekends.

We were great mates – we even shared a bedroom. Mum and Pop had one and Murray insisted on having one for himself. There were only three bedrooms, so Lillian and I were lumped in together. It worked pretty well and we respected each other's privacy.

I enjoyed my life on the farm. It was hard work at times, but I didn't mind that. I liked working with the cows, in spite of being regularly sprayed with cow shit. Cows are indiscriminate when it comes to emptying bowels and bladder. Many times, when I was tying the leg rope or squatting to put the machines on the teats, and wasn't quick to dodge at the first hint of a movement, I got splattered or drenched. One of the hazards of the job! The yard where the cows waited their turn was always a mess, awash with cow shit mixed with urine. Again, it was a part of the job.

Early in July, I was settling into my bed when I was struck by a sharp pain in the middle of my chest. It was very uncomfortable and I spent much of the night pacing around the room I shared with Lillian. She was disturbed by my movement.

'Are you alright, Ian?' she queried anxiously.

'No. I feel pretty crook, but I'll be alright soon. Go to sleep.'

But I wasn't alright soon. Nor was I for the next day, and the next. The pain persisted and I felt pretty sick, unable to face food or to get much rest, even though I continued to do my work around the farm and the house.

'I think it could be the pickles you had last night,' suggested Mum when I told her on that first morning, and she made me a drink of water and carb soda. 'This will fix it if it's indigestion.'

It didn't fix it and I continued to nurse the pain and misery.

Come Saturday night and it was the time when Murray regularly took me in his lovely car to the pictures in Warrnambool. He had bought the car on his eighteenth birthday, with a bit of help from Pop, and it was his pride and joy.

I had been looking forward all the week for the screening at the Capital theatre of 'The Great Dan Patch', the story of a champion American racehorse. Like Murray, I loved horses, and there was no way I was gong to miss this movie, even though I felt very sick.

Alas, I had to leave the theatre and Murray halfway through the picture. The sickness had taken a real grip on me and I felt awful. I spent the next hour walking up and down Liebig Street as I waited for Murray to leave the theatre.

The next day was the eighteenth of July, my fifteenth birthday, and I felt even worse. Finally Pop put me in the Chevrolet and took me to Warrnambool to see Dr Brauer. Dr Brauer had earlier operated on Mum and had treated Pop for pleurisy at that time.

'Have you ever had rheumatic fever, Ian?' He asked. I told him that I'd had it when I was seven.

'I'm afraid it has returned, Ian. It sometimes does. It's straight into hospital for you I'm afraid. Mr Rae, will you drive Ian up there, and I'll ring the hospital to tell them you're on the way.'

So I spent my first day as a fifteen-year-old stretched out on a hospital bed in a large public ward with a dozen men.

There was still no cure for rheumatic fever. All that could be done was to give doses of a vile mixture, which the nurses called sodi sal, actually sodium silicate or similar. I don't think it did anything, except perhaps help relieve my joint pain.

The bed was made up with no sheets – just woollen blankets. The idea apparently was to keep the body as warm as possible. I was not allowed a pillow and was forbidden to even sit up in bed.

Dr Brauer called in to see me, checking my heart with his stethoscope. 'You have to stay in bed, Ian. No getting out at all.'

I really didn't care at that stage. I felt too crook to be concerned with such trivialities!

So I did as I was told. For four weeks I lay there like a log, being fed by a nurse, getting washed all over by a nurse and obediently swallowing my regular doses of the dreaded sodi sal. The resident doctors regularly checked my heart for damage, and to my great relief, at the end of the four week rest, told me that they could find no lasting damage.

The young doctor, who was the one looking after me the most, listened to my heart. 'You can sit up now, Ian, and if you continue to improve we may get you out of bed in a couple of weeks.'

Of course I was pretty pleased to be told that and could hardly wait for Mum and Pop to come visit me. It was 1.30 when they arrived, Mum carrying a paper bag filled with lollies and apples. Visits were allowed only from one o'clock until three o'clock, and this was strictly enforced.

'Mum!' I had almost yelled at her as she appeared in the doorway. The doctor says I may be allowed home in two weeks.' I just couldn't keep such good news to myself any longer. Mum, of course, was pleased, and gave me a hug, while Pop had a big grin.

I don't know how I would have managed hospital if it hadn't been for Harry who occupied the bed opposite me. He was the only man in the ward who talked to me. He did this almost constantly, brightening my day with a steady flow of jokes and tall stories. He was a rough looking Aussie, a labourer with the shire council, about fifty years old, and lived just down the road at Dennington. I don't think he ever stopped talking. I didn't know until some time later what ailed him.

'I worked for the butter factory for fifteen years, but things got a bit slack a couple of years back and they put me off. I was lucky to land a job with the council. I'm pretty well set up now as me missus has just got a job as a machinist with F.J. Just as well, cos we ain't got no HBA to pay for me in hospital. It's gonna cost a man a bloody fortune.'

He was referring to his wife's job with Fletcher Jones, the menswear king of Australia. Everybody knew him simply as F.J.

Fletcher Jones was a much loved local and employed several hundred people at his plant at Pleasant Hill and several stores across the country.

Harry was a godsend to me. I didn't know how to make conversation with grown men – didn't have a clue what to talk about – but Harry made it easy to talk to him. He was forever firing questions at me, questions which required an answer, so I had to talk. When he wasn't asking me about myself and family, he was telling me about his exploits and his family. For instance, I knew that he had two sons and a daughter. His sons worked at the butter factory as labourers, and his daughter had just begun in the factory office. She was his baby at seventeen.

I really liked Harry and I reckon he liked me. At any rate I have to thank him for making my hospital stay pass pretty quickly.

We all dreaded the daily inspection by Matron, a hard looking woman about sixty years old. She strode into the ward like a general commanding the troops. A nurse trailed slightly behind her. From time to time, Matron would fire questions at the nurse, her attitude demanding immediate and accurate answers.

We knew that the nurses also dreaded the inspection and were nervous, so we were on our best behaviour when Matron came to call. Even Harry fell silent and respectful.

'And how is Ian today?' Her question took me by surprise. She had never spoken directly to me before. I managed to stammer, 'I am well thank you Matron', before she whisked herself to the next patient's bedside.

Her eyes darted in all directions, checking for sloppily made beds or perhaps an unemptied urine bottle. Most days she didn't have any reason to growl at her nurses, as they really were very thorough. Everyone, nurses especially, heaved a sigh of relief when inspection was completed and Matron strode off to the next ward.

We had three shifts of two nurses each day, and I got to know them all fairly well. They were, without exception, warm and caring women – some still girls of maybe sixteen. The lone night nurses usually had little to do but keep an eye on the patients. If someone was having trouble sleeping they would often sit talking quietly to the patient. Some of my companions in the ward rarely, if ever, had a visitor and I am sure were pretty lonely.

One nurse spent a couple of hours with me one sleepless and frightened night. I was scared that I would not get well and I welcomed her thoughtful assurances. 'Of course you will get well, Ian. You'll be home again before you know it.' She was right.

One morning, the fourth week of my stay, the resident doctor stopped in to examine me, as he did every day. I was thrilled when he said I could not only sit up in bed but I could get out of it into a chair and go to the toilet and have a shower.

I got quite a shock when Nurse Hadley helped me from the bed for the first time. My legs would barely support me and I almost fell when I tried to walk. Even after such a relatively short time in bed, the muscles in my legs had wasted. I virtually had to learn to walk again, which I did very quickly with the steadying hands of Nurse Hadley. I think her given name was Maureen, but I wasn't sure. In those days nobody ever addressed a nurse by her name. It was always 'Nurse' or 'Nurse Hadley'. As for addressing a doctor by name, it was unheard of – always 'Doctor Brauer', or whoever the resident doctor was; or less formally it was plain 'Doctor'.

It was a happy day when I said goodbye to Harry. Pop called to pick me up and loaded my gear into the back seat of his lovely Chevrolet. It was a bit hard leaving Harry as he was such a good bloke and so much a friend to me.

Doctor Brauer had called in to see me that morning, and after a good listen to my heart, he said, 'Alright, Ian. I am satisfied with that, so you can go home next time your parents come to see you. But when you get home you must stay in bed for at least two more weeks. You can only get up for a visit to the lavatory or to have a bath. Do you understand that? You need a bit more recovery time yet. And you must not do any sort of work for another six months. No work alright? Your heart needs time to fully recover.' I readily agreed and was delighted to be going home.

I waited anxiously for Mum and Pop to visit me, hoping it would be that day. I was disappointed when they did not appear by the end of visiting hours, which ended at three o'clock sharp. They did however arrive at one o'clock the next day, and before they had time to say as much as 'hello', I began piling my bits and pieces into my small suitcase. I had already got fully dressed in anticipation and was ready for a quicker getaway than a Chicago gangster.

Back at home, I did as I was told and straightaway got into bed. I was determined to obey the doctor, even using a discarded milk bottle to pee into so I didn't have to walk to the thunderbox down the yard. I amused myself by reading any book I could get my hands on and listening to the wireless. I loved the wireless and was a constant listener to local station 3YB. My favourite announcer was a young man named Ron Cadee. He worked as a duo with another man whose name I have forgotten. They were a great team and laughed and sang their way through three hours each morning. Ron played the piano in the studio, and he and his mate sang lots of old-time songs, not very well, but enough to entertain me and many others. Ron eventually moved to radio in Melbourne; 3KZ I think.

I had been relaxing at home for about ten days, feeling quite good but a bit concerned with the small white flakes that floated in my urine. My pee bottle was clear glass, so I could easily see this. I felt okay so put the worry aside.

On the afternoon of the eleventh day, I was suddenly stricken with a devastating attack of breathlessness, accompanied by a raging thirst. It was awful. I called for help to Mum who was in the kitchen, even as I struggled to get enough breath. I gulped down glass after glass of water that Mum brought to me. She was very upset and at a loss about what to do. Pop and Murray then appeared from somewhere.

'Quick Gil,' cried my distraught mother. 'Bring the electric fan. It may help.' Pop disappeared and quickly returned with the fan from the kitchen. He plugged it in and directed the air into my face in an effort to send more air in my direction.

All the while, I was thrashing about, arms and legs flying this way and that as I fought for breath. I felt sure that I was dying.

'Gil!' shouted Mum. 'Go to Jimmy's and get an ambulance. Hurry.'

Pop left the room, mounted the Ferguson Tractor which was parked in the backyard, and dashed off to Jimmy Phillips's home to use his telephone.

It was at least half an hour before the ambulance finally arrived. My straining for breath, gulping of water and thrashing the air continued unabated. The two ambulance men quickly placed me on a stretcher and wheeled me out the front door, onto the veranda and down the steep steps into the yard.

Mum climbed into the ambulance with me and one of the ambulance men, and the driver sped off to Warrnambool hospital. It was a terrible time for Mum, as I'm sure she also thought I must be dying. Nothing the ambulance man could do stopped my gasping and frantic, involuntary movements.

Finally I was wheeled into the hospital where two young doctors were waiting. One of them quickly listened to my chest, took my arm and drove a hypodermic needle into it. Almost immediately I passed into oblivion.

When I woke up, some unknown time later, my thirst had gone and, apart from a few twitches, my raving movements had ceased. It was amazing. I didn't really feel that bad now, but was very tired.

The doctors were by my side and prodded and poked me in all sorts of places, while listening with their stethoscopes. One placed his hand flat on my chest. Puzzled he said to the first doctor: 'I can't detect any thrill or anything there. I don't know what this could be. I have no idea.'

The other doctor questioned me. 'Do you ever drink milk that hasn't been heated properly?' I had to agree that I had. We always took milk direct from the big vats at the shed for the house.

'Maybe it's some sort of infection from the cows,' said doctor number one.

'Could be,' the other agreed. 'Maybe it's a form of St Vitus dance.'

The doctors were obviously very unsure of my condition and its cause. One took my hand and pressed on a fingernail. I don't know what he was looking for but he seemed satisfied. 'Hmm. That seems okay.'

'Well, Ian, you certainly have us puzzled. We don't really know what caused you to be so sick. Whatever it was, you seem to be alright now. We cannot find too much wrong with you, but maybe it's a form of the rheumatic fever. We'll keep you here for a week or two just to see that you are okay.' The two men left and shortly after Mum and Pop departed too.

So here I was again, back in the hospital, but this time in a two bed ward. Once more I was not allowed to leave my bed nor to sit up. I had to lie flat on my back as motionless as I could. The nurses removed the bed sheets and replaced them with woollen blankets. I never understood why, but it was part of the treatment.

For the first two days I was alone and enjoying the quiet, but didn't enjoy being back on regular doses of the dreaded sodi sal though, or the daily all over wash-downs by the nurses. Being a fifteen-year-old I was prone to easy excitement and the girls had quite a bit to contend with at times. I think they were almost as embarrassed as I was, but theirs could not possibly have been equal with mine. When a nurse approached carrying a dish of water I knew what I was in for.

Apart from those incidents, nothing much happened for the first week. Then an ambulance crew appeared in the ward and loaded a man aged about forty into the bed next to me. He had smashed his car into a fence, and although not badly injured, the doctors were apparently concerned, as he had hit his head very hard on the steering wheel.

He lay there quietly for a couple of hours. He said not a word and appeared to be asleep. Suddenly he sat bolt upright, stepped from his bed and removed his pyjamas, standing stark naked.

I didn't know what I should do.

'Are you alright, mister?' That was all I could manage. The patient completely ignored me. I don't think he heard. He stared straight ahead.

Next thing, he ran out the door, past the nurses' station and into the big ward where I had been previously.

I got an account of what happened next when I was transferred to the big ward the following day. To my joy, one of about a dozen men there, my old mate Harry was propped up in the bed right opposite me.

'What are you doing here,' I said, surprised. 'The last I heard you were going home – later the same day as me.'

'I did go home, but I was back a week later. It seems I have had the same as you, rheumatic fever, and it's come back again. Not the first time for me. It happens to me all the time, so I'm bloody well used to it.'

Interspersed with his huge laugh, Harry related the story of yesterday's event. It was visiting hours and the ward was packed with men, women and children who watched in amazement as the naked man ran through the room and eventually out the door into the garden. Following close on his heels was the male ward attendant.

'Christ it was bloody funny. Here's this bloke, starkers, runnin' around the beds, with this bloke after him. They was up and down the ward, in and out of the beds, pushin' past the visitors, and there was a lot of yellin' goin' on as well. This went on for about two minutes before the loony joker spots the opening to the veranda and the door into the garden. He made a beeline for that and out he ran, like a racing greyhound, the other bloke after him. I dunno what happened – if they caught the naked bloke or not, but I s'pose they did. It sure brightened the day up a bit for us lot in here! Wonder what got into him?'

Harry sat thoughtfully in his bed, pondering the answer to his own question. 'Christ, I'm a bit like that bloke. I wish I could get out of here. Sometimes I feel like doin' what that bloke did and bolt.'

He reached into his cupboard drawer for a cigarette, lit it and pushed his head into his pillow. He fell silent after that.

I don't know what happened to the man who shed his pyjamas and scared the hell out of a lot of people. He didn't return to my ward. I suspect that the hit to his head caused a temporary loss of sanity!

An interesting young man was twenty-five-year-old David who occupied a bed two down from mine. He was partly paralysed following crashing his light plane and was at the complete mercy of the nurses at bed-bath time. Amongst other functions, he apparently had uncontrollable erection ability and was sometimes in this state during bath time. One day a nurse gave it a solid wack with her pencil. 'Don't wave that thing at me!'

He shrieked in pain. 'You bugger,' he cried. 'I think that hurt.' He had no actual feeling below his waist, but he still had his sense of humour! It caused a lot of laughter in the ward.

The days dragged on, and visiting hours were the highlight of our day. Only a few got visitors every day. I wasn't one who did, but I enjoyed listening to the other patients' visitors talk, and some would even come over and talk to me

'What are you here for? You don't look very sick?' said one old lady.

'Rheumatic fever I think. But they aren't sure.' I replied.

The mirror told me that I didn't look sick. I didn't feel very well but looked okay, with colour in my cheeks. Appearances are sometimes deceiving.

Doctor Brauer said to me one day, 'Ian, you are a pretty sick boy and we must take good care to get you well again. Lots of rest is the best treatment we have.'

Pop was too busy on the farm to come into town every day – he, with Mum, managed about every third or fourth though, which was pretty good. They would bring me pieces of fruit and an occasional bag of barley sugar twists which I loved and was pleased to get. The barley sugar didn't last long. By the time I'd shared them with some of the other blokes and the nurses, the bag was nearly empty.

Harry always had visitors, his wife never missed a day, and weekends all the kids turned up. He had a great family, and I was a bit envious I suppose.

One day, a boy aged about fourteen rolled up to my bedside in a wheelchair.

'I don't really need this wheelchair,' he said, 'but I like scooting about in it. It's fun. I'm in the ward out on the veranda, it's good out there, just three of us. A nurse told me we had the same name. I'm Graham Braybrook and I reckon we may be related. Wadda you reckon?'

I looked at my visitor. He was a skinny kid with a narrow, smiling face topped with dark hair. On the right side of his head was a huge swelling. It looked awful, red and weeping some sort of ghastly looking fluid.

I spoke shyly to him. 'I suppose we could be related. There's not a lot of Braybrooks around that I know of.'

I really wasn't that interested at the time. 'What's wrong with your head?

'I dunno exactly, I think it's some sort of growth or somethin'. They reckon they are going to cut it out in a few days.'

'Is it sore? It looks like it is.'

'Nah. It hurts a little bit, but it's alright. Not as bad as it looks. Do you want some peanuts?' He produced a crumpled brown paper bag from his dressing gown pocket and reached into it. I happily accepted the handful of nuts he transferred to my hand. We didn't worry a lot about transferring germs then.

Graham and I got on very well, and we spent many hours talking about all sorts of things. You know, the sort of rubbish that teenage boys talk about: girls, movies, cars, horses and more girls mostly.

Graham lived in Warrnambool with his parents and two brothers. I didn't ask any more about him or his family, but I found out thirty years later that he was indeed a relation – a second cousin in fact.

One day they took him away for surgery. He gave me a cheery wave and yelled goodbye as he passed my bed. He didn't come back to the ward, which worried me, but I found out later that he had been put in a different ward and was quite okay. I never saw him again.

I dreaded bed-bath time, but had to submit to it every morning. It was so bloody embarrassing, exposing my 'thing' to be washed by women and girls. Some of them took pity on me and let me reach beneath the blankets and wash the bits myself.

I will always remember one blonde-haired woman saying, 'I've washed up as far as possible and down as far as possible, now you wash possible'. She was a good scout, and I really appreciated her regard for my modesty.

One of the young nurses was named Maureen, about sixteen years old and a dark-haired beauty. She caused me considerable difficulty at times. I didn't tell her, but I was smitten by her beauty. I reckon I fell in love with her!

I managed to keep this to myself, but two years later, when working at a shearing shed in the district, I rang her at the nurses home and asked for a date. I hadn't forgotten her, but she certainly had forgotten me and politely declined my invitation. I was crushed. However, I quickly recovered and crossed her off my very short list of 'Possibles'. My (always fruitless) search for my first grown up, close and passionate engagement with the opposite sex continued. The relief option was risky, known to turn one blind.

Time went by, the monotony of the long days relieved by the visits from Mum and Pop, and sometimes Murray. Murray always brought me a bag of lollies and a western paperback to read. I must have read a dozen of them as I passed the weeks away. It was a big day when the doctor said I could now sit up in bed, but had to stay put. No getting out for toilet or shower.

Harry was terrific to me. He talked to me for hours every day, endlessly telling jokes and tall stories. I think he made up most of them as he went, but anyway I liked him very much.

When the doctors finally allowed me to get out of bed, three weeks later, I had to repeat the process of learning to walk. For a start, I staggered like a drunk, held upright by a nurse, but in a few days I was okay again.

Okay,' said Doctor Brauer one morning, you can go home anytime now. But there's a bit more to be done yet, so you will need to come back in a few weeks. Meantime, I want you to go to a dentist and have your teeth checked thoroughly. When you've done that, come and see me, and we'll get you back here and take those tonsils out. Alright?'

It wasn't 'alright' of course. I dreaded the dental treatment and the thought of an operation, but had to agree.

'It's to make sure you are properly cured and won't get any more attacks. You understand?'

'Yes, Doctor Brauer. Thank you,' I replied meekly.

Chapter Thirty-Three

Tonsils – tin baths – Radio 3YB – leaving Purnim West.

The next day, Pop came for me. I had to say goodbye to my friend Harry, and to the nurses who had looked after me so well. I had to fight back some tears as they had become a big part of my life by then.

Pop didn't muck around. He put me in the Chev and right away took me down town to a dentist. 'We may as well get this done. No point in waiting.'

The dentist was an aging man with white hair, dressed in a suit and tie beneath a large white gown sort of thing. He peered into my mouth, this way then that way, prodding with a metal probe.

'Hmm. There are four there that need attention. The best thing I can do is extract them. If I fill them they'll only give you trouble later on. Open wide.'

He stuck a needle into my gums, both sides. The pain was pretty intense, but necessary. After about five minutes he commenced work. He struggled as he twisted and tugged on his extraction implement.

'Your teeth have pretty good roots on them but we'll have them out soon.' The tugging, twisting and grunting continued. After what seemed hours, his dreadful work was done and four of my teeth lay in the stainless steel bowl beside me. I was bleeding a lot and the dentist stuffed cotton wool into the cavities.

'That'll hold it. Leave the cotton wool pads in place for half an hour or so and it'll be alright, son.'

Pop paid the bill and we left for home. The pain went away in a day or two, and I began the road to full recovery. Mum fussed over me for a few days, bringing me soup, mashed potatoes and peas.

'I think I'll make you some barley broth, too,' Mum said. 'It is really good for you and easy to get down.'

Yuck! I remembered it from earlier days and loathed the stuff.

For the next week almost every meal was barley broth, mashed spud and green peas, but I survived and soon felt well again. Mum said it was probably the barley broth.

Two weeks later, I was back in Warrnambool Hospital, not in the large ward this time, but alone. The morning after my admittance, it was off to the operating theatre where Doctor Brauer was waiting, sharp knife at the ready! God what an experience it was. Helplessly stretched out on the operating table I was stiff with terror. This was a new experience, one I would rather not have had. A smiling doctor, whom I didn't know, placed a mask-like thing over my nose and mouth. He carefully dropped a foul liquid onto the pad inside the mask. I went weak and don't remember a thing about what came next. I know I awoke in awful pain and discomfort. My throat was so bloody sore, I couldn't swallow, and as for talking, it was out of the question. At teatime, a nurse brought me a bowl of red jelly and ice-cream. I tried to eat some, but it was too painful. I went to sleep instead.

After a week in hospital, during which I was constantly vomiting, overwhelmed by the lingering taste and smell of ether, I was sent home for more rest. Doctor Brauer's warnings were still ringing in my head.

'No exertion. No work for a year. Plenty of rest.'

'Yes, Doctor.'

It was great to be home, and life resumed much as before. Washing dishes, sweeping floors, peeling spuds, plus helping Mum in the kitchen and washhouse. I was not expected to work in the cow yard or otherwise help with farm work.

On washing day, Mum had to boil the copper which stood in the corner of the galvanised iron shed that we called the washhouse. I used to fill it with water and get a fire going beneath it. The washhouse also housed the tin bath that we each had a turn at once a week. Usually Lillian and I would share the same tub of water – heating large quantities of water was too difficult to then waste it on just one person's wash! It was all pretty primitive, but not a lot different to many homes at the time.

One of my light jobs was feeding the poddy calves their milk at the new bails Pop had made for the purpose. The bails were similar to those we used to hold cows still in the milking shed, and the principle worked just as well on the 'juniors'. To my knowledge, no other dairy farmer used this method at the time.

The calves stood lined up at the bails, and before them was a long trough half-filled with milk. With a little training they quickly learned to drink from the trough. We trained them by inserting two fingers into their mouth, replicating a mother's teats. The calf sucked on that, and as it did, we immersed their mouth in the milk. After a few lessons they drank without the dummy.

Pop was clever and innovative, like his decision to plant a large field of turnips to use as green feed for the cows. The cows loved turnips, and our milk production increased by a third! The only problem was that the milk smelt strongly of turnips! It did not effect the quality of the milk however, but in fact did the opposite. Our butterfat content soared, and with it, the money Nestlés paid the farm.

In another different move, made before I arrived home, Pop had planted about five acres of potatoes and a couple of acres of Queensland Blue pumpkins to earn more money. Unhappily, it was a dry season, and the spuds were invaded by potato grubs, and only a quarter of the crop was saleable, but it returned enough to cover the costs. It was a similar result with the pumpkins. Pop had a heap of these vegetables stored in a hay shed, and spuds and pumpkin featured in almost every main meal.

Pop could be cruel at times. He often kicked cows hard in the guts or belted them around the head with whatever was handy if they gave any trouble. One day, as I was tending the calves, he walked by carrying an axe. 'One of the cows is down with milk fever or something over behind the hedge. I'm gonna have a look at her and see what I can do.'

He returned a short time later. 'Nothing I could do for her. She's had it,' he said, as he walked to the woodheap, axe over his shoulder.

After I had finished with the calves, I went to check on the sick cow. I was horrified to see that she lay in a pool of blood, her throat jaggedly cut. Pop had done this to her with his axe! I was mortified.

I was pottering about one afternoon alone, because Mum was having a short spell in hospital for treatment of a sickness, the nature of which I was not informed. Lillian was at school. Pop pulled up at the yard gate. 'Give me a hand to unload this box from the car,' he called.

I hastened to respond and there was the 'box' hanging from the back of the closed car boot. The box turned out to be a brand new AGA washing machine. 'Gee Pop, Mum will be so happy with this. I can hardly wait for her use to it,' I said.

'No need to wait. Lillian can learn to use it and do the washing when she comes home from school, give it a trial run.'

And so we did. Lillian was rapt and as soon as she changed from her school clothes she started the lesson. Studying the instruction booklet, she quickly learnt how to operate the machine.

'This is just wonderful, Ian. It is so easy to use. Look, it even heats its own water. And it has its own wringer'. Lillian was excited and very, very happy.

The AGA was indeed a marvel and Mum was rejoicing, too, when she eventually got around to using it. Pop was pretty good at times.

A week later, a similar thing occurred. Again I was asked to help carry in a 'box' from the back of the Chev. This turned out to be **the greatest machine of all time**. Well, I thought so. Pop had bought a magnificent, brand new, Classic Radiogram.

The Classic Radiogram was given pride of place in the kitchen, alongside the wood stove, perched on a small table to make it easier to load with records and turn the dial. It was, to me, the most wonderful thing – a piece of the very latest electronic wizardry. It was definitely the top of the range, the ultimate of what was available in 1952.

The Classic Radiogram, enclosed in a beautifully crafted cabinet, made from the most exclusive timber, had a booming, clear and lovely tone. It not only had a radio that brought in a crystal clear radio signal it also had a record player. And not just any old record player. Our new Classic had a turntable capable of playing ten records at a time. It took ten records at once, stacked one upon the other, and it automatically changed from one to the next.

I had never seen such a glorious machine and certainly never expected that we would have such a thing in our house. But there it was, sitting majestically against the wall in our kitchen.

It was amazing and I loved Pop for buying it for us. The old wind-up gramophone that Murray had bought was now redundant.

The only records we had at the time were Hillbillies, mostly Slim Dusty and Buddy Williams. All country and western music was then called Hillbilly, but they sounded so much better with the modern 'needle' – or so we believed.

Pop certainly could be kind and generous at times, but quite unpredictable. Soon after I got home from hospital, it was time for harvesting hay for storage, and Pop got me to help with it. Murray had cut the hay some time before, proudly driving the new Ferguson tractor. The cut grass would lie to cure for a week or two before being pressed into bales. When it reached that stage, Murray pulled the converted horse-drawn hay rake with the tractor to drag the grass into windrows, ready for pressing. Early automation had come to Purnim! The Ferguson made our two draft horses almost redundant. No more would I drive them to the blacksmiths for shoeing. The smith operated from an old shed at Woodford, about five miles on the Warrnambool road. I can still see him pumping the huge bellows to fan the coals in the forge, and with a large hammer, shaping the steel into correct fitting shoes for each foot. Such hot and hard work.

Jim Phillips and his wife, a middle-aged childless couple, were the farm's owners. Scottish blood ran thickly through the veins of Jimmy and he declined Pop's suggestion that he buy a new Ferguson tractor. Jim's Scottish blood would not allow such extravagance. Pop said we needed one to compete, so he went and bought one brand new himself. It was one of the first 'Fergies' in the district.

Both the grass mower and the hay rake Pop had converted to be drawn by a tractor, not our draught horses as previously. He had fitted timber drawbars and I had strong memories of my experience with Mr Johnston at Drouin South.

My job was helping to pick up the pressed bales left in rows by the baling machine. Again, it was the first such machine in the district owned by a contractor hired by Pop, and we were pretty impressed with it. Whereas in the past we had hand forked the hay from the raked windrows onto a horsedrawn wagon for stacking by fork, this machine picked up the hay, pressed it into bales secured with wire and dropped them in rows ready for picking up. And we now had a tractor-drawn wagon as well!

I did the work with a lot of fear in my heart. Hadn't I been told not to work for a year! But I couldn't say no to Pop – no way.

One day about that time, Murray, Pop and I had spent a couple of hours at the Bush Inn hotel at Bushfield a few miles along the Mortlake road. I drank sarsaparilla, not beer like the other two. Pop said I was too young for alcohol, and I respected him for that. On the way home, we stopped on the roadside for a pee, and as we stood side by side, Pop made an announcement. He always called Mum Vera.

'Vera has to go to hospital tomorrow for a big operation. She should be alright, but it's a big job, so fingers crossed, eh?' He told us no more and I didn't know till years later that she probably had cervical cancer.

I know that if Mum had been at home, Pop would not have had me helping with the hay harvest; me picking up heavy bales and loading them onto a trailer. It was very hot, hard work.

Lillian kept us supplied with cordial in water to replace the sweat we lost.

'You shouldn't be working like this, Ian,' said Lillian quietly, as she filled a mug of drink for me. 'Look at you. You are all sweaty and red in the face. See if Pop will let you rest for a while.'

'No, I can't do that. I'm not game. You know what Pop's like. He works hard all the time and expects everyone else to do the same.'

Somehow I got through the harvest without ill effects but I was frightened and worried all along.

When Pop wasn't milking cows he was doing all sorts of jobs around the farm. He was, in fact, a brilliant farmer, ahead of his time in many respects, but never seemed to quite make enough money to buy his own property.

As Mum was recovering in hospital, Pop was taking advantage of her absence and spending quite a bit of time in the Caledonian Hotel in Warrnambool. 'Everyone's pally at the Cally' was their slogan, broadcast regularly on radio 3YB. It was a bit too pally for Pop it seems.

One afternoon, making his way home, he lost control of the Chev on a sharp bend and sideswiped a huge electricity pole. Luckily he was not seriously hurt, except for very sore ribs. He managed to drive the badly smashed Chev home. When he pulled into the yard, Murray, Lillian and I stared in horror. Our beautiful Chev was a wreck, the driver's side was crushed from the front mudguard to the back. We

Pop's 1937 Chevrolet Master Deluxe at Dixie, 1950. I loved this car.

were far more concerned about the car than about Pop. He seemed to be alright anyway, as he grumbled his way toward the cowshed.

'Come on, Murray, it's bloody milking time – and you come too, Ian.' He was pretty pissed, and I was surprised that he ordered me to work at the milking. But I had to do as he told me.

'I'll get the car fixed tomorrow.'

He wasn't badly hurt, just the bruised ribs, a lucky escape. However, the next day he felt really bad and Murray drove him to the doctors. Doctor Brauer diagnosed pleurisy and ordered him straight to hospital. He wasn't seriously ill, but needed hospital treatment for a couple of days.

Mum was lying in her bed in Ward 7 when she heard a familiar voice coming from Ward 6 next door.

'That's my husband,' she almost shouted to the woman in the next bed. 'I'd recognise his voice anywhere. What's he doing here?'

If Pop had any intention of hiding his presence, and maybe concealing the wrecking of the car, the jig was up. On the upside of this, Pop was able to visit Mum in the next room over the next few days of his stay. Mum was discharged several days after him.

Mum never spoke to me about her illness. Whatever it was, she fully recovered, and the Chev was restored very well by a panel beater in Warrnambool. Both Mum and the Chev looked as good as ever!

There was great excitement when Jimmy Phillips turned up at our house one day with his brand new car – a 1952 Standard Vanguard. We all gathered around and ogled the magnificent machine. It wasn't at all attractive in design; it looked like a large, clumsy beetle. The car's most memorable feature that I recall was its turning indicators – little arms that popped out from the front door pillars. Jimmy took great pride in demonstrating them. Me, I still preferred the 1937 Chev Master Deluxe!

Jim Phillips was a good man. His only failing was that he played the bagpipes! Almost any evening we could hear squawking and screeching as he played the instrument on his veranda. Obviously

Mrs Phillips had banned them from the house. The noise wafted easily over the quarter mile distance that separated our house from his. Pop loved the sound and sometimes sat on our veranda with a bottle of beer, enraptured.

Jim was particularly fond of Murray, as he clearly demonstrated not long after I had come home from hospital.

Without warning or any apparent reason Pop gave Jim two months notice and promptly organised a clearing sale. We were thunderstruck – talk about coming from left-field. Soon the sale was over; many of the household possessions and all the farm equipment sold. Even our Classic radiogram went, along with the AGA washer.

One day Pop went off in the Chev and returned late at night announcing that he had bought a house in Daylesford. I'm guessing that Mum had an influence in his choice of Daylesford.

Jimmy Phillips was devastated by Pop's move and did all he could to get Pop to change his mind – to no avail.

One morning, Jimmy called Murray over to his house. He told Murray how much he liked and admired him, thought of him as the son he didn't have.

To Murray's astonishment, Jimmy then asked him to stay on and run the farm, adding that, if he did, the farm would one day be his! Murray could scarcely believe his ears. The farm would be his! This magnificent farm! It was a fantastic offer, which Murray, only just 18 years old and still a boy, agonised over for days. Pop and Mum left it to him to decide. A most difficult decision had to be made. Finally, to Jimmy's utter disappointment, Murray declined and opted to stick to Pop. It was a decision he regretted the rest of his short life.

Chapter Thirty-Four

Daylesford - a long walk - Lismore - Williamstown

The house at Daylesford was an old miners cottage, perched on a steep hillside in aptly named Hill Street. We had no sooner moved in when Pop and Murray headed north to Redcliffs, near Mildura, to pick grapes.

This left me with Mum, Marion, Ken and Lillian. I shared a small room with Ken whilst Mum and Lillian had their own rooms. The house was nothing flash but it was better than some we had lived in. It had no sewerage or septic system but at least we now had a pan service. Once a week the sanitary collector called, took the can away and replaced it with a clean one. This was a novelty.

Lillian was now fourteen and eligible to look for a job. For the first couple of weeks she and I helped Mum settle into the house, looking after Ken and Marion as well. Pop had told Lillian to get a job, but for the first few weeks she didn't try. There were very few jobs in Daylesford anyway, and she was far too shy to present herself.

Mum decided to take off to visit her sister Phemie in Melbourne, leaving Lillian and I alone. We had a great time, sitting or lying in the sun, sleeping or just taking it easy. The housework went undone and the beds unmade.

The light bulb in my room went pop, so I found a replacement and proceeded to make a change. As I stood on a chair and reached for the offending bulb I received a most awful electric shock. There must have been a bare wire in the ancient wiring.

The force threw me to the floor where I lay a quivering heap. My heart jumped and thumped, almost bursting out of my chest.

My first thought was for my heart. No exertion, the doctors had warned. My god, this was extreme exertion, surely. To my surprise

I didn't die. Lillian came rushing into the room 'Ian, Ian, are you alright? What happened?

'I'm alright I think, but I feel awful.' I began to shake uncontrollably, but that stopped in a minute. Before long I felt fine, but the light bulb remained unreplaced

We resumed our life of ease. That is, until Mum came home.

'Get yourself to the woollen mill and get a job before your father comes home,' Mum ordered Lillian. 'He'll have a fit if you haven't at least tried for a job.'

Poor Lillian! I went with her to the small knitting mill downtown, there were two in Daylesford then, and lo and behold – she was hired. So began her working life, working drearily on a weaving machine and sorting and inspecting various lengths of cloth.

* * *

'Hey Mum,' I announced. 'I'm going to go to Barry's Reef and visit Joe Callaghan.'

'And how do you propose to do that? There's no train or bus going that way. What are you going to do, walk?' The latter she said in jest.

'Yes, I am walking – well hitchhiking really. I reckon I'll get a ride or two and be there in no time.'

Basalt Hut, 1960. Ian, Veronica and Frank Braybrook lived there, c. 1950.

Mum reluctantly agreed. 'I suppose it's better than having you hanging around the house. And it'll be good for you to see Joe again.'

The next morning, I was away. Mum made me four pickle and cheese sandwiches and filled a large Mosley's lemonade bottle with water. I tied a woollen jumper around my waist in case it got cold later. My plan was to hitch rides to Barry's Reef via Ballan and Greendale and stay the night with Joe. I don't know why I chose that route when going via Trentham was probably shorter.

'I'm sure Joe'll let me camp the night, and I'll walk home through Trentham tomorrow.'

It was a warm, sunny day, but not too hot for walking. Off I went, making good time till I got near Sailors Falls. A bloke stopped and drove me for about five or six miles. 'This is as far as I go, mate. Good luck with the rest of the trip.' He moved off down a side road. No more cars came along. I kept walking. One driver sped past, but no other car appeared for a few more miles. I finally caught a ride into Ballan, by this time having covered twenty miles, and proceeded down the hill onto the Green Hill road. No cars came my way; there were far

At Joe Callaghan's house shortly before it collapsed, c. 1980.

fewer cars on the road in 1952 than today. After about a half hour of ceaseless plodding – getting slower now – a driver roared past in a big flash car, ignoring my signal, staring straight head.

I eventually passed through Greendale, there was nothing there except the pub, and there was no stopping there for me. I was too young to buy a beer and had no spare money anyway. In any event, I was far too shy to ask anybody for help.

On I trudged, up the big hill toward far-off Blackwood. Another car whizzed past, this driver also ignored my signals. I was becoming more desperate now. I had already walked over fifteen miles and was very tired. Sometime later, I finally entered Blackwood. It was getting late by then and the dark of night was not far off.

I kept right on, very weary by now. By the time I made it to the top of the hill to Barrys Reef post office it was dark, very dark; the pitch black that quickly descends in the forest. It had also become very cold, as it can at night, even in the Summer in these mountains. The only way I could tell I was on the road was by the crunch of gravel under my feet. I was really very scared now.

The bush is full of sounds at night, the screeching of night birds,

The headstone of my childhood best mate Joe Callaghan in the Blackwood cemetery.

the bounding, thumping sounds of kangaroos and wallabies, the creaking of the trees; all sorts of odd noises that are never noticed during the day. I had no idea where I was and all I could do was keep walking. There was not a glimmer of a light in any direction – complete blackness. The prospect of any motor car coming was practically nil. On and on I walked, becoming more frightened with every step. I really had no idea where I was, except that I was still on the road.

Then, in the darkness, I recognised a small group of houses on the roadside as being the tiny township of Newbury. I realised then that I had walked right past Joe's place. I had missed him completely in the black of the night.

Not a light showed from any window at Newbury, so I kept going and, to my relief, eventually made it to Trentham. I don't know what time it was, I had no watch. I found my way into a shed behind the empty Cosmopolitan Hotel. There was some straw piled on the floor, so I covered myself with it and soon fell asleep.

Daylight came. I drank the last of my water, ate the remaining small piece of sandwich and set my path to Daylesford, fourteen miles away. Cars were rare back then and none passed me as I wended my

Cosmopolitan Hotel Trentham, 2013.

way through the forest. I arrived home near lunchtime, totally worn out and very distressed. I had walked about fifty miles in total, and I hadn't even seen Joe, the purpose of my journey.

I stifled a sob as I told Mum my story; miserable and depressed. I never did get to see Joe again. He died in 1953, less than a year later.

* * *

Six weeks after they'd left to pick grapes, Pop and Murray returned. It was a Saturday. As we sat eating our lunch Pop turned to me, 'Murray and me have got a job down Lismore way and you can come with us. A man can't have you sittin' around on yer arse. It's time you did something to earn your keep.'

Mum protested. 'He can't go to work, Gil. You know what the doctor said. It could kill him if he works.'

'Bugger the doctor. He doesn't have to keep the boy.'

The matter was closed, but I was shocked and frightened for my life.

Late on Sunday I found myself camped in a shearers hut at Berrybank Station near Lismore in Western Victoria. Our job was to shovel sheep shit from beneath the shearing shed into bags. It was a stinking, filthy job. The sheep manure had been accumulating for years, and it was foul. The shearing shed holding pens were slotted; there were gaps every inch to allow waste to fall into the space beneath the floor. Our pay was five shillings for every used superphosphate bag we filled.

The work was hot, hard and cramped, as we were beneath the shed. The stench was almost overpowering and sweat poured from me. Every half hour or so we crawled out into the fresh air for a spell and to gulp the air.

By the end of my first day, I was very tired. The only compensation was that I earned fifty shillings – very good pay for the time. I was too tired to eat my tea, a rough meal of mutton chops and boiled spuds, prepared by Pop in the hut's kitchen.

In bed that night I felt miserable, the only company was the pulsing of my heart. I wondered if it might stop at any moment

I managed to survive eight days under the shed, long enough to collect my pay of twenty-four pounds. Greg Gillespie was the owner of Berrybank and as he handed me my pay he thanked me for my work, adding, 'I will have you back here one day'.

It was a prophesy that came true, because two years later I returned as part of Tiger Dorron's shearing team.

As we drove through Ballarat on our way home, I called on Pop to stop near the railway station.

'I'll get out here, Pop. I'm gonna go to Melbourne and get a job. There's nothing for me at Daylesford.'

There was no argument from Pop. 'Alright. Off you go. I'll tell your mother.'

So I went to the station and boarded a train for Melbourne. I had no idea what I would do in the big smoke or even where I would live. I only knew that Frank was living in a boarding house at Newport, near Williamstown, and I hoped to join him there.

Frank was pleased to see me again and introduced me to his landlady, Nanna Bridges. It was to be the start of a long association with Nanna.

Nanna's – as it is now. From Google Maps.

Nanna Bridges' boarding house and Mr Berry's corner shop. Douglas Parade, Newport.

Nanna was very English, a widow aged about sixty – maybe seventy. She greeted me warmly.

'I think you will be happy here. My boys are all very good and you'll get along well with them.' She had a rather posh English accent.

Nanna cared for the lads who boarded with her, 'my boys' she called them, and was a 'mother' to all the younger boarders. She was registered for accommodation with the Railway Workshops, and most of her boarders were apprentice boys from the country, almost all of them away from home for the first time. They needed someone like Nanna, so did I, and we loved and respected her. I didn't learn a lot about her background, except that her husband had died some years before, and she had to take in boarders to earn a living.

Her home was one half of a two-storey double-residence building. The other half comprised the mixed business-cum-milk bar and residence of Mr Berry. I eventually got to know him pretty well, although we were never close. He had a thirteen-year-old daughter, Kathy, and as I got to know her a little, she used to tap on the wall that divided her bedroom from mine. A sort of code, I suppose, and a way for this shy girl to communicate with a boy. Some years later she

Lunch time at Nanna Bridge's boarding house. Frank, Nanna, Wally ?, and Eric (Nester, I think).

was murdered while collecting mushrooms from a paddock around the outskirts of the western suburbs. Her killer was never found.

Nanna's building was on a corner in Douglas Parade and was home to six other young men, boys really, four of them apprentices at the Newport railways workshops. There was Wally, an always smiling young man, Bill 'Snowy' Jensen a sixteen-year-old from Noojee, a timber town in East Gippsland, Eric Nester a one-armed pensioner in his forties, two young brothers, Noel and Len Farrer from Forrest in the Otways, and there was my brother Frank. I was in company that I felt very much at home with – all boys from the bush.

I managed to find a job at Henry B. Smith's in Williamstown. It was shift work, rotating in turn from day, afternoon and night. My job was wheeling bales of greasy wool from a large store to the various scouring and carbonising machines. Here, men fed the wool into hoppers that led to the huge washers that cleaned the grease from the wool and removed such things as burrs and grass.

At Nanna's, I got to know Danny Sheedy, the boot repairer in the shop on the corner diagonally opposite. Danny was about fifty years old, of Irish parentage and a good, fair dinkum bloke. Being on shift

Boot repair man Danny Sheedy. I spent many hours with Danny. He was an important friend for me. His shop was diagonally opposite Nanna Bridges 239 Douglas Parade.

work, I often had hours of daytime to fill. I spent a lot of that time talking with Danny as he busily repaired boots and shoes. In those days, repairing boots and shoes was common, unlike today where we buy cheap footwear and throw it away when it wears out. I'd sit on a stool, and we'd talk for hours. I was fascinated, as I watched him grab a handful of tacks and throw them in his mouth from where he took what he needed to fix the soles and heels to the shoes. How he never swallowed one I don't know, but it would have been bad news if he did.

Danny's shiny, bald head was often bent over an electric high speed rotating machine that ground off excess leather from his repairs, and another part, fitted with brushes, polished his finished jobs to a bright shine. I loved to watch him at work as we conversed over the noise of his machine and his rapid hammering. Danny Sheedy felt a bit like a father to me, the father I still greatly missed, and I admired him very much.

Nanna took in a small family of a Mum and Dad and two young daughters. They lived in a bungalow in the yard. Nanna said that they had been kicked out of the house they rented and had nowhere to go. They could stay until they found something.

One of the girls, a thirteen-year-old, apparently took a shine to me and followed me around all the time. I was a bit uncomfortable with her constant attention and copped a big ribbing from the other boys.

One night I lay in my bed, Frank was asleep in the bed opposite. In the darkness I felt someone getting into bed with me. My God! It was the girl. I didn't know what to do. So I did nothing!

I lay beside her, petrified. What if her father came looking for her? What if she got too friendly with me? She tried. If Frank woke up he wouldn't be very happy, no doubt thinking I had arranged a rendezvous!

The girl was determined, but somehow I found the strength (or, more likely, felt the fear) to resist her urgent demands. She lay there anyway, me wishing she would go away and leave me alone.

Eventually we both went to sleep, and when I woke, the sun was peeking through the window. I lay there very quietly figuring out what I should do when, would you believe it, the door slowly opened. Struth! It was Nanna coming to call us for breakfast. Christ. My goose was cooked. She'd never believe my story. She would chuck me onto the street.

'Come on boys, it's time to get up.'

'Okay, Nanna,' I mumbled from beneath a pile of blankets, hoping that the girl was completely covered. Nanna quietly closed the door.

The girl opened her eyes and smiled as Frank awoke and looked across at the tousled long hair and wriggling form in my bed.

'Shit! It's her! What is she doing here? You'll get in deep shit if you get sprung. Get her out of here quick. I'll go down for brekky and keep Nanna busy. You sneak downstairs and out the front door.'

The plan worked, with my companion slipping quietly out the door into the street, through the front gate and into the bungalow. Her parents were still asleep, thank God!

Each night from then on I was nervously awaiting a repeat performance, but it didn't happen. I was relieved when a few weeks later the family found a house to rent and moved on.

I am almost certain that Nanna saw the girl in my bed, but to her credit, she never mentioned it.

From then on the boys called me 'Spunky Dick'. Make of that what you will. It was an experience that went into my expanding book of knowledge.

Chapter Thirty-Five

LOTS OF JOBS ~ SHEARING SHEDS ~ MUDDAMURRA MICK ~ OLD COBRAN ~ DENILIQUIN.

Frank had a job driving a truck for Bill Murphy at Yarraville, which he liked. However, I was unhappy with shift work so I quit my job at H.B. Smith's and answered an ad in the Footscray Mail for a labourer. I scored the job helping a concreting contractor from Kingsville. My first job was at David Camm's home at Monbulk. He was a member of a long-established family of jam makers of Monbulk Jam, E. Camm and Sons. It was a long drive to Monbulk, the other side of Melbourne, where we were putting a concrete floor in a large garage.

When that was finished, the boss showed me a huge pile of bricks in his yard. 'I haven't got much on at the moment. You can have a go at cleaning these until we get another job.'

So there I was, cleaning the mortar from second-hand bricks. It was bloody hard work that tore the skin from my hands. But the work got even harder when the boss scored a new contract with a builder. From then on I was digging the footings for new houses, all with crowbar, pick and shovel. All of this hard yakka was a worry to a boy who had been told by doctors not to do any work for a year.

I soon left that rotten job and went to work as a bricklayer's labourer. This was frantic, very hard work; mixing mortar (known in the trade as mud) by hand, keeping the supply up to a small team of bricklayers, running up and down ladders to the scaffold where the men worked.

When that job finished, I found work as a labourer for Holland Constructions, who were building a large addition to Swift Meatworks in Newport. It was in the days before pre-mixed concrete, and my main job was shovelling screenings, sand and cement into a giant concrete mixer. I teamed up with Alan, a bloke ten years older than me. We worked well together.

We were working three floors up one day, within the new lift well, stripping the forms from some concrete poured two days before. We stood on a timber platform set on metal scaffolding.

'Did you feel anything move?' queried Alan.

'No, I didn't notice anything.'

We continued with our work. A minute later without any warning the scaffolding collapsed beneath us.

'Shit! The f...n thing has collapsed,' Alan had time to yell.

We both fell, in a scatter of metal and timber bits and pieces. It was a helpless, awful feeling. I had no time to say anything.

I fell into a corner of the shaft and was showered with debris which completely covered me. I don't remember anything after that, just a vague memory of falling metal and timber.

Sometime later, I opened my eyes. Alan was nowhere to be seen, there was nobody about. I had to claw my way from beneath the pile of scattered debris. I dragged myself up and over the rim of the pit, which went about a yard below floor level, and staggered into the open. I was still a bit groggy when the foreman approached me. He didn't look very pleased.

'Where the hell have you been?' Seeing I was not very aware and bleeding from a head wound he asked, puzzled, 'were you in that fall?'

I agreed that I was.

'Shit. We didn't know you were there. We took Alan to the hospital and didn't have a clue about you. Didn't see you. Sorry. Are you okay?'

I nodded, 'Yeah, I think so.'

'I'll run you to the hospital for a check-up anyway. Hop in me car.'

He drove me to the Williamstown Hospital where I was gone over by a doctor.

'Looks like you haven't done much damage, Ian. You were pretty lucky though. Falling in the corner you missed most of the stuff that fell. The other man is in the wards and has broken an arm and a leg. You'll be alright to go back to work.'

So I followed doctor's orders – went back to shovelling gravel, cement and sand into the concrete mixer, none the worse for my experience. Alan, on the other hand, spent several weeks in the hospital and didn't return to work in the time I remained on that job. In the long term, I subscribe my fear of heights to that experience.

Meanwhile, Pop and Murray had also landed at Nanna's boarding house, along with Gilbert junior, my stepbrother. We always called him 'young Gil'.

I went back to Henry B. Smith's to seek a job there, and I was hired as a shift worker again. My job was the same as before. I still found shift work difficult to cope with, but stuck it out. My stepbrother Gil also had a job at HBs, as we all affectionately called it. HBs was a haven for a lot of men. I know of no other employer like it. Most times they would find a job for anyone that asked.

Pop and Murray didn't hang about and went back to work somewhere in the bush. But not before Murray took to me one night and gave me an awful beating. He came into my room where I lay on my bed reading, and without warning, belted me in the face and around the head. I do not know what provoked this attack; as far as I know I did nothing wrong. I think maybe he was vicious by nature and was looking for someone to hit; maybe he was drunk. I was very badly beaten, with both eyes blackened and closed and bruises all over my face, along with a split lip.

There was nothing I could do but cop it sweet. I hurt like hell but in a week or two I was healed. I was always wary of Murray after that.

One of our favourite recreational occupations at Nanna's was duping passers-by. We would place a fat-looking wallet on the pavement outside the building. Any innocent person passing by had no idea that the wallet was attached by a fine, almost invisible wire. We dangled this from the open window above. As soon as a person swooped on the attractive looking wallet we would hoist it quickly upward to where we stood. We'd double up with laughter at the look on the face below. We did this often and got a lot of well-deserved abuse in the process. But we were safe on the first floor, and no way the victim could get at us. Just as well! It was a rotten thing to do, but filled in many a boring Sunday for Noel, Wally and me.

I didn't enjoy the shift work at Henry B. Smiths, it was not hard, but it was constant; opening bales of wool and, by armfuls, feeding the machine. There was no respite, except when the machine broke down, which was rare. The worst part was that I was on rotating shifts – day shift for one week, afternoon shift the next and then night shift. I found it hard to handle the changes of shift. The night shift, 11 pm to 7 am was especially hard. I liked to go out at night chasing girls, mostly unsuccessfully. I spent my meal break sleeping on a pile of wool bales. My boss, Dave Palmer, was a good bloke and let me sleep a bit longer sometimes.

Not long after Pop and Murray departed from Nanna Bridges, my brother Maurie arrived – it was a real family affair. Maurie got work at Smith's as well.

All this time, I was growing up. I was a seventeen-year-old, looking to what seemed a distant day when I turned eighteen and old enough to have a car.

Meanwhile, Frank got into strife at his job. His boss, Bill Murphy had just bought a new car, a beautiful Chevrolet sedan, his pride and joy. One morning, Frank climbed into his Ford tip truck preparing for another day carting bulk raw sugar from the Yarraville wharf to the nearby sugar refinery. Bill had parked his new car in the yard as he went into the office for some reason. Frank, unaware of the car's presence, put the Ford into reverse to back from the shed and went straight into the side of the magnificent Chevrolet.

Bill Murphy heard the noise and came charging from the office. When he saw his new car, badly bent, he flew into a purple rage. He hurled abuse at Frank, and my poor hapless brother was sacked on the spot. He was devastated.

'I didn't do it on purpose, Bill. I'm very sorry,' he tried to explain. Bill ignored him.

There was a happy ending however, as a few days later, after he had cooled down, Bill sought Frank out and rehired him. Frank was a good, reliable driver, hard to come by, and Bill Murphy knew it.

*　*　*

It was August 1954. I had had enough of city life and longed to go back to the bush. Maurie and my stepbrother Bill Rae (Splinter, to all of his mates, because he was tall and thin) were shearing at Gnarpurt, a station I think was owned by Sir Chester Manifold, one of the Western District aristocracy. Frank decided to take us for a drive to visit the boys, so we'd taken a 'sickie' from our jobs. On Friday we set off on what was a long journey in a 1930 DeSoto, Frank's latest vehicle.

Maurie and Bill were working for Tom 'Tiger' Dorron, a popular shearing contractor. I knew Tiger, as he worked in the off season as a wool classer at Henry B. Smith's. Didn't everybody work there? It seems so!

We met Tiger at the shearers huts where he was in the kitchen talking to the cook, Artie Woods. He welcomed us with a big grin.

'Go up to the shed and tell them you're here. Stay out of the way though. The shearers'll knock yer arse over head if you get in the way. Then come back for a cuppa tea and some smoko. You can stay the night if you want to. There are plenty of rooms, and we have blankets.'

It was our first visit to a shearing shed and Frank and I were impressed by the speed involved. Everybody seemed to be in a hurry and the place hummed with activity. The shearers moved rapidly and smoothly as they removed the wool, and just as quickly, the shed hands, known as rouseabouts, picked up the fleeces and hurled them onto a large slotted table. Here other rousies removed any bad bits of wool and rolled the fleece into a large, rough ball which they passed to the wool classers' table. The classer quickly examined the wool for quality and placed it with others of the same type in a large bin. It was great to watch.

We walked gingerly down the board to where Bill and Maurie

toiled side by side. They were surprised to see us and stopped for a quick yarn as they finished off the sheep they were working on. As we talked, they rolled cigarettes in greasy hands and mopped sweat from their heads with dirty looking towels.

After a quick drag on a smoke Bill said: 'We'll catch you at tea time. Right now, we gotta keep at it. It's ewes and lambs and we gotta make a quid while we can.' He reached into the sheep pen and dragged a hapless animal onto the stand. The machine engaged with a whir and he was into the belly wool in a flash.

'I've gotta go too,' said Maurie. 'See you back at the huts at knock-off time, and we can have a couple of beers before tea.' We called the evening meal 'tea' in those days, before we got flash and called it 'dinner' like only the toffs did then.

Back at the huts, Tiger introduced us to Artie Woods the shearers cook. He was sweating over a huge wood-fired stove, stirring some sort of concoction destined for the evening meal. Artie didn't match the image of the TV cooks we see today. He was dressed in baggy, dirty, green trousers, wore a once-white T-shirt and a grubby grey-looking apron. On his head perched a dirty black beret and on his sockless feet was a pair of filthy sandshoes, plimsolls he called them. From his mouth dangled a soggy roll-your-own cigarette. He was not the sort of chef you would find at the Crown. Artie made us tea in a huge teapot from which he poured a very dark brew into large enamel pannikins.

Artie Woods, shearers cook extraordinaire. A portable radio in front. About 1954.

The kitchen was a treasure, virtually unchanged since it was built a hundred years before. On one wall was a giant wood stove, about eight feet wide, a fire glowed hot inside. Its top was fully occupied with large blackened pots and pans, bubbling away with what Artie called 'succulents' for the shearer's tea. Beside this was the bread oven, recessed into the massive chimney.

Artie, Frank and I sat at the scrubbed pine table and yarned all afternoon. He was a Pommy. 'I came out here about thirty years ago.'

He told us he had been a horse trainer 'back home' in England. 'A bloody good trainer I was, and a bloody man finishes up a bloody poisoner for this lot of ungrateful bastards,' he grumbled, a big grin on his wrinkled face. I judged him to be at least sixty years old.

Soon after five-thirty, the tired shearers and rousies trooped in, their day's work done. Their day started at seven.

'Give me a cup of tea, you Pommy bastard,' shouted one of the men, but he said it with a grin and a slap on Artie's back. He was a big man, about six foot two and built like the proverbial brick shithouse.

'G'day, I'm Bob McShadder.' He crushed my hand in a grip of iron. Frank winced too as he seized his hand in a huge paw

'I'm only joking, Artie. Stick your tea up your arse. I'm gonna crack a couple of bottles with Splinter and Maurie; Ron Lyons, too if I can convince him. He's sworn off the piss since last night.'

He turned to Frank and me, 'Better come and join us.' His invitation we happily accepted.

Ron Lyons proved to be a giant too. He had apparently sworn back onto the piss, as he joined us. Ron was aged around forty, over six feet tall and at least fifteen stone. He was also a gentle man who greeted us warmly. 'Good to meet youse. Here's lookin' at yer.' He raised a pannikin of beer. We responded in kind.

Just then, Tiger Dorron appeared at the door. 'Ian, can you come out here. I want to talk to you.' I went right away, wondering what the boss could want with me.

Tiger was standing near the meat safe, the fly screened building in which hung the kitchen's supply of mutton. He leaned casually against the wall.

Tiger had the appearance of a cockatoo, his grey hair stuck out at all angles, and on top it resembled the crest of a cockatoo. He had a smiling face with a weak chin and eyes that twinkled blue. Perched on his small, hooked nose were steel-rimmed spectacles. Above all he had a warm heart.

'Ian, I won't buggerise around. Jonesy, me presser, has stuffed up his ankle – broke it I reckon – jumping out of the back box. He's at the doctors and he rang and said he won't be back. I wonder if you would be interested in taking it on for the rest of the run?'

Me a presser? I didn't hesitate. I didn't like the city. 'Yeah. I'll give it a try anyway. See how I go.'

Tiger looked pleased. 'Thanks for that, Ian. I'd be buggered without a presser. Can you go back to Melbourne to get your gear and come back Sunday? I went inside and asked Frank if he would be in it. He readily agreed. 'It's a big drive but it's alright. I'll do it.'

Ah! Hooray for brotherly love.

And that's how I began my career as a wool presser in the Australian shearing sheds.

My newest job was with the roughest, toughest, hardest working, hardest drinking men in the country. But they were men of integrity and honesty, who were good unionists, all members of the AWU, who stuck together like shit to a blanket. They were the salt of the earth. Blokes like Ron Lyons, Teddy Murphy, Harry and Lindsay Castleman, Bob McShadder, Jimmy McIver, Alan Heinze, Jim Welsh, my stepbrother Bill Rae, and of course, my brothers, Maurie and Alan; all good men.

Of the entire team, the presser was regarded as the hardest working of them all. I was soon to find out why.

I settled into my new job and lifestyle pretty well, although I found the first few days exhausting. It was the hardest work that I had done so far in my various occupations.

I learnt pretty quickly, with a lesson from Tiger. He knew how to do it but was well past the age to actually take it on. I was young and pretty fit. Briefly, the job involved fitting an empty jute bale into the front box of the press, an old Ferrier model, filling it with wool, climbing onto it and tramping it down as hard as I could. This was repeated a few times. Then it was the bigger back box's turn; the same treatment, but at least four refills, all hard work. When this was done I would swing on the end of a rope on a pulley attached to the base of the back box and drag its arse overhead until it sat on top of the front box. Then I'd pick up a heavy iron handle to crank the wool from the back and compress it into the front. With the flaps of the jute bale fastened with metal pins, I'd roll the bale onto scales where the weight and bale number were recorded. I'd finish it by branding the bale with the station name and details of number and content with stencils and branding fluid. I was paid eight shillings and ninepence per bale.

It doesn't sound a lot, but I found myself earning on average twenty five pounds a week, tax free, and tucker supplied. This when a youth my age was lucky to get five quid a week!

I was rich beyond my dreams, and I spent money like water. It went mostly on grog, clothes, cigarettes and having a good time. I would have gladly spent it on girls but didn't have the opportunity.

All newcomers to a shearing team faced a traditional initiation ceremony and I had my turn; Nuggeting. It happened on my first night as I was taking a shower. The ceremony involved the application of a liberal coating of black Nugget shoe polish to the old feller and knackers. I struggled violently but it was futile under the weight of Maurie, Ron and Ted. It took a few days to properly remove, but the worst part was the embarrassment!

Our next shed was Old Cobran at a locality named Caldwell, about twenty-five miles from Deniliquin in the Riverina of New South Wales. Old Cobran was a large property, only that year becoming a Merino Stud. It comprised around twenty thousand acres and ran about twelve thousand sheep. It would keep the team busy for six weeks.

I scored a ride there with Splinter and Maurie in Splinter's big Mercury. It was a ten shearer shed, and two pressers were necessary to keep up with the shearers. The other presser arrived in the late afternoon driving a dust covered, black 1946 Vauxhall sedan. To my surprise and happiness, stepping from the car was my brother Alan, just returned from a run in Queensland with Ted Murphy, Maurie and Bryan Young. They were all good blokes.

Bryan was nicknamed 'Bung eye' for some reason. There was nothing wrong with his eyesight; his eyes were firmly focused on the daughter of Billy May, the manager of Henry B. Smith's and they later married. Ted was a softly spoken gentleman and Maurie's best mate for a long time. Ted died too early, found dead in his bed one morning at his home at Cape Clear.

As usual, Alan had travelled alone. He claimed that he had some courting to do along the way – I'm not sure about that.

'Alan, it's terrific it's you!' I was really excited. 'I was wondering who the other presser was. I'm really pleased that it's you.'

He stood with his hands on his hips, the trace of a grin on his face.

Old Cobran Merino Stud shearing shed and huts, Caldwell, NSW, Picture taken by the author 2016.

'Yeah, we'll see. Have you done pressing before? I don't need somebody dragging the chain.' He paused to flash me a smile from ear to ear. He was actually pleased to see me!

'I'm buggered,' he said. 'I just drove this black bitch about five hundred bloody miles, the heap of Pommy shit.' That was his name for the Vauxhall. It was trouble on four wheels.

It was not the cheeriest greeting, but that was Alan. His bark was always far worse than his bite. In fact, apart from occasional serious outbursts of temper, a Braybrook trait, he was a terrific bloke to work with and an all round great person. I loved and admired him, always had and always will.

Tiger had his best team at this shed, a valuable new client. As well as Maurie, Splinter, Ted, Ron, and Bob there was Jim McIver from Daylesford, the Castelman brothers, Harry and Lindsay from around Avoca way and Jim Walsh from Geelong – all top men at their trade. And of course he had two premier wool pressers, Ian and Alan Braybrook!

The shearing went well, and like most of the others, I drank one or two bottles of warm beer before tea – and often, some after. There was no refrigeration, except in the kitchen, so the beer was never cold. I

My brother Alan's Vauxhall. He named it 'Black Bitch'. It was always breaking down.

am not sure if there were such things as small cans or stubbies then, but I always bought boxes of Abbots Lager in large bottles.

This sort of work gave a bloke a big thirst. We would usually sit drinking around the kitchen table where I listened to a myriad yarns from the older men. Their experiences were fascinating. Their stories have stuck with me; stories like this one from Splinter: Working in Queensland he learned of the two shearers who stuffed their ultra-large suitcases with fine wool and carried it home for sale in Melbourne. Remember that this grade of wool was worth well over a pound a pound. Good, easy money by the suitcase full!

Maurie had a good story on himself. Shearing at a shed in remote outback Queensland, he met up with a luscious lass at the races. He decided to try his luck with her. Confident that he was onto a good thing he volunteered to take her home by taxi. 'Home' turned out to be sixty miles away at a place named Muddamurra! 'Bugger the cost,' thought Maurie. 'It'll be worth it.'

On getting there, he got a very definite knock back. Meantime, it had started to pour rain and the entire area was flooded. Water everywhere, all the roads were cut and Maurie was marooned there for two sex-free days. From then on he was known as Muddamurra Mick, a name he wasn't fond of.

On the first Saturday arvo at Old Cobran I went into Deniliquin with a small group of young rousies, five in all. We were driven in Bob Wilson's beautiful, near new Sunbeam sedan. I cannot recall the other blokes' names. Bob was aged about thirty and was new to the sheds.

We had a session at the White Heart hotel for a few hours. Outside was a group of three girls, hanging about and doing a lot of giggling. They had their eyes on us but we tried hard to ignore them. Finally, given the courage that a few beers gives, I approached one of the girls to try my luck. She was a pretty girl, about fourteen maybe, and dark skinned. A half-caste Aboriginal I supposed. Her name was Joanne. I must have made an impression because she agreed to meet me later at a dance being held in a hall nearby.

More than a little inebriated I met her at about eight o'clock, and we went into the hall for a while. I struggled hopelessly around the dance floor to the music of a three-piece band, drums, saxophone and guitar, but not for long. Soon we left and went to a milk bar for a milkshake.

We then made our way across the bridge over the Edward River toward the Aborigines' settlement, a disgraceful collection of tumbledown shacks and humpies that lined the banks. Joanne and I sat together in the dark, chatting for maybe half an hour, when I made my bold move. I put an arm around her and squeezed.

This went on for a while and I grew very bold and kissed her. Her response surprised me a bit. She was enthusiastic and obviously hungry for a bit of excitement.

Shit! I really didn't know what to do, but I eventually managed to perform, albeit a bit limply. This remarkable encounter continued until I heard a gruff male voice calling from not far off.

'Joanne. Joanne, is that you there?' It was her father. 'What are you doing out there? Come in here.' He must have heard our noises.

The lustful tryst came to an abrupt end as Joanne hastily regained her garments. 'I have to go. Dad'll kill you if he catches you. I'll meet you again next Saturday if you're in town. Same place.' She hurried away and I bolted, looking over my shoulder expecting an enraged Dad in pursuit. He didn't appear.

Back in town the lads were waiting for me in the Sunbeam.

'Where the bloody hell have you been?' demanded Bob. 'We've been waiting a bloody hour for you'. He was not pleased. 'Did you go off with that black sheila?'

I confessed that, 'I might have', as I sat in the back seat with two others. 'Anybody fancy an ice-cream?' All agreed, so I went into the milk bar, emerging with five large double-header cones. I eased back into the cramped back seat, handing out the ice-creams.

'How did you get on with the black sheila?' queried someone. 'Did you f...k her?' I remained silent.

Then suddenly, 'You did you dirty bastard,' yelled Bob. 'Christ you ain't fussy are you?'

'You f...d that black gin, touched her up, and then you handed us f...n ice-creams.' He threw his double-header out the window. The other three followed suit.

'You disgusting prick.' 'You bugger.' 'Stuff you.'

There was a chorus of discontent. Me, I just sat back licking my ice-cream, pretty pleased with myself. I never saw Joanne again.

Old Cobran holds some memories for me. One Sunday, four of us went for a walk along the banks of a nearby river, the Wakool I think. Bob spotted a length of wire tethered to a red gum tree on the bank. Attached to it was a drum net. These devices, fashioned from wire netting, were illegal in NSW, but were often used to catch a fish anyway. The idea was, a fish would swim into it and then couldn't get out, trapped.

We hauled the net in, and to our amazement, it contained a massive Murray Cod. We took it back to Artie to cook for tea. He was astonished at the size of the monster.

'I'll put it on me scales,' said Artie as he dug out his kitchen scales from a cupboard. 'Christ, look at that!' Our fish weighed a massive twenty-two pounds! We had no idea how such a large fish could enter the small opening in the drum net. Maybe it swam in as a youngster and grew up in there. I can think of no other

Peter Daire, Maurie, Bill (Splinter) Rae, Brian Young, ? Ross, Picture by Alfie Price at Brunbungle Station, Wannon Falls, c. 1952.

explanation. Fair dinkum. This is not a fisherman's yarn. But I didn't have a camera then.

We cut out from Old Cobran and headed back to Victoria's Western District, beginning at a six stand shed called Brung Brungle in the Wannon River area. From there we went to Minjah, owned by the Affleck family.

Nothing out of the ordinary happened at Minjah except Maurie getting into a big fight in a nearby pub. And what became known as 'the Artie Woods incident' and the attempted rape of an innocent seventeen-year-old boy. Nothing out of the ordinary!

Maurie was always belligerent, and a bloke was silly enough to pick him in the Hawkesdale pub. With much cursing, grunting, gasping and swinging of fists, a battle ensued.

'I nearly shit myself,' Maurie related the event to me later. 'I punched him in the throat, didn't mean to, and the poor bastard nearly choked to death. They had to rush him off to Warrnambool Hospital where he nearly died.'

Artie had prepared a delicious treat for an evening meal. A treasured recipe his dear old mother had invented in 'the Old Country', according to him. It bore the very ordinary name of Sheep's Head Soup.

Everybody hopped into the soup and we all agreed that it indeed

Hawksedale Pub. Maurie had an almighty fight here. Almost killed a bloke. (Stevage, 2008 Creative Commons License.)

was as fine a soup as any of us had ever tasted. Artie accepted the congratulations with dignity, pride and aplomb.

After we had all eaten, Splinter ventured outside for relief behind the tank stand. To his deep concern he espied Artie's discarded sheep's head. He carried it gingerly back into the kitchen where we diners were rubbing our bellies in satisfaction with a fine meal, especially the soup.

Splinter chucked the head onto the dining table where it landed with a enough noise to attract the attention of all.

'Take a look at that. That bloody poisoning Pommy bugger, Artie, has tried to make us all bloody crook.'

We all stared in horror at the grisly object that stared back at us with sightless, cooked eyes. It was indeed a sheep's head. Complete with wool, eyes, and teeth. I am certain I saw the green grass of it's last meal stuck in the teeth. Artie had simply chucked the entire head in the pot and boiled it for the basis of his soup.

If only Splinter had not discovered the discarded object it would have been alright. But the fact that we saw the head in that condition didn't add to the reputation of our cook, nor to our confidence in his ability.

His rock cakes, also from his dear Mum's recipe book, didn't do him a lot of good either. They were as hard as bluestone pitchers and, worse still, he served them for each and every smoko.

In spite of his cooking disasters, we all liked Artie, for example he did his cooking with a soggy, hand-rolled smoke always dangling from his mouth. This often led to cigarette ash falling unchecked into the meal he served. He once dished me up a fried egg; before it hit the plate a big blob of ash fell from his cigarette. Artie didn't hesitate – he tossed my egg on top of it.

It's doubtful if he washed himself more than once a week, and I doubt that he ever had a shower. Hygiene wasn't in his dictionary.

One time, the property owner ventured into the kitchen for some reason and sprung Artie with his weapon in hand pissing into the slops bucket. The boss was outraged and told Artie in no uncertain terms that he was sacked.

'You filthy swine! How dare you urinate in that bucket. How dare you urinate in my kitchen! You are sacked, you disgusting old man. Sacked, Do you hear me. Sacked.'

'You can't sack me, Sir,' protested Artie. 'I'm on a contract with the shearers.'

'We'll see about that,' roared the boss.

Artie was right, it was not within the owner's realm – it was up to the shearers to decide Artie's fate. Under the contract agreement, it was them that actually employed Artie. They chipped in a fixed amount from their earnings to pay the cook – standard procedure in the shearing sheds then.

That evening after work, the shearers met in the kitchen with Artie and had a vote. Splinter was the Australian Workers' Union rep and he put Artie's future to a vote.

'All those in favour of sacking Artie, put up your hand.' Not a single hand was raised. 'Well that's it then,' said Splinter, 'No need for another vote. Artie you stay, but don't piss in the kitchen buckets again.'

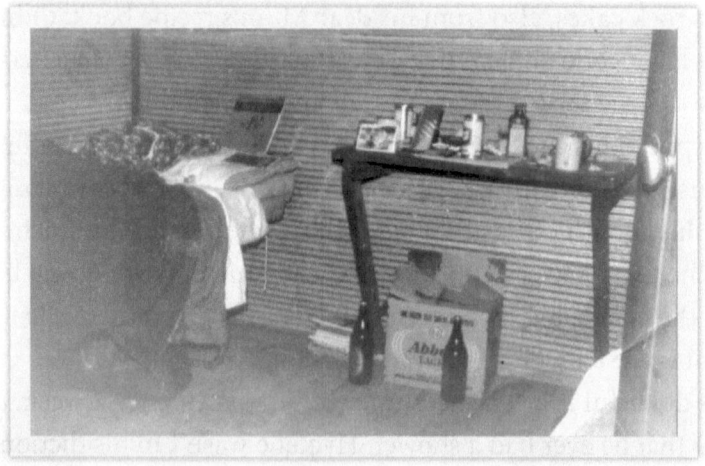

My room in the shearers hut at a property in the Western District of Victoria, 1954. Note the box of Abbott's Lager – my preferred drink at age 17.

The matter was thus settled democratically and a grateful Artie never peed in the kitchen receptacles again – as far as we know.

My room mate, The Duke, and I, knew that Artie always took a five pound jam tin into his bed to pee in during the night. He would chuck the contents out of his hut door in the mornings. One day we sneaked into this hut, took the tin and punctured it with small nail holes.

That night we listened intently until at last we were rewarded by curses and threats emanating from Artie's hut two doors away. It was good fun. Not such good fun however, was my next experience with The Duke.

We called him The Duke because of his aristocratic airs and graces. He was a big man, at least a hundred kilos and about twenty-five years old. He was one of the roustabouts. The hut we shared was typical of the time; unlined corrugated iron, two cheap beds topped with even cheaper mattresses, a small bedside table and large nails hammered into the walls here and there for use as coat hangers. We had the luxury of electric light. Neither of us wore pyjamas and slept nude or in our jocks.

This night, as I lay asleep, I became aware that I was not alone in my bed. The Duke had pulled down the blankets, along with my

At Cardross. Blockie Bill Rouse (with back to camera) and two unnamed helpers at the caustic soda grape dip, c. 1954

underpants, and was doing his best to mount me with a rigid rod. I was horrified. I really had no inkling that this sort of thing happened between men. I had dismissed such talk as bullshit.

He was on top of me and his one hundred kilos pressed down on me. He said not a word, just grunted. I struggled and called for him to stop.

'What the f...k are you doing? F...k off you bastard. Get off me. Go away. Leave me alone!' The grunting and thrusting continued. I put up a mighty fight.

No way was I going to let anybody do that to me. I was fighting like never before. Thank God I was pretty strong for my age. It saved me from certain rape. I really didn't expect anything like this. I only knew that he was not going to put that object inside me. I felt the Duke's rigid rod pressing into the crack of my arse.

He smelled of beer and sweat. I struggled on, calling for him to stop. He persisted, obviously determined to mount me. I was just as determined that he wouldn't. It was all I could do to finally push him away and send him falling heavily to the floor. The Duke then picked himself up and without a word went back to his bed.

I had some trouble sleeping from that night onwards, but he never tried it again.

I didn't mention the attempted rape to anyone. If I had told Maurie and Splinter they would have all but killed the perpetrator, and he would have been sent down the track, broken and in shame and humiliation. I was ashamed to even think about the incident and never told anybody, until now. I suppose that if it happened today it would have made me rich!

From Minjah I made my return to Greg Gillespie's Berrybank Station where I had shovelled shit with Pop and Murray a couple of years before. Greg actually remembered me. He was one of the good, often maligned, Western District squatters.

There were no outstanding events at Berrybank except my visit to the footy at nearby Cressy on a Saturday arvo. I always got dressed up to go anywhere, including the footy; jacket, neat trousers, shirt and tie. It was what I was raised to do. This day, two local would-be thugs approached me as I left the kiosk with an Eskimo Pie in my hand. One sneeringly grabbed my necktie and pulled it tight. I dropped my ice-cream.

'What have we got here? Some sort of poofter, eh?'

'No, I'm no poofter, mate. I'm one of the blokes shearing at Berrybank, and I suggest you piss off and leave me alone. I've got me mates here.'

With that news they immediately backed off. The thought of tangling with a team of shearers was too much for their little hearts! I was actually at the footy with only Alan that day, and at the time he was on the other side of the ground.

On a Saturday night, Alan drove me to Warrnambool for a bit of a night out. I felt quite honoured to be in his company. He was my model brother. At a small hall we noted that a square dance was under way. Neither of us had a clue about square dancing, or any dancing for that matter. We decided to have a punt, mainly to check out the sheilas who might be there.

We entered into the frolicking affair with gusto. As I stumbled about the floor, dosidoing and alamanding left and so on, I tripped and fell. Not to the floor, but directly on top of a rather obese lady who happened to be my partner at the time. The woman cried out and struggled to get to her feet as I valiantly lifted her up. It was an embarrassment

Maurie on the shearing board at Glengower Station in 2017.

to say the least, and Alan and I quickly slunk out the door. It was his and my first and last square dance. I believe the poor, traumatised woman eventually recovered after a number of professional consultations.

My time at Clarke's Glengower station in the Clunes district was more memorable than most. To begin with, Maurie crashed his 1936 Silver Streak Pontiac coupé into a power pole and probably should have been killed. He had only bought the car in the break between sheds and it was his pride and joy.

With a couple of mates on board, he had driven an SP bookie home to near Newstead from the nearby Black Duck Hotel. The Black Duck was Glengower's closest neighbour – still is.

On return from Newstead, Maurie had planted the foot. A couple of hundred yards from the Black Duck, and the same from the shearing shed, one of his passengers said, 'I reckon this car could do a hundred miles an hour.' Maurie apparently thought so too. 'It's doing eighty now,' he cried.

Then he lost control on a bend and the car careered through a barbed wire fence and slammed violently sideways into the power pole. Miraculously, nobody was injured, but the Pontiac Silver Streak was in a bad way. It was to be a month before Maurie could again get his hands on the wheel as the Pontiac languished in Cusack's Castlemaine garage and repair shop. It emerged as good as new and Maurie emerged from the experience a poorer and wiser man.

Before we left, I adorned the

Alan Braybrook and two workmates on Sunday washing day at Lawrenny Station.

shed wall with my name and date stencilled on the whitewash. It remained there intact over sixty years later when I visited there with my son, Glenn. The shed has been abandoned since the 1970s and is in very bad condition. The Black Duck pub still operates over the road.

My name is one of the hundreds stencilled on the wall by workers from as far back as the 1880s. I believe that the wall, if not the entire shed, is a heritage treasure. In 2017 I advised the local heritage person, David Bennear, of it's existence and need for preservation but received no response. I guess it will crumble away.

Our last shed for the year was at Lawrenny Station, a large property near Caramut. It wasn't very eventful, except that Maurie got into a big brawl at the Caramut pub. I was there, but I don't know how it started, but in those days it didn't take a lot to set Maurie off. First I knew was a lot of cursing at the other end of the bar, followed by a God almighty fight. Two locals got into Maurie – but he beat them both. The fight ended when one of the blokes cried out 'Enough'. Maurie had a few cuts to the face but was okay. The other blokes were bleeding pretty badly and went home.

Several of us blokes went into Caramut pub every evening. Six

Ian poses beside Gil's Morris convertible, North Road, Newport, about 1954.

o'clock closing was the law then but was widely ignored by pubs in small townships.

There must have been something in the water at Lawrenny because Maurie went into Warrnambool on a Saturday morning and returned with a motorbike. It was a beauty, a BSA Golden Flash. Maurie had been in a two-up game on the Friday night and, pissed of course, discovered in the morning that he had won over a thousand pounds. Hence the motorbike purchase. He rode it home when the shearing cut out but never rode it again. He claimed later that Pop had sold it when he left it in the shed on the farm, and pocketed the proceeds.

A local man I met at the Caramut pub was selling his motorbike, a BSA 250cc, for one hundred pounds. I had plenty of dough so I bought it. I rode it up and down the property's lengthy driveway and taught myself to ride.

When the shed cut out, we had a big celebration, free beer supplied by Tiger, at the Caramut pub – no fights this time. Lesson: never give free beer to shearers. It was late the night we packed it in. Splinter and Teddy decided to drive to Warrnambool for the night. I thought it a good idea and headed off in front of them on my BSA bike. It must have been near midnight and I was far from sober. Light rain began to fall when I had ridden maybe five miles, Splinter not far behind me, right up my rear end. I steamed along at about fifty miles an hour – pretty fast I thought.

Suddenly, without warning, the motorbike stopped dead and went into an almighty skid. The motor had ceased, causing the rear wheel to lock solid. I lost all control and careered off the road, down an embankment, finally coming to a stop with the bike on top of me. I struggled to get out from under it but the weight was too much. Luckily, Splinter had seen me crash and he and Teddy ran to my aid. They lifted the bike off me and I was able to stand. My right calf hurt like hell. The very hot exhaust pipe had badly burnt my leg and I was in great pain.

'By God,' said Splinter. 'You're bloody lucky you weren't killed.

Christ you were going pretty fast and shot off the road like a rocket. Thought we'd find you dead.'

'I'm alright, but I think I need a doctor.' I was very shaken.

'Hop in the car and we'll take you to the hospital,' said Splinter, and he and Teddy helped me to the car.

I spent the night in the Warrnambool hospital, emerging in the morning heavily bandaged and with my good trousers in a pretty bad state. They had cut them off me. But I was not real bad and, as Teddy and Splinter said, I was lucky to be alive. I fitted myself out in a new pair of Fletcher Jones Plus 8s and was soon back in good form.

While in Warrnambool I rang the nurses' home and got connected to the young nurse, Maureen, that I had my eye on when I was a patient two years before. I don't think she remembered me and politely declined my invitation to accompany me to the movies. I guess that having seen me naked when I was her patient she was not impressed! So I moved on, crushed, but still determined to get my hands on a sheila one day.

I never saw my BSA motorbike again. Possibly it still lies rusting away in long grass on the side of the road near Caramut.

Chapter Thirty-Six

My first car – grape picker – truckie and more.

I went back to Nanna's boarding house, my city home, and to work at Henry B. Smith's. I had just turned eighteen and thought that a young feller like me needed a car if he was going to have any luck with the girls. I found exactly what I wanted. For my first car I chose a beautiful 1926 Chandler tourer. I answered an ad in the Footscray Mail. The bloke wanted twelve pounds for the machine, but readily accepted the ten that I offered him.

'You're getting a bargain mate. She's in bloody good nick. All she needs is a new battery and away she'll go.'

Frank drove me to a garage where I got a battery for two pounds ten. We installed it in the Chandler, gave the carby a couple of tickles, and the old darling roared into life. She was beautiful – or so I thought. The only thing she needed was a paint job, the grey was faded and a bit shabby.

The remains of my first car, a 1926 Chandler. Picture taken at Barrys Reef about 1956 after Pop acquired the car to make a sawbench. Ken is in the car. I named it Genevieve, from a movie I'd seen.

I rushed down to the hardware store and bought a tin of red and a tin of black – good quality enamel – a paint brush, some sandpaper and some turpentine. By this time I had returned to live at Nanna's, and out in Douglas Parade on a Saturday morning, aided by Frank and a new tenant, a bushy young bloke named Ray, we painted the Chandler.

She emerged a gleaming black with a red lightning bolt down each side. She sure looked good. We were very proud of our work.

I waited impatiently for the paint to dry so I could drive around town to show off my lovely new car. Look out girls, here I come!

By the evening, Wally and Eric decided to go to the flicks at Hoyts theatre in Ferguson Street, the main drag of Williamstown.

'I'll give you a ride,' I volunteered.

'But the paint ain't nowhere near dry yet,' ventured Ray.

'She'll be right,' I said. 'Just be careful getting in and out, she'll be right.'

We made our way down town. I pulled up outside the theatre, planning to take a spin up to Titter's Milk Bar, to check on the talent (girls) there. The boys climbed gingerly from the back seat and I gave a wave as I moved away.

Age 17 – unloading a cargo of beer from the boot of Jim McIver's new Ford Consul, c. 1954.

I hadn't travelled more than a hundred yards when a cop stepped out from behind a car, his hand held in the stop position.

Struth, here's trouble. I'm in strife. I hadn't yet bothered to get a driver's licence.

The cop was young and officious. I had put the canvas top down, so he was able to lean on the door sill and look closely at me. 'Do you know you are driving without lights on this heap of rubbish'?

Oh Shit! I had turned the lights off when I dropped the lads off and forgot to turn them on again. This means trouble!

'I'll have a look at your licence, please, driver.'

Uh-oh! Big trouble now. 'Ah, Hmm. I don't actually have one.'

'No Licence, eh? We are in trouble aren't we?' I dunno about the '*we*' but *I* sure am, I thought.

I stepped out of the car. 'I haven't been able to afford the cost of the driving school so I have put it off until I get some money. I spent what I had on the car and stuff today.'

The cop sat down on the running board, casting a contemptuous glance at my car. He commenced writing my ticket, leaning back on the freshly painted door.

'Here you are.' He handed me a page from his book. 'You'll get a summons in a day or two – to appear in court.'

He must have felt a twinge of sorrow for me. 'By rights I should make you leave this awful thing you call a car and walk home, but you can piss off. Don't drive again until you get a licence.'

He left the scene of the crime and stepped onto the footpath where he watched as I pushed the starter pedal, turned on the lights and drove carefully away.

A week later I appeared in the Magistrates' Court in Williamstown, and was fined ten shillings for having no lights and a pound for driving without a licence. I told the Magistrate I didn't have money with me so he gave me a month to pay. It's a bit different today.

I have often wondered what the cop thought when he discovered his lovely, neat uniform covered in what looked like red and black paint!

Two weeks later, I hired a driving school to take me for a licence test in a lovely new Holden at the Motor Registration Branch in Carlton, where I passed with no trouble. I hadn't needed to take any lessons, having had previous experience!

I wanted to get out of shift work at Smith's, so I soon went job hunting. I thought I would have a go at truck driving, and ignoring my lack of a experience, I somehow landed a job with H.A. Chalmers in South Melbourne.

I seem to have been drawn to jobs that spelt hard physical work. My job at Chalmers was collecting pig iron from huge piles on the wharf and delivering it to a variety of foundries around Melbourne. The pig iron came in large pieces, a bit like a basket ball cut in half. It was heavy and rough on the hands, and I had to load and unload every bit by hand. It was back-breaking and I wasn't happy with it. The only good part about it was that I drove a beautiful Reo Speed Wagon, the only one in Chalmers' fleet and quite a rare vehicle. It was magnificent. But it required more than that prestigious honour to keep me at Chalmers for long.

So I went to work with Frank at E. Murphy and Sons of Yarraville! (I never found out who the 'E' was in E. Murphy and Sons.)

At Murphy's, I was assigned to driving an Austin tip truck, a vehicle much despised by the other drivers. This job was a new adventure for me, because it required good driving skills. As I was a former driver for H.A. Chalmers, Bill Murphy was glad to hire me. Obviously I was a top driver to be engaged by Chalmers. Bill didn't know I'd only worked there for a month. Was I up to a job that required skilled driving?

The job was to collect raw sugar from a ship tied up at the wharf and move it to huge storage sheds. I'd pull up beneath a hopper which poured several tons of sugar into the back of my truck. It was just a short drive of about five hundred yards to the storage shed.

It got a bit tricky here. The stored sugar was piled high – a massive heap that you would not believe. I reckon it was about thirty feet to the top. I had to reverse the truck up narrow planks as high as I dared and tip the load onto the ever growing pile. One slip here would mean tipping arse over head and who knows with what consequences. I reckon we drivers were pretty skilled, doing that. No doubt it was dangerous work.

When there was no bulk sugar to unload, I was given a tray truck, a Ford V8, to deliver bags of sugar to factories and shops all around Melbourne. Some of the drivers had a great scheme to subsidise their income. They loaded huge rocks into the truck cabin for when they weighed in to the sugar works. At the wharf they would tip them into the river which meant that when they weighed out they had an extra bag or two of sugar – roughly equal in weight to the rocks they tipped in the river. They tared out okay and took their seventy pound bags of sugar to sell to regular customers – usually grocers.

I drank a fair bit of beer when at Murphy's. Every night after we knocked off, a dozen of us drivers adjourned to Charlie Sutton's pub a few doors down from the depot. Charlie was a popular bloke. At the time he was coaching the VFL team Footscray after a long career as a player. He attracted a big crowd to his pub because of this. We all liked Charlie, one of the good blokes.

Smoko in the grape vines at Cardross. Pop, Murray, Eric and Gil Jnr, c. 1954

It wasn't a bad job at Murphy's, but I tired of it and wanted to move on. So I went back to Henry B. Smith's, this time in the store, stacking bales of scoured wool ready for export.

* * *

When I had returned to Nanna Bridge's boarding house after the shearing I was warmly welcomed by Nanna and the boys I had got to know pretty well. In a way it was good to be 'home'.

Pop had partnered with Murray and bought an ancient Ford Blitz Buggy tip truck, a leftover from the war. Pop had it neatly sign written on the driver's door, 'G. Rae and Son, Contractors'. They intended to get contract work with it, but alas, it didn't last long. Work was hard to find, and the Blitz was not very good. In fact, it was an unreliable heap of junk – a 'bomb' in the language of the time.

It wasn't long before Pop and Murray departed Nanna Bridges, going bush again. Around that time, my brother Maurie arrived – it was a real family affair. Maurie got work at Smith's as well. All the time I was growing up.

* * *

Murray came back to stay briefly at Nanna's. 'I'm going to Redcliffs grape picking with Pop'. he announced. 'Any of you wanna come, too?'

Picking grapes sounded pretty good to me, so I handed my notice to Dave Palmer at Henry B. Smith's. A few days later, with Eric Nester, (we called him 'Wingy' because of his one arm), young Gil, Pop and a recent arrival at Nanna's, Frankie Burton, a brash young pommy, we set off. I travelled with Eric and Frankie in Murray's 1947 Ford V8 and Gil with his father in his 1935 Ford pick-up. We formed a sort of convoy and drank large quantities of warm, long-necked bottled beer along the way.

We eventually arrived without incident at Bill Rouse's grape block at Cardross, just out of Redcliffs, on the Murray River. Pop and Murray had worked there the previous season so, being good, reliable workers, were welcomed back by Bill and his son George.

Bill Rouse was a returned serviceman from the first war who was granted a block by the government, as were many others. It was more a sentence to sweat and toil than a gift, but a lot of men were glad to have the opportunity to be independent. Bill's next door neighbour was his son George and wife Nancy, who, of course, also grew grapes.

George, a short man in his seventies, with skin burned dark brown and a smiling face beneath a battered, sweat-stained felt hat, was pleased to see us.

'It's good to have a strong team of pickers here. We have a good crop, and with a bit of luck and hard work – we should all do alright this year. Come along and I'll show you the hut. Three of you can stay in it and the rest can go to the hut at George's place on the next block'

It was a hot 38 degrees as Bill led us down a bit of a track for a couple of hundred meters, past the grape drying racks. There stood

Frankie Burton outside the steel grape pickers hut at Cardross, 1953.

Shower time for Frankie Burton at Cardross fruit block, c 1954.

what was to be our home for the duration of our stay. Sitting in the middle of an open space, shimmering like a mirage in the hot sun, and perched on a patch of dusty red soil, was the tiny hut I was to share with Gil and Frankie Burton for the next four or five weeks. It was made from steel – walls, roof, even the door – it had one small window, steel-framed of course, and at one end a wood stove with oven. There was a small table, a set of drawers, an old wardrobe and four tubular steel chairs. There was a cold water shower nearby, set in an old corrugated iron water tank. It was a delight to step under it after a hot day in the vines.

There was not a tree in sight; nothing but red soil and row upon row of grape vines. The hut proved to be an oven – all steel set in full sun, with temperatures always around the thirty-eight degrees. It was almost intolerable and extremely uncomfortable. We soon moved our steel stretchers outdoors and usually slept there. I'll never forget that all-steel hut, the very latest concept in prefabricated housing.

'Why in Christ's name would you put a bloody steel hut out here in the bloody stinkin' hot sun?' asked young Gil.

Frankie Burton, a fresh faced, light-skinned, newly arrived pommy was perplexed. Nobody could answer Gil's question. Frankie felt the heat more than us.

The steel pre-fabricated hut at Rouse's fruit block, Cardross 1953.

What with the heat and the flocks of mosquitos that descended every night, life wasn't pleasant. And the days were as hot as Hades. Frankie elected to be our cook and he turned out some pretty passable meals, mostly canned spaghetti, Imperial Camp Pie, baked beans and sausages. Sometimes there were some green veggies and even some mashed spuds and gravy. Considering it was a wood stove and it was stinking hot in the all-steel hut, he didn't do too badly.

While we struggled with heat and poor tucker, the rest of the crew luxuriated in the relatively cool mudbrick hut and were served their meals by Nancy Rouse at the house.

Frankie reckoned he was a 'shit-hot' cook. 'I shoulda jolly been a chef,' he said. Frankie was a bit of a wag and loved to sing old songs from his memories of England. He was an East Ender, a Cockney and I'll always remember his favourite song, he sang it so often.

> 'All my life I wanted to be a barrer boy,
> A barrer boy I always wanted to be.
> When I wheels me barrer, I pushes it with pride,
> 'Cos I'm a coster, a coster from over the other side'.

I don't know who or what a 'coster' is but I believe a 'barrer' is one of those large wheelbarrows they seem to push around the streets of London.

Frankie had turned up at Nanna's one day, unannounced, seeking a place to stay. Someone had pointed him toward Nanna's and she took him in. He was a merchant seaman, attached to a Norwegian freighter anchored at Williamstown. He brought a Swedish man with him who turned out to be good bloke, we named him Johnny. Frankie liked what he had seen so far in Australia and had decided he was not going home. So he jumped ship. He was a happy, smiling young man, twenty-two years old, covered in tattoos, sporting a fashionable duck's tail haircut and full of life and energy. Small in stature, he nevertheless was afraid of nobody.

Frankie oozed confidence in himself and was handsome enough to draw women to him. He was accepted as one of us and was at home in our company. He never returned to England and I last heard from him in 2005. He was living alone in a caravan at Daylesford. 'Temporarily', he said, and I guess that would be so.

I found picking grapes hard going. I didn't like the heat and I couldn't master the art of picking, even though the grapes hung suspended in vast quantities and it didn't take many bunches to fill a bucket. The fierce heat really got to me, and after filling a few buckets I'd take a spell in the shade beneath the vines for a couple of minutes. I still quietly worried about my heart.

Eric had trouble, too, especially with his one arm. He approached me one afternoon. 'How about we join as a team, you pick one side of the row and me the other and we split the tally?'

I readily agreed. 'That's okay with me, Eric. Together we may even make a bloody quid.'

On the first day we picked 45 buckets all up, which was hardly a thing to brag about. On the second day, after a big night at the Redcliffs pub, we managed just one bucket. It was a record never to be equalled.

'One bloody bucket,' laughed Gil. 'I can't believe it! One bloody bucket between two blokes.' He walked away shaking his head.

He could laugh as he was a gun picker, regularly doing 200 buckets a day. In fact he went out at night picking in the moonlight while Frankie, Eric and I were at the pub with Pop and Murray! Gil was there to make money – and he did.

Eric and I copped a real teasing from the entire crew. 'I don't think I ever had a team of two picking together before,' said Bill. 'And for sure I never had one that picked only one blasted bucketful!' Everyone roared laughing.

Also working with us were a married couple, European immigrants. They had a son, nineteen-year-old Rudolph and sixteen-year-old daughter, Annie. Annie was the one who took my eye, and somehow I found the courage to ask her to go to the pictures with me on Saturday night. To my surprise she accepted. She didn't look that good but the main thing was that she was a girl!

I got a real ribbing from the other boys, especially Gil, who mimicked Annie's accent. 'Oh mine Iank, mine darleenk, you are such lovely boy.' Then he put on a pathetic male voice. Me. 'Oh Annie, you are soo beautiful. I love you I am thinking. Would you give me even a little look at it please?'

Of course I was embarrassed by all this and glowed red.

Come Saturday night, and Murray, with his Ford loaded to the hilt with young men, dropped me at the appointed rendezvous, The Busy Bee Café. There, waiting for me, was Annie. There were gasps of disbelief. Before us stood a vision of loveliness, Annie had transformed from a frumpy, dark-haired girl dressed in boots and dirty overalls into an absolutely gorgeous beauty. The boot was on the other foot for the other blokes now, and they were green with envy! I had scored a ripper!

Annie and I had a good night filled with ice-creams and lollies. I walked her home, and we sat in her father's Ford Prefect sedan in the driveway, where we exchanged a couple of shy kisses. I was too shy to even contemplate further advances.

I had to get a taxi back to the hut, which sent me broke, but I felt it

Drying racks at Cardross. We spread the grapes on them after dipping in caustic soda solution and they were sun dried.

was money well spent! It was worth it just to see the looks on the lad's faces as they stared in disbelief at the gorgeous sheila I had scored!

Saturday morning and we were making our way to Mildura. As we approached the township of Redcliffs we were confronted by a long line of stationary cars, and police cars with lights flashing all around. We had completely overlooked that our new British Queen and her Duke were visiting the district and they were about to arrive at Redcliffs.

'I don't give a stuff about the Queen,' muttered Murray as a policeman approached the car.

'You can't go on through to Mildura, mate. You'll have to follow the crowd onto the footy ground. The Queen is going to be there in a few minutes, so we need to move along.'

Murray complained, 'I don't wanna to see the Queen. We wanna go to town. We don't care a stuff about the bloody Queen.'

The cop glared at Murray with a look that suggested he believed the complaining driver was a disloyal, treasonous, contemptuous and disgusting bushwacker slob, deserving of a good flogging. With a grimace of distaste he waved Murray on and we were forced to follow the train of cars ahead. There was a huge crowd of excited people assembled around the oval; men, women and children, all lined up as close as they could to the fence to get a glimpse of the royal couple.

A great cheer went up when Elizabeth and Philip appeared on the footy ground standing in the back of a Land Rover. Children waved ribbons and flags and the mums were just as excited. It was all very jolly.

Murray had climbed up a nearby tree to get a good look. 'If I've gotta see her I may as well get a good view,' he said as he climbed upwards onto an overhanging limb.

Suddenly there was a tremendous crashing sound as his perch snapped. Murray, the reluctant observer, crashed heavily to the ground. He lay motionless, crying out in great pain, his face contorted in agony.

'I've buggered me back. I reckon I've broken something.' He was obviously very distressed. Somebody ran to a policeman who rang an ambulance. We stood around helplessly.

It took half an hour for the ambulance to arrive, the driver having to force a way through the crowd. The crew quickly got Murray onto a stretcher and whisked him away toward Mildura and hospital. It was to be his resting place for three weeks as he had surgery where some damaged bones in his back were set in plaster. He was waist to upper chest in a solid cast. Other than that, he was relatively uninjured, but he sure got a big fright.

We were working on George's block. Overall, the team members were doing well, keeping 'Spider', the bloke driving the horse-drawn pick-up trailer flat out. Eric and I contributed little to his load I'm afraid.

'When are you two blokes gonna pull the finger out?' joked Spider.

'It's too f...n hot for me. I can't hack the heat,' said my one-armed picking partner.

I struggled on, hating the job. Then one morning, George approached me. I think he'd had enough of me dragging the chain. He was a kind man.

'Ian, I think you'd do better working on the dip, so go and see Bill. He'll fix it up. It's a wages job, twelve quid a week.'

It was a lot better working on the dip. Hot and constant, it involved dipping buckets of grapes into a large tank filled with a weak solution of caustic soda and water. It was a lot easier and I was actually making money!

After we submerged the grape-filled buckets in the solution for a few minutes, ten at a time on a winch, we carried them to the nearby drying racks. These racks were four tiers of wire netting, about fifty yards long, on which the grapes were spread to dry, in a few days becoming delicious sultanas. The worst part of the job came with every little scratch or cut causing pain as the caustic mixture found its way into the wound.

When we finally finished the picking season, I actually owed George and Nancy seven pounds, money I had overdrawn, but they let it slide. Instead they handed me a twenty pound note.

'You'll need a bit to see you into another job back in Melbourne, Ian. You can give it back from your pay when you come here next year.'

I never did return – nor, I'm sorry to say, did I repay the advance.

When it was time to leave, Murray had still not recovered from his injuries. These good-hearted people took him into their home while he recovered. He was their guest for two months – no charge. George and Nancy treated him as one of their own, and Nancy acted as his nurse. He was later able to join us in Melbourne, travelling by train, as he had entrusted young Gil with his precious Ford V8.

It seems that Murray was destined to die by an accident involving a tree. When he was just thirty-one, he was struck on the head by a falling branch as he worked at his job felling red gums on the Rufus River just out of Mildura. He lay there dead for several hours until his girlfriend went looking for him, because he was late for his evening meal. He is buried in the Mildura cemetery.

I travelled with Pop back to Nanna's, and Gil drove the others. Pop and I didn't talk much on the long journey. I was always a bit afraid of him and didn't quite know what to say, although by this time he was quite good to me. We stopped only once, for petrol and a few plonks for Pop at a wine saloon in the main street of Wycheproof.

'I'm gonna get a drink. Do you want one?' I didn't drink plonk but went with him into what was like stepping back fifty years into a shanty. I sat on a stool while he polished off a couple of glasses of red wine. I reckon it was likely to have been one of the last wine saloons still in existence.

The drinks finished, we set sail for Nanna's and arrived early in the evening. Nanna, as always, welcomed us back, but she had no room for us. 'That's alright,' Pop said. 'I'll go and see my brother Tom at Colac, then see Vera for a while.' And away he went.

Nanna, as usual, was helpful. 'Young Gil has got a room at a place in North Road and you may get in there.'

She gave me directions. It wasn't more than a mile away, so I was able to walk there, lugging my old suitcase. Sure enough, Nellie, the generously proportioned, aging landlady, had room for me in her two-storey home.

'It's five quid a week up front.' She held out a hand for payment which, thanks to my former boss, I was able to produce. I scored a bed in young Gil's room, a sleep-out in the yard. Murray joined us at Nell's six weeks later, still on crutches, when he had recovered enough to travel.

I went back to Henry B. Smith's and, once again, was given a job. I have lost count of the number of starts Henry B. Smith's gave me over the years. This time it was day shift. I was helping in the store, stacking bales of wool and loading trucks for the wharf.

It was pretty rough at Nell's boarding house. The meals were terrible, and that's what counted for me. One night, as I lay half awake, Gil brought a female companion with him, one of the local prostitutes. He had a wow of a time as I lay listening to the proceedings. Not a good experience!

But it wasn't all bad. Gil had bought a nice looking Morris 8 roadster, and we used to cruise around Williamstown looking for girls. No

My 1934 Chev roadster with mate Dave Williams at Williamstown, c. 1956

Luck! But it was fun. I loved this little car with the top down, and decided I needed one like it.

For seventy-five pounds, on twenty deposit, I was able to buy a 1934 Chevrolet roadster, complete with upholstered dickie seat. I used to cruise around Willy with the Chev overflowing with my mates from Nanna's and the (very) occasional girl. It was fantastic fun, especially with the top down.

I loved it – a fantastic car. A slight problem was that it had next to no brakes. One day, loaded with two girls, Joanie Hayes, Betty Flood, and a mate, Dave Williams, I was tootling behind a bus in Douglas Parade. I wasn't concentrating properly when the bus came to an unexpected halt. I had no hope of avoiding a smash. No bloody brakes! I rammed into the large bumper bar on the rear of the bus at twenty-five miles an hour.

The four of us, jammed into the front seat of the Chev, got chucked about, but nobody was badly hurt. Joanie bashed her knee on the dashboard, but it wasn't serious. However, my beautiful Chev was practically destroyed. It was the end of her road and I got a tenner

The workers at Henry B. Smith, Williamstown about 1961. I have many names on file.

for her from a wrecker. It was back to walking again. By the way, Joanie Hayes was later to become my wife.

A week later, for a hundred pounds, on twenty-five deposit, I was able to buy a black 1934 Chevrolet sedan. It was really in good condition – a bit of class – or so I believed.

I hadn't had my '34 Chev more than a month when it vanished from my parking spot in a lane across the street. I reported it to the police but held out little hope that I would ever see my car again. Two weeks later, two cops came to the door carrying an oil-covered crown wheel and pinion in a hessian sack.

'This is part of your missing car. Can you identify it? We need that identity to charge the bloke we've got hold of. We know that he's knocked off a lot of cars but can't pin anything on him. Is this your Chev's crown wheel and pinion?'

How the bloody hell would I know. One crown wheel and pinion looks the same as another! I barely knew what a crown wheel and pinion was, except that it was part of the differential.

'I can't be sure. I can't really say, but it could be mine I suppose. I really dunno.'

'Come on, you must have a pretty good idea. Does it look like yours at all?'

Nanna Bridges, unknown, Joan Hayes (later my wife) and Frank Braybrook, c. 1956.

I had to agree that it did look like a crown wheel and pinion and maybe it was from my Chev.

'That'll do us,' said one of the cops. 'We'll be calling you as a witness in court before long. Thanks for your cooperation.'

Away they went. I heard cop number two say quietly to his mate, 'We've got the prick this time'.

Apparently all that could be found of my Chev was the crown wheel and pinion! Whatever happened to the rest is a mystery.

A week later, I was subpoenaed and appeared in the Footscray court. I was pretty frightened by this. I had never been in a courtroom as a witness and never given evidence – in any event, I was not sure the car parts on display in the court were actually from my car.

I guess my evidence was not very convincing because the offender was pronounced not guilty by the stern looking magistrate. I can't recall what I said in evidence, but it earned the ire of the two arresting policemen and the one who was the prosecutor. As I went to leave the building the leading cop called to me.

'Just a minute. We want to talk to you.' I was led into a large office in the police station next door.

'Sit down here,' said the prosecuting cop, indicating a chair set in the middle of the room.

'You laid down on us you prick, didn't you?'

I had no idea what he meant.

'No, I don't think so.' I was genuinely puzzled.

'Come on don't give us any bullshit. We know you got together with Madigan and cooked up that bullshit story. Tell us the truth. I can tell you we are not bloody happy. We put a lot of time into getting that bastard and you got him off with your f...n lies'.

I was almost shitting myself by this stage. I could do nothing but deny what they were saying. I had never set eyes on the bloke until that day and had never said a word to him.

'Look, if it was him who pinched my car I want to see him get put in jail. I don't know if it was him or not.' I felt trapped, ringed by three cops standing over me as I sat in between them. It was like the third-degree, and I was completely innocent.

'I swear I didn't work out anything with that bloke. I never did.' I was getting pretty scared now.

'Well we *know* you did, and we think we might charge you with conspiracy. What do you think of that?' said the prosecutor. The others nodded.

Posing with a Ford Zephyr (not mine) to impress a young female pen pal from Louisville, Kentucky, c. 1955

'You know that's serious don't you. It means jail time buddy!'

Jail time! Christ. I was there to help put the crook that had apparently pinched my car in jail, and now it looked like he was set free and I was going to jail. I could scarcely believe the turn of events.

Thank God it eventually turned out alright. After making me sit and stew for another five minutes that seemed like an hour, the leading cop said. 'Okay. You can piss off and try to stay out of f...n trouble.'

The bastards had only been putting the shits up me, they were just dirty on missing a conviction. I got out as fast as I could and made my way back to Nanna Bridges' by bus.

I didn't have a car these days!

Chapter Thirty-Seven

A HIDE OUT - A BROTHER MARRIES - BACK TO THE BUSH FOR GOOD.

About this time, I can't recall why, I moved with Maurie and Gil to a boarding house in Yarraville. It wore the grand title of 'Hyde House', due to its location on Hyde Street. We called it the Hideout. It was a large old home with a long passageway, off which were five bedrooms. Each was fully occupied.

Our landlady was old and very small, quite ugly and heavily addicted to booze. The food was awful. There were twelve of us in total and each meal time we sat around this huge table. It was difficult to reach the bread, salt and Daffodil margarine, stuck in the middle of the table. Maurie coined the phrase 'Boarding House Reach', which was appropriate. One large feller, named Charles, was a glutton. He stuffed himself with food and finished each meal with bread smothered in jam. Maurie named him Monbulk, after the popular jam brand.

Hyde House boarding house. We called it the Hideout. Hyde Street, Yarraville.

Another guy wore a suit, tie and a felt hat; he was aged in his forties. He would slink about the building in the dark of the night, his felt hat pulled over his eyes, saying quietly, 'I was a communist for the FBI', to anybody who would listen. He was weird. 'I was a Communist for the FBI' was a film doing the rounds about that time. Another bloke used to dust the filthy collars on his white shirts with French chalk to conceal the dirt and save washing them.

One night we had a big drinking session in our room and I was busting for a pee. As we all usually did, I went to the open window and let it go, one of the advantages of being male. There was an almighty female shriek from outside. Our landlady had been lurking below eavesdropping on our talk!

'You filthy bastards,' she cried. 'You f…n well pissed on me. Get out you dirty bastards. Get out. All of you go. Go now, before I call the police.'

We went. It was not late, so Maurie, Gil and I went down to Nanna's. Thankfully she had vacancies and welcomed us back. She was a darling. I felt at home there.

* * *

Frank and Lillian wed at Frankston. I'm the best man.

Time went by. Maurie turned up one day with a new girl on his arm, Joyce Tuckwell, a lovely brunette who hailed from Tottenham, a western suburb. It wasn't long before they decided to marry. It was a spendid wedding and all went well. Joyce was lovely in her white wedding dress and Maurie was looking grand in a new suit.

The wedding ceremony went smoothly and there was much joy. However, it was a little different later at the reception. This was held at the home of Joyce's sister, Edna, and her hubby Ray, at the rear of an old bakery in Newport.

Whatever was in the grog, or the finger food, set off a series of fights. In fact at one time it seemed that everybody was fighting someone. Pop was there and he got stuck into Murray, young Gil was fighting one of the guests, and other guests I didn't know were swinging punches as well.

Then Frank, who never threw a punch in his life, got stuck into me. I don't know what I did to antagonise him, but he sure was angry – or mad with the grog perhaps – he rarely drank. He landed one mighty punch on me that sent me flying. I crashed through the open window and landed on the cobblestone driveway, dazed and bleeding from a cut on the mouth.

I admit I was pretty drunk. Through the fog, I saw a group of guests take hold of me by the feet. They dragged me down the drive onto the street; my head bobbing and bashing on every join in the cobblestones, Frank supervising. They bundled me into the back seat of Frank's car and left me. I was too stupid to fight back and stayed put on the back seat until the party was over. Frank then drove me back to Nanna's and I went to bed.

It was a memorable wedding and we all grew to love Maurie's bride. Sadly, Joyce died from cancer in 2017.

Life went on for me much as before. Working at Smith's, chasing chicks, drinking a lot of beer at the Vic Inn and eating dim sims and short soup at the Chow's on Nelson place. When not doing that, I was washing down banana splits with milkshakes and spiders at

Titters Milk Bar at North Willy station or Mr and Mrs McKenzie's Milk Bar in Ferguson Street.

One night at the Chow's on Nelson Place, Frankie picked a fight with someone for no known reason. He was a belligerent little bastard. They fought their way around the café tables, knocking over chairs and sending condiment containers and serviettes crashing to the floor. It was like a bar room brawl in the Wild West. The angry owner rang the police. I saw and heard him and called to Frankie, 'For Christ's sake, Frankie, knock it off. He's called the bloody cops. Let's get out of here fast'.

Frankie ceased pummelling his unhappy opponent, and we bolted onto the street. Just at that moment the bus to Newport was approaching. I frantically hailed the driver and we quickly got on board.

'Shit. That was close,' said a smirking Frankie. 'But I fixed that smart bastard.'

I agreed, but had no idea what he'd fixed him for. We hadn't travelled more than a few stops into Ferguson Street, when a police car drew alongside and pulled the bus over. We had been sprung.

Ian at Nanna Bridge's, 1957.

Two burly cops stepped into the bus. Their eyes fastened on Frankie. They had got a good description of him from the Chinese owner.

'You can come with us, sir,' said one, producing handcuffs. They took the culprit away and charged him with disturbing the peace or similar.

Frankie was bailed by Nanna that evening, and when he fronted the court a week later he was fined five pounds. It didn't do anything to stop his future belligerence.

But times were changing. Young Gil had met and married Meredith, a girl from Kangaroo Island who was now living in Williamstown. Most of my mates now had girlfriends. It was different now. I had a girlfriend too, Joan Hayes from the Chev smash incident, and fell head over heels in love with her. We all called her Joanie.

I left Nanna's and went to board with Mrs Johnstone in Williamstown. She was the mother of Sandra, the best friend of my girlfriend. Sandra suggested it would be handier for me in my courting, being in the next street. I moved there but was never happy in that environment – not relaxed enough, but I stayed until I finally left for the bush.

In due course, Maurie and Joyce introduced their son Colin into the world. Soon after this event, they moved to the tiny township of Fern Hill, near Trentham, the heart of spud country. Maurie was digging these plump tubers for a living, and I was a bit envious, not with his job, but living in the bush.

I was now nineteen, almost twenty, grown up, and decided to leave Henry B. Smith's and move upward in my career by becoming a spud digger! Maurie and Joyce agreed for me to become a boarder. One Saturday morning I loaded up my new car, a 1930 DeSoto, purchased from Frank, and said farewell to my friends and Joan, promising to see her every weekend. I made my way up the Calder Highway via Woodend to Fern Hill. The tired old car crept along at a steady forty miles an hour. I was feeling pretty happy. In an hour, if the DeSoto made it to Fern Hill, I would be back in the bush.

However, it wasn't long before I was overcome with missing Joan so much that I gave up my career as a spud digger and returned to Willy and Henry B. Smith's. I was a young man desperate for stability and love in my life, and I soon proposed marriage to Joan. At the same time, even though I adored the girl, I wasn't sure I was doing the right thing. I wanted my father and his advice. Alone in my room, I spoke to him. 'Dad, why aren't you here? I want to talk to you, to ask you what you think I should do. What should I do, Dad?'

Of course there was no reply, but I really meant what I said to my father. He was often in my thoughts. I don't think I ever fully recovered from his death.

Joan and I married in September. I was just twenty and she eighteen.

Joan Hayes and me in 1956. We married the next year at Congregational Church, Williamstown.

We were very happy together in our small rented home behind Litchen's Dry Cleaners in Douglas Parade, Williamstown. Eventually, two wonderful sons, Glenn and Dale, and eight years later, I made it back to the bush where I always wanted to be.

Joan and I took the plunge into the unknown and rented an old house in Stanbridge Street, Daylesford. I had first lined up a job at the newly opened 'Spud Factory', where they packed potatoes into paper bags. It was a lousy job, but I was happy.

Four weeks later, the business shut down and I was unemployed. As a husband and the father of two boys I was in a pickle. No job meant no money.

I was lucky, as I managed to quickly find a job driving a semi-trailer truck to and from Melbourne for the Sampson brothers, who also had the Esso service station. It was a shit job, 5 am starts and late finishes, six days a week, with lousy pay, but I had paid work!

Best of all I was with my family, back home in the bush where I have always belonged.

The End